Double-Click Velocity

Sharon E. Harris

First Edition

PAGE PUBLISHING, INC.
Conneaut Lake, PA

First originally published by Page Publishing 2020

ISBN 978-1-64701-738-5 (pbk)
ISBN 978-1-64701-739-2 (digital)

Printed in the United States of America

Contents

Introduction

"My legs! My legs! I've lost my legs!" he hollered. Someone shook him by the shoulders.

"It's all right. It's all right." It was a voice that wasn't familiar, a feminine voice well intentioned. She kept shaking him gently, trying to wake him from a nightmare, but he only faded back into a deep sleep.

Back at the cabin, heavy wind and rain beat against the structure of the building, making her shudder. She sat at his bedside and waited, watching the clock and noting how long it took him to wake up—two hours and fifteen minutes. He fluttered his eyes open and looked around the room. There she was, sitting on a wooden chair at his bedside, peering into his face. "Hello?" she said. He didn't answer, just stared back at her with glossy eyes. She wondered what type of state he was in this time. At least he was calmer. He woke up without making a sound.

This book is action packed and transcends time. Well plotted dramas unfold with each chapter, increasing the appetite of its readers to wanting more. If you love mysteries, you won't be disappointed. There is never a dull moment in your reading adventure in this book because, as an avid reader from a child, I appreciate a book that keeps your interest as it stimulates your vivid imaginations. I do not wish to give a lengthy introduction, for the sake of not keeping you from starting on your journey. Mysteries to be solved, beaches to explore, adventures to experience and much more, are all awaiting you as you open the door to *Double Click Velocity*. Come on in and welcome to *Double Click Velocity*.

Chapter 1

Two of a Kind

Squawking overhead, king of the sky, an eagle glided at treetop level, glaring down at the man standing motionless below. Looking up at the predator, hands in his pockets, the man focused on the wind that whistled past his ears. *How lucky you are to be born with wings,* he thought, shifting his gaze to the horizon that bestowed everything it touched with a straight boundary line.

Controlling his emotions no longer, he shouted to the heavens, "Freedom!" raising a clenched fist, the wind carrying his voice to the distance and beyond. Inhaling long and deep, he filled his lungs with a purity of air known only to those who exist free in uncharted wilds.

"Freedom!" he shouted again, an inner surge of pride overcoming his emotions.

The eagle squawked once more, head tilted downward, viewing all below. Wings stretching eight feet or more, it glided with power and full command of all it surveyed, defying the wind itself. With acute, piercing vision, the predator searched for the slightest movement.

Suddenly, the eagle spotted an imperceptible something below, unsuspecting and innocent in its awareness. The predator's head jerked downward, eyes riveted on the target as it increased in velocity with uncanny agility. He watched as the eagle raised its head with a bird pierced in its claws. The eagle soared again until it was out of sight.

"I believe I can fly," he said, his voice escalating in volume. He raised his hands to the sky, leaned his body forward, and closing his eyes, pretended to soar like the eagle.

He felt light, the fresh, crisp air baby soft. Its clean scent lingered in his nostrils. He turned and viewed everything in sight. From the top of the world, everything looked beautiful, a stillness of nature that provoked serenity—a faint blue mist draping the atmosphere. He flew on and on like the eagle and searched for him. "See, I can fly too!" he yelled, informing the king of the sky in no uncertain terms.

"I am a fighter!" he further declared. "I have strength! I have power! I have endurance! I must hold on to hope!" he shouted.

A suddenness of purpose coming upon him at once, he caught sight of something just ahead, but before he could halt in midair, a black mist enveloped him and he awoke, walking, to somewhere, somehow. Where was he? Where was he going? He hadn't a clue. His beady brown eyes scanned the surrounding area frantically, his heart pounding wildly in his chest as if he'd all of a sudden realized his plight. He was in trouble and he knew it as he opened his mouth to yell for help, but his tongue cleaved to the dry roof of his mouth. He continued to stagger through the hot desert in his search for water. His dark skin burned from the glaring sun. He pulled off his jacket and tossed it aside, his short-sleeved shirt saturated with sweat, revealing the contour of his body.

The sound of his unbuckled sandals caught his attention, and he stared down at his feet with an unsure look, then raised his head as he continued to scope the surrounding area for signs of life, any life, anything moving at all.

Sweat streamed down his face. He pulled off his knitted hat to fan his face, and a bundle of something fell loose from beneath. "Aah!" he hollered in anguish, brushing his head frantically with his hands. But whatever clung to his head was there to stay.

"Uh, dreads?" he muttered in confusion. The thought of having dreads had never crossed his mind. He pulled on them with a slight tug, and sure enough, they were real. They dangled in thick chunks down his chest. He pounded on his arm with his fist, and sure enough, it hurt. That eliminated the possibility that he was either dead or sleepwalking.

He analyzed his circumstance. To have gone to bed without dreads and woken up the next day with them in the middle of nowhere wasn't at all possible. He was like a man whose mind had been wiped clean. No traces of what had been familiar. He knew nothing but the language he spoke.

Amid the glaring sun and in a situation that seemed not of his making, a feeling of abject horror came over him as never before. A man that didn't even know his name was like a piece of rubble, unrecognized and fit for nothing. He had no wallet, nothing that could identify him or even provide an address.

Maybe he was about to get a break. He spotted a truck in the distance.

He staggered along the steaming sand and stood directly in its path. He mustered up his strength to wave his hands. Though he didn't have to, the driver of the truck came to a sudden halt, a lone man wearing a knitted sport shirt and sunglasses. He tilted back his wide-brimmed hat and smiled friendly-like out the window.

"Hey! Hello! How did you get out here, on foot no less?" the driver said.

"Agishia neba fueba oye, oye, oye?" He was shocked at the words as they proceeded from his own lips. Or did they? He looked to the left, to the right, and then behind him. It was just him and the driver. His language sounded similar to Christian people speaking in tongues. What language was that, and what had he said?

"Ah, sorry, but I don't understand what you said. Do you speak English at all?"

He nodded and attempted to speak again, but only this time he was sure he would speak in English.

"Guanduvisa skibee wuga woah," he uttered, frightened by his own voice.

The man beckoned for him to get in the truck, noting it was useless to communicate with words. He reached behind him and pulled a bottle of spring water from a cooler and handed it to him.

"Maybe the police might be able to help you," he told him and then pulled off.

What in God's green earth is going on? he thought to himself, grateful that the man had picked him up. Was he experiencing reincarnation? Had he been someone horrible in his previous life and had been rewarded a life of confusion in this one? Or had he been great in the previous but now had to learn suffering so he could understand both? He looked up into the great blue sky and demanded an answer, but only to himself.

His mother's voice jolted him. *Boy, is that what you read in the Bible? Did you ever find a statement about reincarnation of human beings in God's Word? Snap out of it!*

He fell backward with a thud in the jeep.

"Are you all right?" asked his new friend. He nodded but dared not open his mouth to speak. It was funny how he couldn't speak English but could understand it. How could that be? It was a psychological breakdown, he figured. *But who can and will help me?* he thought as the Jeep whizzed over the rough, parched ground. He knew he had to take it like a man because nothing, he was sure, lasted forever. No circumstance, situation, or problem was ever here to stay, and he knew that today might just be his day of final victory.

His mind went on relentlessly. *One day, out of the blue, you realize that you're at a certain point in life. Is this all there is? For instance, you're born not knowing you even exist. Then one day you see yourself, the person that makes up you, and realize that you're here. Then what? Wait for a determined appointment to die and then go back to where you came from in the beginning? Is that all there is?* he thought to himself.

Where did we come from, and where are we going? The tone of his thought was as authoritative as it was indeterminate. He looked up into the bright blue sky again and demanded an answer from the man upstairs. *The man upstairs?* His mother would have slapped his mouth shut had she even known that he had such a thought. *The good Lord in heaven...He holds your breath. He could just take it, you hear? He is God. You better show Him reverence.*

His eyes dropped from heaven to the ground in an instant. His spirit connected with something, but he just couldn't put a finger on it. *I wish I could fly, then I'd be free,* he thought. *Free forever.*

*****

Estelle slowly wobbled her way into the living room, where her husband, Cedric, sat perfectly still, like a "propped-up corpse" still. Only about twenty minutes ago, he'd made his way to his La-Z-Boy chair, where he plopped, waiting for the six o'clock news.

"It's time," she said faintly. He pretended not to hear her, or so she thought. Then suddenly something sharp and piercing cut through the air and jolted him to an upright, rigid position. It was her voice. She'd uttered his name in a shrill-sounding grind.

He swirled around breathlessly and saw her standing by the door that joined the living room and the kitchen. He had no idea when she'd entered the room, but all of a sudden, she was there. With her back slightly bent forward and eyes tightly shut, and with head down and one hand on the doorpost and another on her stomach, she panted. Her face was tense, almost like that of a porcelain doll, as if every muscle had been frozen.

Cedric jumped to his feet. "Yes," he said, almost in a whisper. She pointed at her stomach, and he knew from all the physical evidence that she was in labor.

Despite Estelle's sudden plight, though, he had to take the time to review his last I-don't-know-what-in-the-world-is-going-on-with-me plight. He ran his fingers through his hair, and a feeling of relief swept over him when his fingers slid through strands. He couldn't live with himself with a head of hair that was entwined in thick, heavy chunks.

"Thank God!" he muttered. The pictures were vivid, a dream within a dream.

He was lost again in his thought world, and it had seemed so real. His living room had suddenly become the Sahara Desert. He wasn't the least bit thirsty, he wasn't wearing sandals, and he wasn't wearing a jacket. There was no other person in the house besides him and his wife, and whatever language he'd spoken, he had no clue. How could he not have been able to speak the English language? Why had he been having dreams?

Maybe he needed to see a shrink about his episodes, but he hated the very thought of lying in a black chair in front of an old man with gray hair and glasses hanging from the tip of his nose whose intention was to probe into his mind to see what was *wrong*.

Maybe his lapse into the unreal world had something to do with some kind of trauma he'd experienced during his childhood of which he had no memory. He couldn't remember a time in his life when he'd been dreaming and had woken up from a dream into a seeming reality when indeed it, too, was a dream.

He heard his name echo again from one end of the house to the other. He had never thought that a woman of such petite stature could speak with such volume. Well, he guessed that when a woman is in labor, anything's possible.

Okay, now that he knew that she was in labor, what was the *first* step? He'd gone to those time-consuming Lamaze classes but hadn't paid much attention.

His mind was fuzzy. His wife stayed in her position, immobilized by pain, while he waited for his mind to clear. "What should I do?" he asked boldly.

She slowly raised her head and glared at him. Certainly, she was going to tell him what to do, he thought to himself. But something strange happened.

With a raised hand, she pointed a shaky finger at him. "You did this to me!" she said. He saw her lips move to form the words, but he knew the feminine voice his wife possessed was nothing compared to the deep, husky, monster-sounding voice he'd heard. Something wasn't adding up. His beautiful wife had been transformed into a monster.

He didn't respond to the accusation and figured it was a smart idea. He stood firm and stared at her with pity.

"Could you call Madeline, please?" she said in a calm tone, a vast contrast to the way she'd spoken just a moment ago.

Cedric ran past the telephone, past his wife, and slid right into the kitchen. "Who moved the telephone?" he asked like a man in authority. "It was right here the last time I used it!"

It dawned on him suddenly. There was never a telephone in the kitchen. He hustled back into the living room.

His mind went blank again. He'd forgotten what he was doing. He stood solemnly and thought for a moment.

"Oh, yes, the midwife's number." He fumbled through the sheets of paper that listed important numbers.

"Here it is." His hands shook as he punched the numbers. He waited. No answer. He panicked. He dialed again just to make sure that he'd dialed the right number. Still no answer.

When the doorbell rang, he literally dropped the phone and ran past his wife, who'd made it onto the sofa.

He swung the door open and hollered, "Praise God!" To his relief, standing on the other side of the door was Madeline.

"God sent you! I know He did!" he declared and yanked her inside. She grinned.

"It's good to see you too, Cedric. I just wanted to check—"

"Perfect day to check," he interrupted. "She's in labor!"

Madeline hurried into the living room and knelt down beside the pain-stricken Estelle.

"Well, hello, Ms. Estelle," she said in her French accent.

Cedric's head pounded. He knew that his pressure was elevated. That was just too much action for him.

"I'll be back," he muttered into the air as he reached for his keys that were lying on the center table.

He felt faint. He knew he had to get out. He slid his hands into his pockets and walked toward the garage.

His head cleared quickly from the fresh smell of flowers from his wife's garden. He sat in his car and leaned his head against the headrest. He closed his eyes and reminisced for a moment. It had only seemed like yesterday when he'd first laid eyes on Estelle and had hoped that she would one day be his wife. Who would have known that in a couple of years, she would actually have said yes to his proposal and become the mother of his offspring?

Daddy—it had a nice ring. He was happy.

He waited in the car for the news of the delivery. But being isolated in one place got the better of him. He pulled out of the driveway and made his way about the city, hoping and praying for a safe delivery. Madeline's years of experience as a midwife gave Estelle assurance that everything would be all right.

*****

The curtains moved gently against a light wind. The afternoon breeze was soothing, giving rise to the tender chirping of a flock of birds just outside the window and adding to the soft and delicate cry of a newborn baby.

Estelle's relaxed body lay still on the queen-size bed as she rested from a long, hard labor. She was exhausted but felt relieved—free, actually. All was well.

The midsize room was fully illuminated by the natural light that came through the windows. The soft color of the mint-green walls held a haven of sweet peace. The colors in the room seemed sharper than they'd appeared before. She smiled as she cast her eyes on the vase of flowers that Cedric had given her the day before. Everything seemed like a fairy tale.

She slept peacefully as her midwife walked back and forth from her bedroom to the nursery room across the hall.

Madeline nudged her. "It's time to start bonding with your precious bundle," she said with a lilt in her voice. She smiled the smile of a caring midwife.

Estelle returned the smile as she cupped her hands to receive her son.

"Oh, Maddie," she whispered softly. Her voice seemed to ripple the atmosphere. Madeline placed the tiny figure in her welcoming arms. She held him up and looked him over. He wriggled his little body and cried delicately.

"Oh, BJ," she whispered softly as she kissed him tenderly. He puckered his lips and searched for a finger to suck. His shiny black hair lay flat on his head, a perfectly round face accented by deep, obvious dimples.

"Ten fingers and ten toes," she said as she stroked his body. She held him close to her body to keep him warm. He was perfect, immaculate in every way.

With legs crossed and hands clasped, Madeline watched with tenderness in her eyes, and Estelle bonded with her gift of life.

After a few moments, Estelle turned to her and said, "I'll hold the other one now." Madeline didn't move, didn't know what to say. Her eyes lowered to the floor. There was a moment of heartfelt, deep silence.

Madeline's expression had suddenly changed to a grim look. "I'm so, so sorry. He didn't make it," she stuttered.

Estelle's eyes narrowed, and her lips curled into a frown. "What?" she said incredulously. A gradual change from a soft and gentle look to anger had covered Estelle's face like a mask. She searched Madeline's face. She couldn't have meant what she'd just said. *Didn't make it?* That just couldn't be true.

"What do you mean?" she asked, her voice quivering.

"I'm sorry," she said again sadly, as if she blamed herself.

Estelle sobbed softly. As much as it was in her to scream her heart out, weakness from her hard labor prevented her.

"Bring him to me, please," she demanded between sobs. To her surprise, Madeline objected.

"It's best that you didn't see him. It would traumatize you even more."

Estelle became agitated. She was in no mood for advice. "I don't care what you think. Just bring him to me," she insisted impatiently.

"All right," said Madeline hesitantly. "After I clean him up."

She took BJ and handed Estelle two capsules that she'd taken from a prescription bottle.

"Take these. They'll help you to relax." Estelle swallowed them and laid her head on the pillow "I'll be right back." Madeline turned and walked out of the room.

*****

Madeline wrapped the baby in a blue-and-white baby blanket. She glanced at Estelle, who was still sleeping. Cedric wasn't home, but she was glad that he'd responded to her paging him. Surprisingly, he was more tolerant of the tragedy that had unfolded in their lives.

"Come home, now," she urged. She didn't want Estelle to be alone for too long, so she hurried out the door and carried the tiny bundle to the car.

Two hours later, she returned and found Cedric's car in the driveway. She was glad that he was home to tend to his wife.

He wasn't there for the delivery, and Madeline was happy about that. She knew that he wouldn't be of much help, anyways.

Estelle sat upright in the bed when she heard Madeline's voice. Madeline walked over to the side of the bed and felt her forehead. With jaw set, Estelle pulled her head from under her hand. Madeline ignored her reaction.

"Your temperature seems fine now. How do you feel?"

"Where's my baby?" she demanded as she keenly watched her face. Madeline placed her purse on the little table in the corner. She slowly walked over to the chair she'd sat in two hours ago. She studied Estelle's face before responding.

"You fell asleep, and I didn't want to disturb you, so I took him to the hospital. I couldn't keep him too long. I had to bring him to the hospital. The law is very funny, you know."

"She's right, darling," Cedric said to his wife, who stared wide-eyed at her midwife. "The law is very funny. We wouldn't want to fall negligent. If the hospital will take care of the burial, why not let them?"

Madeline was relieved that at least someone was on her side. Estelle completely ignored her husband, as if he wasn't even in the room.

"I'm sorry, I was just looking out for your well-being," she defended.

"I'm not an invalid! I know how to look out for my own well-being. That was my child!" She roared, stressing the point. "Why didn't you wake me up so I could look at him? So I could hold him and tell him what was in my heart?" She moaned weakly, as if her strength had just been zapped. Madeline handed the death certificate to Cedric.

"The hospital will take care of the burial," she said again. Cedric sat on the bed next to his wife and buried his face in guilt. He knew that what he'd said weren't exactly the perfect words that should come from the mouth of a father who'd just lost a child. He was saddened but couldn't express his grief any other way. He knew that he should have also been there with his wife through the whole labor. But what guy had guts enough to stand through the whole ordeal of his wife's labor?

Estelle couldn't believe Cedric could be so cold and insensitive about their son and her feelings. Overcome by emotion and grief, Estelle threw her head on the pillow, covered her face with the covers, and cried bitterly.

*****

As time went on, Estelle seemed to have somehow been able to pull herself together and accept the loss of her baby. Cedric was grief-stricken, but he was able to adjust from the agonizing loss much sooner than she had. *God knows why,* he thought. *God knows why.*

As he bounced BJ on his knees, he couldn't shake Brandy from his mind. He stared at him from head to toe and back again. It wasn't hard to picture Brandy since they were identical twins. Cedric grieved silently.

BJ cooed and wriggled in delight as he peered into his father's face. He cuddled his only son and rocked him back and forth in his strong arms.

It had been a few months since BJ was born, and Cedric struggled to keep up with his financial obligations. One day, as he sat and mused on how he was going to manage in the days ahead, someone tapped on his office door and told him that Ted McVaine would like to see him in the personnel office—not a good sign.

He had a gut feeling that it wasn't going to be a good meeting. He was right. Ted handed him a slip and apologized with sympathy that he and six other employees had to be laid off from the landscaping plant. He could hardly pay his mortgage as it was, and to be out of a job would sink him even lower.

"Things aren't going too good with the plant," Ted told him and shook his head in sorrow. "I hate to have to let you go. You've been a good worker. I'd be more than happy to write you a good recommendation whenever you need one—"

Dumbfounded, Cedric stared at Ted and hoped that what he'd heard wasn't true. At this point, he welcomed one of his fantasy dreams. He hoped that he would wake up and find it was all a dream. He really didn't expect to be laid off even though the possibility was on his mind, slacking business and all.

"I know," Ted said with empathy and patted him on the shoulder as he noted the disappointed look in his eyes.

"How much time do I have to find another job?"

Ted lowered his voice and whispered with a quivering voice, "You have to leave now." It was obvious that it was hard for him to let him go, but as a director, he had to do what was necessary for the business. Ted sighed deeply.

"Now?" Cedric echoed to Ted as if they were sworn to secrecy.

Ted nodded. "I can't explain. I'm not allowed to."

Cedric walked out of the personnel office and gathered his belongings, got in his car, and without looking back, drove away, and circled the city a few times to gather his thoughts.

Finally, he took the road that led to his house. He didn't know how he was going to break the news to his wife but knew he had to tell her straight away. He wasn't worried about her blaming him, but he was worried about her emotions because she had always been a worrywart.

If only he could keep it from her until he found another job, but how would he do that? How do you get up every day and kiss your wife goodbye and tell her you're going to work and, at the end of the week, you don't have a paycheck? What would you tell her? He thought for a moment, but nothing logical would pop in his head.

He had to tell her, and he knew it. Over and over he rehearsed how he would break the news to her and console her that everything would, in the end, be all right.

A delicious aroma greeted him as he opened the door. Estelle was wearing a flowered apron and a pair of kitchen gloves.

"Good timing," she called as soon as she heard the door open. She was in a good mood—a great mood, he thought—compared to other days.

BJ sat in his high chair and banged his bottle on the tray. His milk-mustached face was round, plump, and smiling as he held his bottle upside down, watching the milk drip out.

Cedric sat at the dinner table, but with a finicky appetite. He wasn't in the mood to eat, but he didn't want to disappoint her. She'd worked so hard to prepare his favorite dish.

Estelle noticed his unusually quiet mood. "How was your day?" she asked for the second time. BJ tossed his bottle, and it landed in Cedric's plate.

"I was laid off," he blurted out without any acknowledgment of BJ's action. He picked up the bottle and sat it on the table. BJ squealed for his "baba." Estelle reached for it and handed it to him.

That wasn't exactly the way he'd rehearsed it in his mind to break it to her. It was evident that deep in his subconscious, he'd wanted to get it off his chest.

He braced himself for her reaction and felt the crusty feeling of embarrassment enveloping him. There was no reason to be embarrassed, but of course, he was, as most anyone would be. How was he going to take care of his family? He would be less than a man he thought if he couldn't take care of the basic need of his loving wife and son.

Her fork went halfway to her mouth and then was on its way back to her plate with the mashed potatoes and steak still attached to it. He avoided her gaze. She was silent. Cedric hated the silence because he wanted to know what she was thinking.

As she watched her from the corner of his eye, the clicking sound of the knives and forks seemed like hammering cymbals. It lasted only seconds, but those seconds seemed like eternity.

She raised her head and looked at him. "What happened?" she asked softly.

He took a deep breath and began, "They had to lay off a few workers because of some undisclosed problem at the plant." He breathed.

"Oh, that's terrible!" she exclaimed. "Well," she continued after a brief pause, "I know that it's disappointing news, but try not to worry about it. You'll find another job soon enough."

He looked up from his teacup to see the expression on her face. The worry machine had just told him not to worry.

"I've been thinking," she said in an almost-cheery tone. "We spend too much of our time worrying about things when we should try to enjoy every moment of our lives. Things will always work themselves out."

A sigh of relief escaped his lips. He felt relieved. She'd changed. Normally, she would have cried and fretted and asked him over and over what they were going to do, but Estelle was very optimistic today. Will she be like this tomorrow? he wondered.

His taste buds finally acknowledged the delicious meal. They chatted and made plans about their future. "Things are going to work out," he said with great relief.

*****

The next day, he drove to town. *Milolta County Department of Social Services* read the huge sign on the front of the welfare building. Cedric felt like a lowlife. He was ashamed. He'd really wanted to be the one to bring BJ to his pediatric appointment while Estelle applied for welfare, but she insisted on bringing him because, according to her, he never remembered what the doctor said and he never asked any questions.

The waiting room was no less crowded than he had imagined. He looked around, and to his relief, there were no familiar faces. He'd never set foot in a welfare office before today. He felt horrible. They took his fingerprint and his picture, and it made him feel like a criminal.

"It's just to make sure that clients aren't getting benefits elsewhere," the clerk told him. It only made him feel worse.

"I wouldn't commit a welfare fraud," he defended.

"It doesn't matter. Everyone has to be finger-imaged." He must not usher his son into such defame. Cedric hoped he would find a job before the eligibility appointment.

After spending almost half the morning going through the welfare ritual, he finally left with a handful of papers. He had no intention of returning for the eligibility interview; he would leave that up to Estelle. Already he had done more than he'd wanted.

He thought about his unfulfilled ideas or dreams and came to the conclusion that everyone had them. But whatever the case might be, with a wife and a son, he had no time to be an airhead. No way was he a space cadet, and he had no intention of initiating such a trauma to pass on to his son.

He must be manly—rough, ready, and prepared for the future. He wasn't born in a wealthy family, so he knew that he had to push, pull, and drag to make a good future for them.

There were the T-ball games, the baseball games, soccer, basketball, and the whatevers, he thought. BJ would probably prefer to play basketball, judging from Cedric's love of the game. *They say the apple doesn't fall far from the tree, or he's just a chip off the old block,* he mused.

Whatever he had to do, he would do in order to make sure their future would be comfortable. Being a recipient on the county's welfare program wasn't a very good start into a bright future. He swallowed hard, having trouble believing he'd just come from the welfare office. *I have to make a move for the better,* he resolved.

*****

Mrs. Dunns, one of Estelle's neighbors, stood in the living room with a brown paper bag in her hand, then set the bag on the table. Estelle opened it and took out the four sweet potato pies that she'd made for them.

"Oh, Mrs. Dunns, thank you!" she exclaimed, pulling a white sheet of paper from the bottom of the bag.

"I thought you would love to have that," said Mrs. Dunns as Estelle read the recipe out loud.

"I'll give it a try, but I don't think I can make them as good as you," she said with a grin.

"I wish I could do more, but that's all I can do. I sure wish you didn't have to go."

"We wish so, too, but that's the best thing to do right now," explained Cedric. "It's hard for me to find employment here," he continued, "and the job offer that I have in the South is too good to give up. It's a great opportunity, and we must take it."

"I'm going to miss you terribly," sighed Mrs. Dunns.

"We'll miss you too. We'll keep in touch," Estelle promised as she picked up her son and cuddled him a bit. BJ smiled as she planted a kiss on his soft, chubby cheek.

Estelle walked through the house and checked all the rooms to make sure that they'd cleared out all their belongings. It was empty, as empty as it was the first day they had walked its hallways.

She stepped out the door and stood on the lawn of the house they'd called their own. She bit down on her lip as she tried to hold back the tears. Milolta had been home all her life.

She feared the unknown. She'd never been to the South. She had no idea what lay ahead, but she knew that they had to take the chance.

She reminisced on the great memories that they'd shared in the house. It was the first thing that they'd made a decision on, together, as a couple.

"Let's go, Estelle." Cedric was impatient and fighting his own brand of heartache at leaving.

"I'll be right there," she said as she took one last look at the house.

She walked stiffly to the car and sat down next to her husband. She stared him in the eye without saying a word.

Neither spoke until Cedric finally broke the silence. "I know." That was all he said, then he drove away. Estelle reached over and caressed her son's cheek, contented he was with his pacifier. A year ago last Tuesday, she brought him into the world in the house that now got smaller and smaller in the rearview mirror, headed as they were for a new life in the South.

Estelle didn't say much, but several questions were foremost. Were they doing the right thing? How did her husband really feel about the move? Had he expressed exactly how he felt, or was he trying to simply keep her from worrying?

His freshly cut hair and white shirt gave his face an angelic glow. He looked even more handsome than ever. She glanced at his big strong hand that held the steering wheel. He rested his left elbow on the door and cupped his chin with his hand. His relaxed shoulders pressed back into the seat.

"Cedric," she said softly. He gave a quick glance in her direction.

"Yeah."

"What if things don't work out? Would you choose to come back?"

"Just take one day at a time," he replied as he kept his focus on the road. "We'll see. We can't make decisions today for the future." Then he added, "At least not like that."

BJ sneezed. Estelle smiled. "Is that for good luck, pumpkin?" she said in a stronger tone. Maybe that was a sign, she told herself, that everything was going to be all right, so taking one day at a time wasn't a bad idea after all.

*****

Nineteen hours later, Cedric pulled up in front of his uncle's house. "Well, here we are."

"Finally," said Estelle. "Flying would have been less tedious, but it's not bad," she said as she stared at Uncle Cornelius's house.

Cedric assured her, "There's plenty of room for us until we find a place of our own. We'll be just fine."

Agreeing, Estelle said, "And if things don't work out as we hope, we'll just work out our problems and survive."

*****

Estelle gently rubbed the spot on BJ's thigh where he had gotten his vaccination. It was a hard lump, and the pain reliever she'd given hadn't seemed to help because he'd been crying for what seemed like hours. Naturally, she was frustrated. Her baby was in agony, and she couldn't do anything to relieve him of distress.

Cedric insisted she call his pediatrician, and Estelle finally agreed.

On the phone, the doctor urged her to bring the little boy into urgent care. After examining him, Dr. Penn admitted BJ into Children's Hospital. It ached Estelle to see her son lying in a hospital bed with tubes attached to his little body, but it had to be done.

She squinted her eyes to ease the burning sensation from her lack of rest. She'd spent endless days at his side, watching his every moment.

Dr. Penn walked in while she was caressing his feet. He shook his head and explained to her that BJ needed a blood transfusion as soon as possible. His vaccinated area had gotten infected, and the infection had traveled into his blood. "We can't make any promises, but we're doing all that we can," he tried to assure her.

Estelle felt numb because to her the news seemed so much worse than she had expected. Not her BJ. She couldn't lose him. She knew she just couldn't.

Her mind reeled the thought over and over that her beloved BJ could die. The thought of him dead erupted a sudden bad feeling in her stomach.

"To lose one child is horrible, but to lose another, after we've bonded with him, is dreadful!" she complained to her husband.

She stared at her son. She wanted to hold him but couldn't. She placed her middle and index fingers on her lips, then placed them on his.

Cedric reached for her hand as they walked out the door. BJ was alone, and she hated it but didn't argue with her husband when he firmly told her that they needed to leave and freshen up.

Estelle finally sat down to write Mrs. Dunns a short letter, but as suddenly as she'd thought about it, she changed her mind.

"I'll do it another time," she muttered to herself and rose to her feet. She took a peek into BJ's unoccupied room, and a shot of pain ran through her heart. She hurriedly closed the door and, in despair, slowly walked to her room, her head hanging in torment.

*****

Mrs. Dunns pulled out a letter from her mailbox. She'd finally gotten a letter from Estelle. She held it tight, as if the wind might snatch it away from her. It was her first time hearing from her since they'd left. She cast a glance over at the For Sale sign on their two-bedroom raised ranch. It was partially covered with snow.

She read the letter wide-eyed and frowned. "Oh, BJ, dearest BJ, how sad!" Her voice quivered in sorrow. Tears welled up in her eyes. She brushed her eyes clear and walked toward the house as she shoved the letter in her pocket.

Jiggy ran to meet her and licked her legs. She patted him on the head, and they walked to the porch together. She sat in her favorite chair and rocked the hours away.

*****

As the years passed, on occasion Estelle would pop into her mind and she'd think and wonder for a long while about how she was getting on with her life. She had replied to Estelle's one letter but hadn't heard from her since.

Estelle would always be the daughter she never had because she'd felt a connection with Estelle and treated her as if she were her very own. Often she thought, *I hope all is well, Estelle. I pray to God it is.*

Chapter 2

A Brush with the Past

Life is a cycle, Mrs. Dunns told herself, a never-ending story. We wake up, do our routine, go back to bed, sleep again, wake up again, and so the routine goes on. Even in the change of nature's seasons, mankind's routine changes not as we experience the different seasons of our lives. Life simply goes on, unhindered, pleaded with, but immovable. In the summer of our lives, all seems to be going well—new job, new addition to the family, or whatever it is that makes one glow with happiness and fulfillment. But then comes the fall, and the green leaves turn to brown and eventually fall from the tree, where everything seems to go wrong. Bad luck and mishaps become our companions, and our spirit falls into a state of gloom. The winter seems the ultimate, though, as if our lives are in ruins and we're at an impassable dead end. Nothing seems to go right, but then one day, new hope, a resurrection of the dead—spring has sprung. Spring leads to a new beginning and brings us right into the summer of our lives all over again. And so the cycle goes on.

"Ah, the smell of Pine-Sol," she said out loud. "A distinctive, wordless statement—the bathroom has been freshly cleaned, and there are no abiding germs."

It was a small bathroom in a two-bedroom house on the odd side of a quiet street. Mrs. Dunns's blue-water toilet, shiny tub, and shiny face bowl were the last of her morning chores. She picked up her big white beads strung by a white cord and her big colorful butterfly earrings that rested in a box of jewelry by the faucet.

She set out to tackle the day with whatever came her way. She stared at her reflection in the mirror. She hated the blue rings around her iris, but she didn't let it bother her too much since there was nothing she could do about it. She placed the beads around her neck and snapped on her earrings.

You look as good as you feel, she told herself with purpose, *and today, I feel pretty good.* She reached for her flowered dress, which she'd hung behind the bathroom door, and slipped it over her head. She picked her hair with her fingers and gave herself one last look in the mirror before she walked out of the bathroom.

Her deep-blue eyes peered out her bedroom window with curiosity. She watched a woman go from house to house, speaking only for a moment to the person who appeared at the door. Obviously, she was intently inquiring about something.

Mrs. Dunns hurried downstairs and out onto the porch, where she casually sat in her wicker chair and waited for the woman to approach her. She opened up the daily newspaper and pretended to be engrossed in it.

She raised her brow every now and then and peered over the newspaper to see how close the stranger was to her house.

She became even more engrossed in the newspaper when the lady knocked at the house right next door. Glancing over her glasses, she was just in time to see Mr. Willis shaking his head. The disappointed woman walked away with droopy shoulders.

"Excuse me, please," the feminine voice said, floating over the air. Mrs. Dunns acted startled and rose to her feet and greeted the woman with as friendly a smile as she could muster. "I'm sorry to disturb you, but I'm looking for a couple," she began with a hint of frustration. "I don't know how long you've been living here, but did you know Estelle and Cedric, who lived at number 15?" She pointed at the gray-and-white house that was five houses away.

"I've been living here for twenty-three years. I might be able to help you, miss, ah…?"

"Oh, Mrs. Applegate. I'm sorry," she said, apologizing.

Mrs. Dunns paused as she folded her newspaper and set it in her chair. "What were the names again?" she asked, as if her mind had just emptied out everything that it had received that morning.

"Estelle and Cedric."

She smiled broadly. "Oh, yes, I do remember them, indeed. They were a fine couple. They had a beautiful baby boy."

Mrs. Applegate's face brightened to a glimmer of hope. Her trip might not be futile after all. "They moved many years ago," she continued.

"Do you know where they've moved to?" she asked anxiously.

Mrs. Dunns squinted her eyes. "No, I don't. I mean, I don't remember," she added quickly.

The woman's shoulders dropped again in disappointment. *No hope*, she thought, *of ever finding Estelle.*

"Let me see." Mrs. Dunns's voice interrupted her thoughts. "I did get a letter once from her after she'd moved south. Yeah, the South," she repeated, as if to convince herself.

"The South?" echoed Mrs. Applegate.

"Yes. Things got hard. They lost the house. They had to move. Cedric's new job at the mattress company was going well." She spoke fluently, as if a wave of memory flooded her.

"Do you still have the letter?" she asked desperately.

"Ah, no, I'm sorry, I don't." Mrs. Dunns sighed. "Are you a relative?" Mrs. Dunns asked abruptly.

"No," she answered softly. "I have some very important information for her, though. I really do need to find her." She paused and took a deep breath. "Do you know what state she moved to?"

"I'm afraid I don't." Mrs. Dunns looked at her with compassion. "I'm sorry, but I wish I could be of further help."

"Do you think there is a chance that you might hear from her again?" Mrs. Applegate's eyes stared sharply into Mrs. Dunns.

"I haven't heard from her in many years, but you never know. I can see the urgency in your eyes. I hope chance will have her contact me. I'd certainly let her know that you were looking for her."

Mrs. Applegate jotted her name and telephone number on a sheet of paper and handed it to Mrs. Dunns. "Thank you for trying," she said warmly. She turned to leave, but then a thought struck her. "Would you be so kind as to give her a specific message for me if fate has it that you come in contact with her again?"

"I'd love to," she replied cheerily.

Maybe a twist of fate would bring her in the presence of Estelle. Mrs. Applegate earnestly hoped for that. Only time would tell if they'd ever cross each other's path again.

As Mrs. Applegate drove away from the quiet residential neighborhood, Mrs. Dunns stared at her departure in anguish. She must find Estelle even if she had to tear her attic down to find that letter. She hurried into the house and began her search for Estelle's old mail.

Halfway through her search, the telephone rang. It was Hattie. "Grandma, don't forget my recital. It's in an hour. Don't be late, Grandma, or you'll miss it."

She did forget. Her visitor had taken every ounce of her attention, but she must divert and pick up *the Estelle matter* later, but even at the recital her mind stayed engrossed on Estelle and Mrs. Applegate until Hattie and her ballet team walked onto the stage.

"That's my granddaughter," she said to the woman at her right as she pointed at the curly-haired twelve-year-old brunette. "Isn't she just a doll? And she dances just as pretty as she looks."

Her son tapped her on the arm and whispered, "Mom, please don't disturb your neighbor."

Hattie and the girls sat poised as they waited for the music. *What strength in their toes,* Mrs. Dunns mused as some of the dancers stood on their tiptoes with arms outstretched and head and body held rigid.

The music started softly, and they glided across the floor in a smooth, rhythmic fashion. As the music rose in sound and pitch, the gracefully balanced movements flowed as they gestured with their head, hands, toes, and entire body. At the crescendo of the music, their bodies increased in virtuosity and the recital ended in an explosion of ecstasy.

"Bravo. Bravo!" shouted Mrs. Dunns. Hattie looked at her family with pride. It was an enjoyable evening for Mrs. Dunns, but all the while she couldn't keep her mind off Estelle. As time passed, she longed for fate to bring Estelle back into her life. She hoped fervently that the good Lord above would just send Estelle her way again so that she could relay Mrs. Applegate's message. She moaned as she rocked herself in her chair and looked deep into her mind's eye at what Estelle's face might look like after hearing the message. She prayed the Lord would intervene.

*****

Hattie and her father came to visit Grandma Dunns. "Why, hello, Dr. Dunns. Making house calls today?" Mrs. Dunns greeted her son.

"Hello, Mother," he said as he planted a kiss on her cheek.

She turned to her granddaughter and asked, "And where are your siblings?"

"They're both out with Mommy," replied Hattie.

"We've come to get you, Mother. We're taking you out."

"Out?" she asked, as if it were a foreign word.

"Yep, out."

"And what did you have in mind to do with me?"

"You'll see, Grandma. Just come with us and you'll see."

"With a look like that, I cannot debate," she said.

Fabian Dunns and his daughter Hattie took Grandma Dunns to Milolta Center Square and brought her into almost every shoe store and department store. She picked out hats and shoes to match and a new handbag. Hattie was the fashion queen. If Hattie liked it, Fabian bought it.

"I haven't had this much fun shopping since I was a teenager," she said, beaming. "Oh, son, thank you for such a beautiful day. And you, Hattie, such taste for a twelve-year-old. Why, you're beyond your years."

"I know," she said bluntly. "But try not to wait so long to get new clothes, Grandma. You've got to keep up with the fashion world."

Mrs. Dunns felt a warm tingle in her stomach. It was a change of pace for her. It was a nice and thoughtful thing for her son and granddaughter to do to break up the routine of her day. The last time she went shopping was five years ago. She had no need to shop because she took great care of her clothes, but just to get out and get something new, she'd forgotten what it felt like, and now she knew that she'd been missing out on one of the joys of being a woman.

*****

Mrs. Dunns called Stella on the telephone and told her about her pleasant day. "What did you do today, Stella?"

"James and I went out to Country Style Buffet for lunch. The food was really good."

"We should go out sometime, Margaret."

"You're right, Stella. I think I need to get out of the house more often. Being out actually uplifted my spirit."

Stella and Mrs. Dunns laughed and thanked God for how their day had gone. Later on that evening, Mrs. Dunns invited her over for tea.

Margaret Dunns sipped her decaffeinated herbal tea while enjoying Stella Levine's company. "I'm glad you came to visit, Stella."

Mrs. Dunns clasped the green teacup in her soft hands and stared deep into it and looked back at something that caused her wrinkles to soften.

The eye, the appendage of sight that has entitled mankind to obtain many of his sense impressions, is far more brilliant than the finest camera, by which tool mankind has used to mimic its radiance but cannot supplant.

From the top of the tea where the steam rose, Mrs. Dunns looked past the steaming liquid into her mind's eye and summoned her recollection.

A smile lingered as she stared deep into the cup. "April 5 has always been a special day for me." Without shifting her gaze from the cup or even blinking, she asked, "You know why, Stella?"

Stella looked over at her with anticipation. She sensed that Mrs. Dunns, a woman that was older than her by just a few years, had something intriguing to share. "No, Margaret, but I'm sure you're about to tell me, right?"

Mrs. Dunns looked up at her, and with a glow in her eyes, she said, "Silhouette." Without hesitation, she rolled on. "April 5 marked the night of a new beginning for me." By now her teeth were exposed and her face had broadened by her flush smile. Her pearly white teeth were closely arranged, and they were all hers. She stared back into the cup as if she were reading a line to a play from inside the cup.

"I was in my early twenties, twenty-one to be exact, and still living with my mother at that time and working at a fast-food place while also taking a few night classes at the local college."

"I never went to college. I never wanted to," Stella broke in, but Mrs. Dunns went on as if Stella hadn't spoken.

"I had worked a few extra hours and was going home, well, kind of." She paused for a moment. "It was about ten thirty, actually. When I got to the porch of our house, I heard footsteps running just beyond the gate of our backyard." She suddenly looked at Stella as if to check the status of her attention. Stella stared back at her, her eyes compelling her to go on.

"Our backyard, you see, was adjacent to a little slope that led to the baseball field. It was a beautiful open space. I must say, the caretakers kept the grass well greened."

"Anyway," she continued, her face taking on a new glow, "I walked quietly to the back of the house and peered toward the baseball field, and there it was, the silhouette of a man running around the small field. I watched him run and then slow to a stride. What really intrigued me were his long graceful strides. I quickly glanced behind to see if anyone was watching, then opened the gate and took a few steps."

She looked over at Stella again, and Stella smiled at her. "Go on," she urged.

"You're a good listener, Stella," she said with grateful eyes.

"That's my middle name. Stella The-Good-Listener Levine." She laughed. "Now, please go on. Weren't you afraid that he might see you and hurt you?"

"Oh, I wasn't the least bit afraid. I don't know why, but I was really curious. I wanted to know who this handsome man was."

"A handsome silhouette? How did you even know it was a man?"

"I just knew." She took a sip of her now-warm tea. "He walked around the field several times, and I just stood and watched. Finally, I walked over to the field and spoke to him. 'Gorgeous night, isn't it?' He stopped abruptly. He hadn't noticed I was there. 'Indeed, it is,' he replied. 'Won't you come and join me?' I didn't hesitate. I dropped my bag, and off I went, taking long strides right alongside him."

"You mean to tell me that a total stranger wanted you to walk around a baseball field with him in the middle of the night and you agreed? Pretty daring, wouldn't you say?"

"Well, I guess, but I didn't care. Anyway, as I strode around the field, and as we conversed, you know, saying our names, our hobbies, and so on, all the while I couldn't help but marvel at his handsomeness.

"'How old are you?' he asked.

"'Twenty-one,' I replied, and then to even the score, I asked him how old he was, and he answered, 'Ah…twenty-one and a half.'

"I was surprised when he told me his age, as I had thought he was much older, so I stopped in my tracks while he kept on going. Then he called back, 'Something wrong?'

"'No.' I laughed and ran to catch up. 'It is just that you acted much older,' I said.

"'Well, I'm older, aren't I?' he replied.

"'Well, yeah,' I reluctantly admitted.

"Mel stopped, and we sat on the bleacher and talked. We exchanged phone numbers and, almost a year later, got married. We had many wonderful years together. But who said life was fair? My silhouette man was taken away from me the day before our wedding anniversary. Just like that, he died. A healthy man went off to sleep and never woke up." She sniffled. Stella sniffled and wiped away a tear that escaped her eye.

"But it's okay, though, Stella. As they say, better to have loved and lost than not to have loved at all." Stella nodded and gave Mrs. Dunns a warm, very brave smile.

Stella Levine didn't mind listening to a good story, whether true or made-up. She was physically and mentally strong and credited her good health to her mother's rich teaching and home remedies. She was convinced home remedies did the trick.

"Well, Margaret, it's getting late, and we've got to go to church tomorrow. We have a lot to be thankful for, don't we?"

"Yes, indeed," agreed Mrs. Dunns.

*****

Estelle stood between the kitchen and living room. Eighteen years ago, she stood in that very spot, immobilized by intensive contraction.

She took a deep breath and let it out slowly, as if she wanted to relive the moment captured by memory. She felt goose bumps all over her body as she reminisced about the memories of the past. She'd never thought that she would be able to see the inside of their first home again.

Estelle treaded the floor of every corner of the house and brought to life the memories of the experiences that she'd had while living there. There were good ones as well as bad ones. She and her husband had made many changes within and without after they'd settled down.

Estelle looked at the couple standing in front of her and smiled. "Thank you," she said over and over. They didn't have to allow her into their home, but they did.

A mixture of happiness and sadness was in the air. She shed no tears, however. She was strong. She cherished the memories of the past, but nothing, she knew, lasted forever.

She was optimistic, always living as if the glass was half-full. She saw the good and not the bad. Among the thorns and thistles in the valley was the sweet smell of roses and other flowers that lifted otherwise-hanging spirits.

It was a way of healing. As she stood in the house that brought back so many memories, Estelle couldn't help but let her spirit go in the bliss of the reunion. A huge part of the void in her life had been filled. She was glad that she'd gotten to see it again.

She walked out feeling like someone who'd left a mind-healing psychiatric session. She felt free. She walked away this time accepting the fact that everything was okay.

Cedric had always told her that everything was going to be all right, and he was right. No matter what it is a person goes through in his life, it is only a test. It is just a test to strengthen the weak and make them into a mighty warrior.

"Oh, Cedric," she groaned. "If only you were here. Why did you have to go?" She managed a smile. *Death is no respecter of persons, occupation, age, or humility,* she silently told herself. *If it's your time, it's just your time. But, Cedric, my love, one day we'll be together again, in heaven.*

Cedric had had a heart attack that gave him no chance to fight. Death, the ultimate weapon in this life, will not hesitate for any race, creed, or national origin.

She took another look at the house. "I feel so attached to this place," she muttered. She looked to her left at the house of the only true friend she'd known.

"Mrs. Dunns," she whispered to herself. "I wonder if she's still living there."

As fate might direct every step, Estelle headed toward the old familiar mint-green house. She opened the gate and walked on the pathway that led to the front door.

She rang the doorbell, and a frail woman in a flowered housedress appeared. Although it had been seventeen years since she'd last seen Mrs. Dunns, she knew that it wasn't her standing at the entrance of the door.

"Yes?" said the woman in a shaky voice.

"I'm sorry, I was looking for Mrs. Dunns. My name is Estelle."

The lady looked at her. Her head shook slightly from an obvious affliction with the Parkinson's disease.

"She's dying. She's in Mercy House. They told us she wouldn't live more than a month." She paused, then added, "I'm her sister, Ruth." Estelle reached for her outstretched hand and shook it gently. "Nice to meet you."

"Would I be able to see her?"

"I think so."

Estelle didn't want to put off any opportunity to see her if she might die. When times had gotten hard, Mrs. Dunns had been a strong support emotionally and every other way. She'd even given them food when there was nothing in their food pantry.

Estelle hung her head in empathy and walked away. "Thank you," she called without looking back. She cleared her throat and walked stiffly to the car with one thought in mind.

*****

As Estelle sat by the side of the bed in the tiny hospital room, she stared down at Mrs. Dunns's frail figure. She lay motionless. Her body was almost as flat as the bed she lay upon. Country music played softly from a tiny pocket radio that sat on a table inches from her head.

The room was hot, almost suffocating, Estelle though to herself. Four little pots of flowers lined the windowsill of the only window in the room.

She pulled her arms out of her blazer and wiped her forehead with the back of her hand.

Mrs. Dunns looked as though she was in a deep sleep.

"Mrs. Dunns," she whispered in her ear. Mrs. Dunns slowly turned her head to the side.

"Can she hear me?" Estelle asked the nurse, who was busy putting in fresh linens in a cabinet.

"Oh, yes, she can hear you. Just give her a few moments to respond."

She waited. She placed one hand on her forehead and gently stroke her cold, feeble hands with the other.

"Mrs. Dunns, it's me, Estelle."

"Estelle?" she said, whispering and motioning with her hands.

"What does that mean?" Estelle asked the nurse.

"She wants the bed raised." The nurse raised it just a bit to put her in an almost-sitting position.

"This is Estelle, Cedric's wife. I was your neighbor at 15 Sherwood Terrace."

"Estelle?" she said again faintly.

An almost-invisible smile changed the contour of her face. She opened her eyes slowly and searched the room for her visitor. Estelle gently guided her head toward her. Mrs. Dunns looked her in the face and smiled faintly and squinted her eyes.

Estelle roamed the room with her eyes for a pair of prescription glasses. She leaned over and picked them up from the little table at the foot of the bed and gently placed them over her eyes.

"I just had to see you. You'd been so good to me. When I heard that you were in the hospital, I just had to come and see you."

Mrs. Dunns gasped. "Estelle," she whispered, as if it had just dawned on her who her visitor was. Her face took on a new look. Her eyes softened and became watery. A look of pity covered her face as she stared into Estelle's face. She raised a finger. "Someone…" She paused to rest. Estelle sat upright and waited for her to go on. "Is looking for you." Estelle frowned in surprise. Mrs. Dunns's speech was slurred as she tried to communicate with Estelle. Estelle had difficulty piecing the sentences together. She finally came to the understanding that someone had tried to contact her. She couldn't figure out who it could have been. She didn't know anyone by the names Mrs. Dunns had spoken.

"Apple," she finally added.

"Mrs. Applegate?" asked Estelle. The name seemed to have fallen off her tongue subconsciously. Mrs. Dunns nodded.

"Important information for you," she said softly. It had been years since Estelle had last seen Mrs. Applegate. She couldn't imagine what important information would cause her to come looking for her after all those years.

Mrs. Dunns was sick, she thought. Dying, for that matter. Maybe she'd exaggerated the importance of Mrs. Applegate's visit, or perhaps it had been nothing more than an illusion. Estelle doubted the credibility of the information that she gave her based on what she saw here.

"When was she looking for me and why?" Estelle managed to say.

With difficulty, Mrs. Dunns tried to relate to Estelle the information that Mrs. Applegate had given her. She'd grown tired, and communicating was even more difficult.

"She had something important to tell you." Her chest heaved. She tried to roll to her side. Estelle helped her.

"Important information..." She shuffled. "It's very important to you, she said. It's about..." She gasped for air. It's..."

Mrs. Dunns lay still. Estelle touched her gently. She gasped again for air. The old woman opened her mouth and moved her lips in slow motion, but there was no sound.

"Nurse!" Estelle yelled. Mrs. Dunns didn't look at all well. The nurse hurried in from the urgency in Estelle's voice.

"I don't think she's breathing." The nurse checked her pulse. There was none. "She's gone," she said without hesitation.

"Gone?" Estelle said, as if she didn't understand the nurse's words. *How could she have died so soon? I just got here,* she only said to herself.

It didn't seem right. The cold hands of death snatched Mrs. Dunns from earth to heaven in an instant, thought Estelle as she rose from her chair. The room was no longer hot. A chill ran up her spine, and she reached for her blazer and threw it over her shoulders. The color of the room seemed to have suddenly changed from a soft baby blue with burgundy wallpaper to a muddy gray-black color of no consequence.

Something smelled awful all of a sudden. She hadn't noticed before the horrible smell that oozed from the room. Had that smell been there all along and had gone unnoticed, or did the smell of death permeate the room as the death angel came and snatched Mrs. Dunns away?

The death angel! If he was there, then perhaps he might be unsatisfied and was looking for someone else to take. She hurried out of the room. Her head spun. She wanted out of the building and away from the hospital.

"Are you all right?" she heard a voice ask from behind. There was no telling how long ago the voice had spoken, but she'd just heard it. It sounded like the deep, slow talking sound from a tape player whose batteries were running low.

She nodded and staggered a bit to the elevator.

As she walked out of the building, she couldn't help but wonder about Mrs. Dunns's information. Was it credible? Was her thinking clear when she had received it?

Her information might have been credible, because Estelle did know a Mrs. Applegate. What important information did she give to her? Did she leave an address or even a telephone number with her?

Mrs. Dunns never got the chance to tell Estelle about the information from Mrs. Applegate, and Estelle had no idea how to get in touch with her. She had a sunken feeling in her stomach.

She was curious, and it was getting the best of her.

*****

Night and day she thought about the last few moments with Mrs. Dunns. What type of information was it, and how could she find out?

As months went by, the curiosity of Mrs. Applegate's visit to Mrs. Dunns seemed to lessen in importance. Estelle continued to look forward to a brighter and better life. She tried her hardest to let go of the past and focus on her years ahead. To her the future could be just what she made it, and she smiled. "I'm gonna make it the best years of my life."

Even though her Cedric wasn't there anymore to share life with her, she was determined that nothing would hinder her happiness here on earth until the day she would meet her beloved Cedric in heaven.

As the years slipped by, the pain from the loss of her loved ones lessened. Their memory lived on in her mind, but not as a loss, but as a gain. Even though roses wither and die, to have had the opportunity to enjoy them while they lasted was better than not having them at all.

She knew that her precious roses were in heaven and someday she would be with them forever. Who knows, she thought, maybe it was God's will to spare them from the awful agony of living in this wretched world.

Chapter 3

An Unusual Event

Brendan walked out of the motor vehicle building with his eyes focused on his temporary license. It had expired just a few days earlier. The officer would have given him a ticket for driving with an expired license, but he'd decided to give him a break.

"Oh, I'm sorry," he said regretfully without looking up. He stooped to the ground and began picking up the contents of the man's wallet he'd knocked out of his hand.

"Never mind," the man said in an annoyed tone. Brendan's eyes landed on a picture that was behind the man's black shoe. It was partially covered by a yellow sticky pad. Before he could reach for it, the man made a sweep and scooped up the remainder of his wallet's contents off the ground and then snatched the rest out of Brendan's hands.

"I'm really sorry," he said, but the man kept his head straight. Brendan could have sworn that he knew the person in the picture. Who was he, and why would he have a picture of her? Maybe it was someone that looked like her, because, after all, the picture was partially hidden. *Who knows?* he thought.

He backed out of the parking space and proceeded to go home, but he couldn't shake the feeling that there was something about the man he'd bumped into.

"Since I have nothing better to do, I think I'll follow him and see where he lives. Let's see how well I can follow someone without being noticed," he said, challenging himself.

He drove to Park Avenue and waited. He sat in the driver's seat with his back pressed against the door and his feet stretched out across the passenger's seat. He watched the six-foot-two-tall stranger with curiosity as he moved stealthily out the front door of the county Department of Motor Vehicles.

The stranger tossed what appeared to be a small black leather bag on the passenger seat as he took one last glance in all direction. He glided around the steering wheel and took off smoothly on the freshly paved road.

Brendan snapped on his seat belt and pulled out hastily onto the rough, winter-beaten road.

"I must not lose him," he counseled himself as he glanced into his left rearview mirror. "That's not the attitude of a normal man. Why would he try to look all around him casually? I knew that there was something about him."

As his subject's wheels rolled north on the one-way street of Hudson Avenue, Brendan drove south hastily on Park Avenue's one-way road. He made a quick left onto River Street and another left onto Pius Avenue. In about two minutes, his subject would be at the intersection, at which he'd have three choices of direction.

He hustled, running a couple amber lights. He made another left turn on Juniper Street and headed toward the intersection where his subject would be, but as he made the turn and got to Bob's Mini Mart, his subject swooshed past him. Brendan turned quickly into the minimart and made a U-turn and proceeded to follow him.

He followed diligently. Every once in a while, he'd pull over to avoid being noticed. At last his subject turned off onto the dead end of Gwendale Road. Brendan stopped and stayed out of view before making the turn. He knew that he didn't have far to go, and there was only one way out.

He made the turn and spotted the car at the side of the road. He pulled into the family health-care center and watched him through his binoculars.

The man pulled off his sunglasses, a mustache, and a thin-layered mask that had changed his features completely.

"Ah!" Brendan said in disbelief. The man carefully put his disguise into his combination briefcase and snapped it shut. He rubbed his face, straightened his tie, and made a U-turn.

"No way!" he breathed out in shock. "I can't believe that man is her father! I knew it! I knew it! My hunches were right. I knew there was something about him. I knew that was her picture behind his heel. He's in some kind of fishy business," he said convincingly. "There's just no way he could be doing all this and is not doing something wrong. Just what was he doing at the Department of Motor Vehicles with a disguise on?"

Brendan grunted out loud. "He seems like a saint, but he is as subtle as a snake. I knew there was something about him, but who would have known that he was the one I was following? What a coincidence!" *I've got to find out what he's up to,* he thought.

Brendan proceeded to follow him again, and this time he went home. Brendan sat in his car and waited. He watched him as he got out of the car and entered the house with the black bag and briefcase.

"I've got to find out what he's up to, even if it kills me," he vowed. Brendan told no one. Before he went spilling the beans, he had to be sure his hunches were right. He knew that if he suspected being watched, he'd make sure he covered all his bases.

*****

A few days had passed since his last discoveries, and Brendan worked feverishly to find out something, anything.

He ascended the stairs to Saint Paul's study (a name Brendan secretly called him because he acted so righteous). He was out of town, and Brendan sprang at the opportunity of searching his study.

He'd always gone to his house because of the close relationship he had with his daughter. Brendan was like a family member. After finding out what he did, he'd wanted to be able to search the house without appearing suspicious.

His daughter had gone to the basement to load the washing machine, and Brendan wasted no time jumping to the task. He must work fast, and he knew it. If she caught him in her father's study, she wouldn't think much of it, though. She would believe that her father had left the study unlocked by accident and she would just warn him of her father's intense privacy about his study. Regardless of how she'd react, he must not be seen in it.

It wasn't hard to pick the lock. He opened it in seconds. The desk drawers were locked. He wasn't surprised. He didn't know what he was looking for, but his mind was open. He searched carefully but thoroughly as he tried to leave things undisturbed. He didn't see anything out of the ordinary, so he gave one last quick search, but then his hand knocked over a stack of disks. They sat in a little case behind the computer. There were six of them with different-color tabs. He snatched them up, put them in his pocket, turned the knob on the lock, walked out, and shut the door quietly.

"Oh, gosh, I hate to do this, but I've got to go," he apologized to her. "There's something I've got to do."

"So soon? But you just got here."

"I know. I know. I'll make it up to you. Maybe later I'll come see you, but now I've got to go."

Anxious to see what was on the disks, he headed straight home, where immediately he inserted the disks into his computer. *Enter password.* Password? he thought. He slid them in one at a time, and all six needed a password clearance. He was at a dead end; disappointment was putting it mildly. He tried for hours to unlock the password but wasn't successful. He didn't know how he was going to get into the disks, and he had no intention of returning them.

*****

In a couple of days, he was back in the study. This time he was there alone. He had to find the password to the disks, and he believed that they had to be somewhere in the study.

I would make a good detective, he thought as he picked up a coin and studied it. There was no apparent significance, per object on the coin, and he turned it over for what seemed the hundredth time in his hand. He had picked it up from the right-hand corner of the middle drawer, the only drawer that was unlocked. *Strange, since a few days ago it had been locked.*

His study was locked, his computer locked by security code because you couldn't log on, and the desk drawers were locked as well. To top it off, he also locked up all his disks with a password. *And you tell me a man with such caution has nothing to hide?* he asked himself.

He looked at the coin and frowned. He'd never seen one like it before. He studied it carefully and contemplated putting it in his pocket.

"Nah," he muttered. "This shouldn't be too hard to sketch." He thought about the disks that he'd taken. He had dinner with his daughter yesterday, and she hadn't mentioned anything about her father searching for any missing disks. He'd walked in while they were eating and had joined them for dinner. All three of them enjoyed a sumptuous meal, and nothing about missing disks was even remotely brought up. *Possibly, he hasn't missed them yet,* he thought.

He heard the rumbling of a car engine. His heart skipped a beat, and he froze in the middle of the floor. He sighed in relief as the sound faded in the distance.

A coin shop should be able to let me know what it's used for, he thought. Maybe it didn't have any significance, but it wouldn't hurt to find out. If the coin was valuable in any way, he knew it would be easy to come back and retrieve it.

He placed the coin back in the drawer, in the same spot where it had been, and walked out.

He had a hunch that the coin had some kind of connection with the disks that he had stolen. He also knew, if he could open the disks, he could put the pieces together and uncover some deep secrets. But the passwords to the six disks prevented any unauthorized opening. How to bypass the password was now the order of business.

He closed the door and casually walked out. He had a lot of investigative uncovering to do, and his mind whirled with anxiety.

As he drove to the coin shop, his mind focused on the password issue. He jotted down a few numbers and letters and hoped he was at least somewhat close, though one digit off was the same as a mile off.

He pulled up into the parking lot of the only coin shop in town. A middle-aged man with sandy hair sat comfortably in a black leather chair behind the counter. When he heard the entrance bell, he peered over the glasses that clung to the tip of his nose.

Brendan pulled out the piece of paper and showed him the sketch. "Have you ever seen a coin like this?"

The man studied it, then shook his head. "I must say that I've never seen anything like it. I've been in this business for ten years, and I'm afraid I haven't the faintest idea. Very interesting, though," he added.

He handed the paper back to Brendan. "Unless it was custom made to unlock something," he called to him as Brendan walked out the door, "you're sure out of luck."

Brendan stopped abruptly. He smiled at the man. "Thank you. I think you've just helped me a great deal."

The floor safe, he thought to himself excitedly. "I've got to get back into the study," he said as he headed to his apartment.

*****

Saint Paul was the subtlest man he'd ever known. He posed as the perfect gentleman. He loved and cared for his family and seemed to be a valuable asset to society, but Brendan wondered how anyone could be so clever that even the people in his house could be so oblivious to his schemes.

The seemingly ordinary man might fool most everyone, but not Brendan, because he, Brendan Jerome Clark, was very observant and knew from the day he met him that there was something different about him. No matter what the price to pay, Brendan would find out what that *something* was.

He worked day and night, and with every spare moment, he committed himself to as much investigating as possible, no matter how small the lead.

Today something was about to take place, and Brendan wasn't going to miss it. He'd overheard him on the telephone, but Saint Paul didn't know that Brendan was within earshot. All Brendan heard in pieces were "Thatcher's Hill tonight."

He jumped at the opportunity and was there at the blink of an eye. As he waited, he scoped out the area keenly for anything that might be of significance. A rectangular metal object about two feet long sat partially hidden in the bushes. It stood upright on one end. A two-inch jagged-edged coin with the symbol of a red dragon was mysteriously welded at the other end of the metal. He picked up the metal and inspected it.

"I knew it!" he said with delight. It was almost identical to the coin he found in Saint Paul's study. The only difference was that there was no picture on the one in the study. He placed it back in its position and waited.

He was excited. He sat in a nearby patch of bushes and waited for some kind of action.

Suddenly, the sound of a helicopter came out of nowhere. Two great lights appeared out of the sky and headed toward his hideout. His heart pounded wildly in his chest.

He knew that something was going on, and he wanted to know what it was, but this wasn't the type of action he was looking for.

"What in the world?" It was coming right at him, and he didn't want to be spotted, but with those lights you could see a pin.

He wasn't about to let anything happen to himself. He had all intentions of protecting his well-being at all costs. Not that he was equipped with any deadly weapons, but he thought, Mother Nature had enough weapons he might borrow. He reached for two fist-size rocks and waited ill at ease.

It was too dark to see anything besides the bright lights that illuminated the skylines.

The helicopter landed in the clearing. Brendan raised his head to take a peek from behind the patch of bush where he'd been hiding. The lights went out, and the beam from a single flashlight came on almost instantly. Four figures dressed in full black alighted from the helicopter. The beam of the flashlight danced in the darkness. The light landed momentarily on the helicopter and revealed its Army colors.

The Army? One of the men pointed in the area of the metal object as if he'd spotted it in the light. Two of them disappeared into the patch of bushes next to the object.

It was too dark to see them clearly, but he knew they weren't up to anything good.

The two men returned to the helicopter hauling something that was apparently too heavy for one man to handle. He got a glimpse when the light momentarily landed on it. It looked like an oversize black chest.

The rambling of their whispering voices didn't give him any hint as to who they were and what they were doing.

They moved quickly. The helicopter lights came on, and they were off again. He thought about going over to the area and looking for some kind of clue, but he figured that he'd seen enough for one night. Daylight would be better anyways, he determined.

With quick steps, he moved toward his car, which was parked about two blocks away. It seemed as if his car had mysteriously moved farther away from where he'd parked it. He made long strides in its direction.

He was finally on his way home. It felt good. It was about 11:30 p.m. and dark, as the moon wasn't out yet. That worked in his favor because otherwise he could easily have been detected.

As he drove past the clearing where the helicopter had landed a few minutes ago, he stopped and cast his eyes in the direction of the bush where the men had retrieved the chest.

Suddenly, he heard the rev of a vehicle and a Jeep pulled up in front of him. Someone stuck his head out the window and shouted, "Let's get him!" Brendan stepped on the gas and swung the car around and sped away like lightning.

The mysterious Jeep took off behind him, hot on his trail.

The road was windy. Brendan drove recklessly in hopes of shaking his pursuers. The windy road was to his advantage, however, and he was able to get a good lead.

He pulled over into a shallow ditch that was off the dirt road and switched off his lights. With engine off and all lights out, Brendan waited breathlessly for the Jeep to pass. Within a few seconds, the jeep sped past the ditch. He didn't waste any time getting out and heading in the opposite direction of the jeep. Whoever they were, he was relieved that he was able to shake them off.

As he lay in bed and thought about the event that had just transpired, his mind recalled every intricate detail.

Did the rectangular metal have anything to do with those men in the helicopter? Was it an object to mark the spot? Who were those men that had chased him?

The coin that he saw in the drawer couldn't have been a coincident to the one on the rectangular object. They were unusual and almost identical.

He knew that the disks that he had had a lot to tell about this particular event. If only he could crack the password barrier.

It was pure luck that he'd found out that something was going to take place that night and in that particular area. What to make of the whole thing was a mystery to him. Curiosity was getting the best of him, and he would not rest until he found out.

*****

"Brendan!" gasped Jeannine Shrouder. "Mrs. Clark, help!" Jeannine dived into the pool and threw her arms around him. She raised his head above the water and dragged him to the edge of the pool. Mrs. Clark came running with the kitchen knife in her hand that she was using to dice green peppers and onions for her stew chicken.

"Jeannine, what's the matter?" she asked, panting.

"Brendan," she gasped. "He...I found him floating facedown in the pool!" she exclaimed in her Jamaican accent. Mrs. Clark dropped the knife and fell to her knees next to her son. Her body trembled with fear.

"Oh my god!"

Just as Jeannine was about to do mouth-to-mouth resuscitation, Brendan popped his eyes wide-open and hollered, "Gotcha!"

"Brendan Clark, you should be ashamed of yourself!" scolded his mother. "You scared me half to death!" she said in disgust and dropped his head.

"Ouch!" he moaned, giggling.

"I can't believe you did that! You are stupid! You're stupider than stupid. I'm soaking wet, and I've got an appointment in half an hour, and besides, you almost gave your mother a heart attack! You're disgusting, Brendan Clark. Next time, when you're really drowning, I'll hold you under with my foot!"

"Bren," said Mrs. Clark, "that was very irresponsible of you." She held her chest, retrieved the knife from the ground, and walked back to the house.

"I hate you," said Jeannine matter-of-factly.

"Oh, but it's impossible to hate me, right?" He laughed mischievously.

"I came over here to ask you if Mr. Pratt gave any homework assignment."

"Yep," he replied. She waited for him to go on.

"Well?" she said impatiently.

"Well what?"

"Well, what was it?" she almost yelled.

"Can't tell you."

Jeannine rolled her big brown eyes at him. "Can't or won't?"

"All of the above."

She took off her shoe to toss it at him.

"All right, all right," he caved in. "Read chapters 11–13 and do the problems at the end of each chapter."

"Can I borrow your notes, please?" she asked on a softer note.

"Only if I know that you're not mad at me."

She rolled her eyes at him again. "I'm not mad," she said, half-lying.

"How do I know that? I need a smile to prove it." She gave him a plastic smile to get him off her nerve. Brendan got out of the pool, and in a flash, he picked her up and tossed her in.

"I know that Jamaican people like wah-tah, mon," he said, mimicking her accent.

She laughed hysterically.

"See? No problem, mon," he said.

"Mrs. Clark, are you sure this is your son? You're too nice of a woman to have a mentally deranged child!" she said.

"Oh, I'm afraid he is, Jeannine," she called out the window. She recalled the day he was born. *He's just about all I've got left,* she thought. She stared at her only son and hoped that one day he would get married and give her a dozen grandchildren. She would like that very much.

Jeannine went straight home after she left Brendan. She changed out of her wet clothes and rescheduled her appointment. She sprawled her books on the sofa with a set purpose to study.

She blasted some reggae music. The windows vibrated at the sound. She flipped through the pages of her textbook.

Ben Shrouder strolled into the living room with one hand in his pocket and asked in a deep voice, "How can you study with so much noise?" His six-foot-two, well-built figure hovered over his daughter's petite body like a towering giant.

As the sunlight glared through the window, it exposed the definition of his well-chiseled face. His big brown eyes narrowed as he stared down at her with tenderness. His perfectly shaped lips curled into a smile, exposing his smooth white teeth. His firm, carved cheekbones were well-defined under his deep and smooth chocolate complexion. He raised his hand and ran it over his coarse hair. "You're amazing," he said.

"That's the best way to study, Daddy. Can't do it when it's too quiet." Her dark-brown eyes stared boldly into his, and her dimples flickered as she grinned up at him. He returned the smile and sat down next to her. He took her arm by his two fingers and declared, "A couple more pounds wouldn't hurt you, J. I can see right through your skin." He chuckled, and she looked at him with narrowed eyes.

"Oh, just teasing," he added quickly. "You're a-okay just the way you are."

The aroma from the kitchen traveled into the living room. Dinner was ready. Ackee and saltfish, dumplings, and yams with freshly made carrot juice were irresistible. Steaming sweet potato pies baked to perfection sat on the kitchen counter. What more was there to think about besides the food that Ida had prepared? Jeannine closed her books and headed for the kitchen, Ben trailing behind.

"I didn't realize how hungry I was until I smelled the food, Mama."

As they entered the kitchen, Ida uttered, "Is that the only time I can get you two into the kitchen, huh?" Her hazel eyes roamed back and forth from father to daughter. Her thin lips glistened from her strawberry lip gloss, her favorite. She smudged her forehead with a streak of flour from the back of her hand. Ben reached out and wiped the residue from her silky-soft caramel skin.

"Of course not, honey. I was in here earlier, getting a glass of water."

She reached out and patted him on the cheek. "I see," she responded and tossed him a wink. "We have to wait for Washburn and Casey. They'll be here in a few minutes."

Casey was the eldest of the Shrouder children. Next in line was Washburn, then Jeannine.

With the money Ben made at his computer-based job, the Shrouders were financially stable. Ben spent long hours in his study on the computer. Ida, on the other hand, would just cruise around the house after work and keep herself busy until bedtime.

Ida picked up the phone to call Casey, but she had already left. Jeannine set the table, and they waited for Casey and Washburn to arrive.

Ida had wanted to come to the United States because she wanted a change of pace in her life. The desire for different sceneries and just to be someplace else for a change drove she and her husband to migrate to America. It had been five years, and so far, even though the cultures were different, Ida and Ben were comfortable as could be expected.

The front door opened, and in walked Casey. Washburn arrived a few minutes later. The get-together was pleasant as could be as it wasn't every day that Ida's children got to eat their mother's superbly prepared dishes. Days like this were precious. The time spent together, the memories they shared served as a guiding light that reminded them of how they came to be, how they made it through life's hard trails, and how they would continue to stand strong—so long as they had one another.

After dinner, Jeannine returned to her studies and Ben wasted no time in locking himself away in his study.

He shuffled the papers on his desk, anxiously searched through the file cabinet, briefcase, and desk drawers, but then came to the conclusion that the disks must have been misplaced somehow.

Lost or stolen? He couldn't bear the thought. He was getting frustrated by the minute as the search proceeded out the study and through the entire house. He couldn't believe they were nowhere to be found.

Neither Ida nor Jeannine had seen any disks lying around the house. The last time he had them was when he'd completed the last of the data entry about a week or two ago. He could have sworn he'd put them in his briefcase.

He felt like the last breath was leaving his body and that he desperately needed oxygen. He knew that he had to find those disks, and that was bottom line.

"I've looked everywhere, Daddy. I'm sorry, but I didn't find them," Jeannine said regretfully. She hated to see her father so disappointed.

The telephone rang, and Ida picked up the receiver almost instantaneously.

"It's for you, Jeannine," she called from the family room.

"I've got to talk to you," said a voice at the other end of the phone in Jeannine's ear.

"Brendan?"

"Yes. Can you meet me in the parking lot across from Lobster House?"

"When?"

"Now."

"That urgent?"

"Yep."

"Okay." She hung up the receiver, grabbed her purse, and headed for the door.

"Where're you going?" her mother asked.

"I'll be back, Mama," she called as she closed the door behind her.

In ten minutes flat, Jeannine pulled up in the parking lot. Brendan hadn't gotten there yet, so she grabbed a novel to keep herself occupied.

"Hey, beautiful," Brendan called out his window moments later, having pulled up a couple of rows over.

"What took you so long?" she complained.

"Traffic. I'll get right to the point because I've got to be somewhere in an hour." He pulled out a tiny gold box from his pocket and opened it.

"An engagement ring?" Her eyes widened. "You're going to propose?" she asked incredulously. She took the ring from its container and placed it on her finger.

"It's beautiful."

"What do you think?" he asked.

"Oh, Brendan, I think you'd make a wonderful husband!" she said with glee. "But," she added on a softer note, "I don't think she's ready for marriage."

He sighed deeply. "I know," he admitted, "but I hope she'll say yes when I do propose."

"Kim does like you a lot, and that's a good start," Jeannine added to console him.

"Is that what you wanted to see me about?"

"Yep."

"That's it? You're incredible, you know that?"

"Yep," he replied with a grin. "I wish we were both going with you to Jamaica, J. It would be so romantic to propose there. I think she'd say yes too. She'd be so mesmerized by the beauty of the island that she'd want to get married there. When do you leave?"

"December 22, and I can't wait."

"Is your father going too?"

"Yes, he is."

He glanced at his watch and said abruptly, "Gotta go. I'll call you later."

"You need to pay me for my service," she called after him.

"You're the best, Jeannine!" He took off out of the parking lot and headed west toward the thruway.

*****

Summer was almost over. Mrs. Clark put finishing touches on the last baby sweater she'd made. The evening air felt good. It was much better than the day had been. A light, cool breeze lingered with her on the porch. She opened up the little metal box where she kept the money she'd made from crocheting, knitting, and tailoring, truly God-given talents.

It had been too long since she'd worked, and she didn't feel comfortable going back into a competing workforce.

She counted up the profit that she'd made from the past month and a half. She was pleased. She was able to save only a little bit, though. Better than nothing, she thought.

"How is my millionaire mother?" Brendan teased as his slender figure charmingly climbed the steps to the porch.

"Oh, dear, I didn't even hear you open the gate."

"Too busy counting your cash flow seems to be the problem," he teased. He sat next to her and scooped up the handful of dollars on her lap.

"We've come a long way, Mom."

The two sat on the porch and talked until it was beginning to get dark.

The night air was filled with bugs and mosquitoes. "Everything has its place in this world," said Brendan as he stared down at a mosquito that sat on his arm. "You don't bother me, I won't bother you," he said as he slapped the life out of it.

"I think it's time to go inside," he said and rose to his feet.

Mrs. Clark pulled out the gift-wrapped package from its hiding place and handed it to her son.

Brendan held his gift up to the light and inspected it. "Is this real gold?" he teased. He hugged her tightly.

"You've got nothing but the best, son," she said as she returned the hug. "Do you like it?"

"Of course I do, Mom. Anything from you is good."

She smiled. "Happy birthday, and many, many more, son."

"Thank you." He kissed her lightly on the cheek.

Mrs. Clark hooked the necklace around his neck. "You look so handsome."

"I know!" he teased.

She handed him a birthday card sealed in its envelope. He opened it, and money fell out at his feet.

"Oh, I get money too? You're the best, Mom!"

"Yes, it's to help pay your rent. I don't know why you don't move back home. You shouldn't have moved out in the first place."

"Mom," he responded, whining at her scolding, "how else am I going to learn responsibility if I don't go out on my own?" He smiled to himself. "I just lost that lousy job at the shipping company a week ago," he said on a different note. "I'll find something soon, though. Besides, I have just a little while left in college, then I'll get a real job."

He picked up his keys and kissed his mother good night.

"When will I see you again?" she asked.

"Tomorrow," he replied in earnest.

Mrs. Clark followed her son out the door and watched him drive away. She walked to the side of the house and turned on the sprinkler.

"How time flies. It seemed like only yesterday that I held him in my arms and welcomed him into my life."

As the rushing water bathed the flowers at the side of the house, she hardly noticed them as her thoughts brought her back a few years earlier, when she became a mother. *He's a good kid.* She took a deep breath of fresh air and let it out slowly. *What a pleasant night it is,* she concluded and retreated her steps into the house.

The phone rang just as she closed the door behind her. It was Ida. The thrill was obvious in her voice as she talked about her upcoming trip to Jamaica. Mrs. Clark was jealous.

"One of these summers I am going to fly with you to Jamaica. As a matter of fact, before I go to my grave, I must see the island!" Ida chuckled.

"Promise?"

The two got to know each other through Brendan and Jeannine.

Brendan and Jeannine were inseparable. Brendan was going to miss her for sure. She was his friend and counselor. Whenever he needed an opinion on anything, he'd turn to her.

*****

Brendan felt the cool air enveloping the city as he left his mother's house; the inevitable winter was just around the corner. Milolta looked still and peaceful. Traffic was light, so it took him only a few minutes to arrive at Remington's house, where his mother greeted him in one of her cheery, irrepressible moods.

"Is that hot cinnamon rolls I smell?" Brendan said as he sniffed his way into the kitchen.

"Indeed so," said Remington as he sunk his teeth into one of them.

When Brendan left Remington's house, he was surprised to find it had rained. He envied anyone who lived on a tropical island, as the cold air gave evidence that winter was really on its way.

Why couldn't I be taking a trip to the island? he asked himself flat out. He was not the type to travel, but he wouldn't mind leaving Milolta for just a couple of weeks during the winter to bask in the tropics.

"It's gotten too cold too early," he whined at Mother Nature. It was just a few hours ago that it was warm, and then all of a sudden it had become bone-chilly.

"Oh, man!" he uttered in disgust as he stepped into a puddle. As soon as he got through the door of his apartment, he slipped off his wet socks and tossed them in the hamper.

It was going to be his first Christmas in his own apartment. That was a positive. His little eighteen-inch Christmas tree glowed from the steady Christmas lights. He flipped the switch on the radio.

"I'm dreaming of a white Christmas…" was the song that greeted him. "I don't think so," he said as he flipped it back off.

There was one message on his answering machine. It was from Kim. He had to call her. That would make his day complete.

He tried in vain to reach her. Marshall's deep, husky voice at the other end of the line interrupted his pleasant thoughts of her.

"Hi, Mr. Futon, it's Brendan. May I speak to Kim, please?" he stuttered unavoidably. He'd almost forgotten that she lived with her father. For some reason, he'd expected her to answer the phone as if she should have been waiting next to it for his call.

Marshall told him that she wasn't home. He was disappointed. He walked into the kitchen and tossed a frozen dinner into the microwave. He watched it rotate until done.

Meanwhile, at the other end of town, the chirping sound from the Christmas tree was the only sound in Marshall Futon's house. It was the housekeeper's day off. Marshall sat and stared blankly at his computer screen. Kim knocked lightly on the door of his study.

"It's open." She creaked the door open and slowly peeked in.

"What's up, Dad?" she said, giving him a tender smile.

"I didn't know you were here, honey," he said in surprise. "Brendan called for you. And oh, yeah," he said after a brief pause, "Ben called looking for Jeannine. He wanted to know if you knew where she was."

She shook her head. "I'm not sure where she is," she responded. Without saying another word, she closed the door and hurried to her room to give Brendan a call.

She dialed his number, and the phone rang twenty times. Brendan was sprawled out across the bed and floating somewhere in la-la land. Kim hung up the phone and dialed again. He didn't budge. He was sound asleep, and nothing, not even the ringing telephone only inches away, was able to cause a stir.

*****

"Tyranny. That's sheer tyranny! Don't you think?"

"Yeah, but who cares?" Remington cast a glare at the heavyweight champ.

"Cut! Thank you. That was good. We'll be calling you."

Remington placed his hand above his eyes to shade them from the glare of the light, so he could see who'd spoken.

"We'll be calling you. Goodbye!" the voice said impatiently.

"All right," he said hesitantly. He met Jeannine in the back and asked doubtfully, "So what do you think?"

"You were great! You'll make a good actor, Remington. How could they not like your act?"

"It was so short, though. How could they even judge my acting from just a few words? I think this is it. I'll never hear from them."

"We'll see. Stop worrying about it. Even if you don't, they're not the only acting studio around."

"I've got to get into acting, Jeannine. Acting is who I am."

"And you will if you're persistent." They left the studio and stopped at a fast-food restaurant across the street for a quick bite.

"I have to go see Brendan. You could come with us to my house. We—"

"Sorry, I have a busy day today. I have to try to get in contact with a couple more acting studios to set up an appointment for an audition. Somebody will like my act and hire me."

Remington dropped Jeannine off at Brendan's apartment.

"Right on time for lunch," he said as she walked through the door.

"Sorry, just ate. Let's go," she ordered jokingly.

"But...but...," he teased.

"I'll wait until you're done eating, but we've got to get going. There are some things that I'd like to do at my house."

"Like what? Paint?"

"Whatever. Hurry up."

Jeannine's father, Ben, had the house to himself, but only for a short while. He sat down around Jeannine's computer and slipped in one of his disks. Despite his exhaustion, he'd decided to run through his files.

The phone rang. He was annoyed and snatched it off the hook. After a brief silence, he snorted, "Can't this wait until tomorrow?" After another brief pause, he pressed the Hold button and sluggishly climbed the stairs to his study.

As soon as he got to his study, Jeannine and Brendan walked in. "I'll be right back," she said and walked into the kitchen. Brendan made his way to the family room and sat down around Jeannine's computer desk.

He touched the mouse, and the screen saver deactivated. Ben's open files appeared. He placed his hand on the mouse and began to scroll through the files. Just then, Ben entered the room.

"What're you doing? That's confidential information."

Brendan apologized. "It doesn't make sense to me, anyway," he confessed.

"Hello, Daddy."

"Hi. I didn't hear you come in, J." He picked up the receiver and said softly, "I'll call you back in two minutes." He closed out the file and retrieved his disk.

He turned to his daughter and said, "I'll be upstairs if you need me."

Brendan stared after him.

Jeannine noticed Brendan's expression. "You'll have to excuse my father. It's company policy."

Brendan shrugged his shoulders and only smiled.

Chapter 4

The Great Beyond

Something highly contagious, affecting everything on Earth, saturated the atmosphere—perhaps from the Great Beyond—ushering in a presence, captivating humankind in its wake, and leaving no one unaffected. Happy faces were seen everywhere as the force took control over lives, as if mystically etched into the atmosphere by the finger of a great artist, faces giving life to an otherwise-dull scenery. The invisible force knew not the boundaries of age, color, creed, or national origin, and all became inaugurated by a spiritual power hovering mightily in the air.

Each person was empowered by such force to *act*. The captivating effect was sensed in every home, every shopping mall, and every pocket of existence. Driven by a force that was not their own and controlled by a great power, the human race fulfilled the law of unselfish love—love without a requirement, like forceful beams cascading from the strength of the sun, penetrating the atmospheric realm, and giving mankind a supernatural power to *give of themselves*, each beam acting as an agent of kindness, gentleness, and peace.

What else could drive humankind to act favorably to one another? The answer was clear: only a force that could alter mankind's inherent self-centeredness.

It was a season in time when differences were set aside, people giving of themselves and receiving of others, when all had one common law, and that was the gift of giving. It was the time of year when those who weren't remembered were suddenly thought about. The ever-powerful spirit of a perpetual Christmas loomed, being flown on the wings of love into the human heart. Christmas carols played softly one after the other as the seasonal music released the essence of unselfish love. The aroma of peace lingered in the atmosphere like the scent of freshly cut flowers, floating in the air and delivering a vibrant ecstasy.

"Last call for Flight 232, boarding at Gate 6."

The heavy traffic of footsteps lent a sort of disconnected cadence to the musical rhythm of the Christmas carols. With just three days left until Christmas, one couldn't expect it to be any less busy. It was the time of year that most people traveled from one end of the Earth to the other. Faraway loved ones and pen pals pulled together by the invisible rope of togetherness that held them close at heart.

Bulky suitcases and luggage of all kinds jittered on the conveyor belt as they made their way to the bottom of the aircraft. From point A to point B, scurrying people made their way about the airport.

"We've got to hurry," called Ben Shrouder, who was leading the way. His hands tingled from a slight numbness from the weight of the hand luggage and coarseness of the straps. As he juggled them for better position, he suddenly became aware that his glasses were hanging from the tip of his nose. He managed to free a finger and adjusted them.

Ben, Ida, Washburn, and Jeannine hurriedly made their way through the traffic of people in search of Gate 6. The honorable *time*, the highly valuable *time* didn't wait for the Shrouders, or for anyone else, for that matter.

"Excuse us, please," said Ida in her feminine voice to a couple that was standing in the middle of the walkway scoping through a magazine. Her knee-length skirt swung from side to side as she hustled along, hoping they were walking in the direction of Gate 6.

"Could you please tell us the direction to Gate 6?" asked Ben between breaths to the young man behind the counter.

"Follow those lines," the young man said, pointing off in the opposite direction of where they were heading. Ben's arms dropped in disappointment.

"Good thing we asked," he said. He turned and looked at his wife, whose face was displaying the burden of the out-of-shape syndrome.

She dropped her bags and placed her hands on her hips, trying to catch her breath before she took another step.

"When you come to the end of the lines," the young man continued, "then make a right and it'll lead you to Gate 6."

"Okay, here we go again!" said Jeannine in a disappointing tone. She feared they might very well miss the flight. Her braids glittered with sparkling glitter. Her velvet pants were about half an inch from the floor. Her sheer open-front, duster-length jacket was beautifully enhanced with baby-blue flowers. Her high-heeled shoes added an extra two inches to her five-foot-five petite stature.

"Jeannine, you and your brother are young and full of energy," said Ida. "Come on, get your feet moving faster! When you get there, just let them know we're on our way. They'll wait for us."

Moments later, Washburn hollered, "Wait, wait!" as the flight attendant readied the door for closing.

"Whew, that was close!" he exclaimed. In the nick of time, they made their flight.

They entered the aircraft with a deserved gratitude. The long narrow aisle finally came to an end as they made their way to the four seats reserved in first class just for them.

A warm tingle lingered in Jeannine's stomach. Nothing could be more pleasant than the feeling of going home to Jamaica, especially after five years. She leaned back on the headrest and closed her eyes.

"Yes, home at last," she muttered as a faint smile broke through the corners of her mouth.

"Sleeping already, sis?" her brother asked, sitting next to her.

She fluttered her eyes open and looked at him. "Nope, just meditating."

"Bet I know what you're thinking about," he challenged.

Jeannine merely smiled at him. Before he could guess, she revealed her thoughts.

"Everything that makes Jamaica what it is. In three and a half hours, my feet will be touching the soils of my home country, Jamaica!" she said enthusiastically.

It was unusually cold for the month of December. They weren't the least bit surprised, however, about the amount of snow they'd gotten, because Milolta had a way of surprising its inhabitants with early snowfalls.

Washburn glanced over his sister's shoulder to take one last look at the winter scene. He had forgotten his gloves, and his hands were numb from the cold as he and his father unloaded the luggage and suitcases from the limousine. It was hardly an issue, though, as warm thoughts of Jamaica kept his mind occupied. Butterflies floated in his stomach as he dwelled on the pleasant thoughts of home.

Jeannine snuggled comfortably in her window seat. *Sweet paradise. I can hardly wait!* She glanced absentmindedly out the window, hardly thinking of how cold it was outside. She barely noticed the snow-covered ground. Her body was in the United States, true enough, but her soul and spirit had already made it to Jamaica. Vivid memories of long ago played in her mind.

She knew that she wasn't the only one who was experiencing feelings of hope and extreme joy at the thought of going home. Perhaps everyone who was on the aircraft had the same feeling.

It wasn't a coincidence that they had chosen to fly to Jamaica three days before Christmas. Christmas in Jamaica was one of the most memorable times of the year.

Ben wiped a bead of sweat from his forehead with a handkerchief. He wasn't doing too badly for his age, he thought. Juggling hand luggage and moving at the speed he was going was pretty good for a man in his midforties who didn't exercise regularly.

Ida took a deep breath and let it out slowly. She rested her head on her husband's shoulder. "We made it," she said peacefully. Ben threw his arms around her shoulder.

"I knew we would." He smiled. He adjusted his seat to tilt back just a bit.

Ida yawned. "I'm ready to go to sleep now." She snuggled closer to him.

No coats, no boots, no heavy clothing. It'll be two weeks of sheer pleasure, Jeannine thought as she stared out the frosted window.

It was beginning to snow again. Flakes dwindled past her window. She knew that when they returned it would still be winter in the States, but she refused to dwell on that thought.

"Warm weather, sunny days, and endless visits to the beach—now that's what I call a real vacation," declared Washburn. "The first thing that I'm going to do when I land is to kiss the holy ground." He rubbed his hands together and gave a chuckle. "Girls, girls, Jamaican girls!"

Jeannine slapped him lightly on the back of the head. "Is that all you think about, girls?"

"No, Mama!" He laughed. "I think about food too. Jerk pork, curried goat, Tastee patties, and mangoes…"

"Relax, will you? I need some peace and quiet," his sister interrupted.

Ida peeked over the back of her children's chairs. "Are you two all right?" she asked. Jeannine nodded. "I wish Casey were with us," she said to her husband.

"Well, you can't find a job that will give you two weeks' vacation after only working there for six months," Ben replied.

"I know, but I wish she'd found it sooner."

"There will always be another chance," her husband consoled.

Four barrels of groceries and two barrels of miscellaneous items packed to capacity sat at the wharf in Jamaica, waiting to be claimed. Ben and Ida had many things to give to their families and friends.

"We have more than enough things for everyone," said Ben.

"I hardly believe so," Ida replied. "Between your relatives and mine, it would be impossible to bring enough things for everybody."

"Every Jamaican who knows someone coming from a foreign land is expected to be given something by the arriving person. Moreover, one couldn't be going home to Jamaica from the States without something for everyone."

"We could," Ida added, "give something to each household we know and not to each individual."

Ben nodded. It sounded good.

Ida looked at her watch. "We should be in Jamaica by one thirty."

Levers, buttons, and lights lined the wall of the cockpit. All the buttons were checked. All gadgets were at their proper functioning level as the pilot competently prepared for the flight.

"Good afternoon, and thanks for flying Air Jamaica." A baritone voice broke through the multitude of conversation. A hush of silence fell abruptly as passengers listened to the information and instruction.

"This is a nonstop flight to Montego Bay, Jamaica. From there the next stop will be Kingston. Please buckle your seat belts and prepare for takeoff."

The cooing of babies and the never-ending questions of inquiring minds lent an added accent to the blended conversation.

A young woman sat perfectly upright in her seat. She reached for her seat belt and shakily snapped it into place. She crossed her slender legs and dangled them nervously. As she gnawed on her nails, her eyes roamed the aircraft swiftly. Her round face twitched every now and then.

"First time traveling?" asked her neighbor.

She nodded without looking at him, as if she was trying not to break her concentration.

She reached for her pink-and-white sweater and threw it over her bare legs, shielding against the cool air.

Her neighbor reached over and held up a tract in front of her. "Peace with God" was sprawled in big bold black letters at the top. Behind the letters was the painted picture of a blue sky with fluffy white clouds. She hesitated, then reached for it.

"Thank you," she muttered. He smiled and looked away, as if he knew that she wished not to be disturbed.

She laid the tract in her lap and continued to dangle her legs and gnaw at her nails.

Peace with God, uh? God. Her thoughts dwelled for a moment on the tract. *Just another fanatic who has nothing to do but throw his life away on a cult.* She frowned. *And if God does exist…*

She cast the thought out of her mind. She needed to concentrate on at-hand things, and that didn't qualify.

"Excuse me. I'm sorry, forgot to introduce myself. My name is Charles."

She sighed silently. *Don't bother me,* she thought to herself. She smiled stiffly and said, "Karen."

"Nice to meet you, Karen."

"Thanks," she replied, trying not to give way to a conversation.

Charles snapped his seat belt on and settled in his seat. He opened up his Bible and began to flip through the pages.

People of all races, color, and creed, and for all different reasons, were aboard the Air Jamaica flight. There were tourists visiting for the first time; others were tourists on a return visit who, from previous experience, were compelled to return to the tropics.

There were also native Jamaicans who were visiting their relatives in the States and their time of visit had expired. Some deemed it a valued privilege to have had the opportunity to be a part of a culture that was somewhat similar yet different from their own in many ways.

"It was an eye-opener," one woman commented, "to have had the chance to experience the American culture."

"I enjoyed my stay," her companion added.

Among the diversity of passengers were Jamaicans who maintained permanent residence in the US while visiting the home country from time to time. Regardless of status, they all had one thing in common—love of the island.

The Shrouders could hardly wait for the plane to get to Jamaica, where they would bask in the warm climate of an island that was well versatile. Warm temperatures all year-round were one of the many attracting features of Jamaica, though some would say too warm and too humid.

The aircraft jolted as its wheels rolled down the runway. In a few moments, the front tilted as it lifted off the ground and soared into the deep blue yonder.

Karen gripped her seat and shut her eyes tight as the aircraft escalated in height and speed.

"It's all right, this is normal for all flights," said Charles, who noticed the tenseness in her face. He handed her a stick of gum. "This will help unplug your ears." This time she didn't mind having a conversation to keep her mind off her fears.

"I always hated takeoff," said Ida. "My ears are so clogged."

"Here," said Ben as he reached into his breast pocket for a stick of gum.

Jeannine was ecstatic. An overwhelming sense of joy flooded her soul. She was really on her way home.

She had no appetite. She was too excited to eat, too happy to even feel hungry.

She was tired, but excitement evacuated sleep from her eyes. She glanced around at the neighboring passengers. Everyone had taken up some kind of hobby that would help pass the time as they patiently waited for the aircraft to reach its destination.

She couldn't help but notice Karen, who was sitting in the center row. What caught Jeannine's attention was her striking resemblance to Kim. Her features and the outline of her face were similar to Kim's, except that she was a little underweight, she thought.

She had a pretty face, but she would look so much better if she had more meat on her bones.

Not wanting to stare directly at her, Jeannine watched her from the corner of her eyes. Karen fumbled through the few pages of the tract as she subconsciously but competently read the tract from cover to cover. She glanced at Charles, who was fast asleep with a little green Bible in his hand. Must be her father, Jeannine thought.

Jeannine thought it odd that she would be so lost in the thought of a perfect stranger.

She frowned as she continued roaming the aircraft with her eyes. The verbal and nonverbal language of the passengers intrigued her.

Some were listening to their headset, some were reading magazines or the newspaper, and quite a few of them were sleeping.

Her attention shifted as she stared out the window, mesmerized by the beauty below.

Beyond the clouds, the plane rode on the wind's wings. The clouds lay pure and fluffy beneath them. The radiance of the sun glowed on the clouds, enhancing their beauty. Before she knew it, she was dozing.

A sudden turbulence awoke her with a start. Her heart skipped a beat. She turned and looked at her brother, who was not disturbed by the sudden rhythm of the aircraft.

"Sleep is kicking in. I've only gotten three hours' sleep last night."

Ben didn't respond. Ida peered over the edge of her reading glasses to see if he was sleeping. He'd heard every word that she'd spoken. He could relate to the fact that she was very tired, but he had no intention of sleeping right then. The scenery outside was too beautiful to ignore. He took one snapshot after another.

"I don't think those shots are going to turn out good, because you're taking them through a glass."

"They will," he reassured her.

"Oh!" Another turbulent jolt sent him back hard against his seat. "I guess that shot won't turn out too well," he said as he placed the camera in his lap.

"Mama?"

"Yes, honey, what do you need?"

"Nothing. Did you feel it?"

"How could we not feel it? That was a huge one. Don't be afraid, though. It's all right. Planes do experience a little turbulence every now and then."

Jeannine tried to dismiss it from her thoughts. She prayed again for a continuing safe flight. She hated turbulences.

She blasted her music and concentrated on her days ahead, trying hard to block out her fears. *Mmm, I wish I could snuggle in those,* she thought as she concentrated on the clouds beneath the aircraft. As she focused her thoughts on the beauty of outer space, she hardly heard a word of the reggae music that was coming from her headset.

Washburn, on the other hand, was in his own little world. Nothing disturbed him. Jeannine was glad that he had finally fallen asleep. She cherished the quiet moment, because she wanted to be able to think.

Karen's nervousness did not allow her to rest. It was escalating. For the third time, she flipped through the pages of the tract. Unable to concentrate because of her nervousness, she rested her head on the headrest and closed her eyes, as if she were begging sleep to take her away. She knew that if she closed her eyes long enough and sat perfectly still with a blank mind, she would be able to fall asleep.

Charles stirred. She glanced over at him and became suddenly aware of the angel-like look on his face. He looked peaceful, she thought. Worry-free. How could anyone be worry-free? Especially when you're thousands of feet in the sky? She shuddered at the thought.

Her eyes shifted to the green Bible he held in his hand so tight as if he were consciously aware of it. She didn't believe in the Bible. A bunch of white men wrote the Bible, she claimed.

She recalled the fear she had when she saw the movie *Burning Hell.*

"There's no place like that," she comforted herself. She remembered the heated discussion she had with a member of the church she used to attend.

"Well, the Bible says there is such a place as hell," the woman had argued.

Karen was angry. "A loving God would not put people through that agony, and besides, one cannot burn forever and ever. They would burn to ashes. They would die eventually. Of course, it didn't have to mean a literal burning and could mean simply a bad physical location," she reasoned.

One way or another, she found it hard to accept the Bible as the word of an infinite, loving God. The Bible, in her eyes, contradicted itself. That brought her to the conclusion that man, the fallible creature, who had been wrong from the beginning, was wrong again even in the question of heaven and hell.

*****

All six disks sat in Brendan's drawer. One after the other he popped them into his computer and fiddled with the keypad, but to no avail.

Where could he have kept the passwords? he wondered. Brendan was sure that he had them written down somewhere, but where? The sooner he solved the mystery, the better it would be. He grunted.

He had almost forgotten about his appointment. He locked away the disks and hurried out the door. It wasn't long before he pulled up in the parking lot of McDowell Computer Systems.

As his best friend floated somewhere among the clouds, Brendan sat waiting with sweaty palms and rapid breathing for someone to appear in the waiting area and call his name.

The wait was almost unbearable. He'd been sitting for a little over an hour.

Among the 110 applicants that took the exam, he was one of the few that qualified for employment. He was nervous.

A man finally appeared at the doorway. "Brendan Clark?" he asked in a husky voice.

"Yes."

He reached out a hand that looked like it was made of metal. "I'm Felix Mathers. Welcome to our company."

His nicotine-stained hand gripped Brendan's seemingly unweathered hand. Brendan grimaced slightly under his firm grip. He returned the handshake with a smile dampened by a discomfort of uncertainty.

Felix Mathers, a five-four stocky man, was the frontline manager. His stocky body fit snugly in his sharply ironed suit, which glistened from an obvious overstarching.

The hard lines around his eyes danced at the movement of his lips. As he smiled, the hard lines increased in contour.

"Thank you. I feel privileged." His heart pounded faster. He didn't care too much that the man's hand was as hard as steel. He'd finally gotten a job in the field of his major. He had always wanted to graduate from college with work experience. His opportunity was knocking at the door, and he was ready.

He was extremely grateful to this man, who saw qualities in him that might be of asset to their company.

He stuck out his chest and, with pride, strutted behind Felix to the conference room.

Felix's stubby arms swung swiftly as he led the new employee to the conference room.

Brendan felt as though he was in heaven, but he had three months to prove himself capable of being a great asset to the company. He was confident he had all the qualities they needed.

*****

It was three days before Christmas, and the malls were crowded; jolly Christmas songs played in stores while people frantically combed through racks and stands to find the perfect gift.

Last-minute shoppers paraded the malls, filling every store, as they spent lavishly on gifts of all shapes, colors, and sizes.

Every parking space was taken as each city and town was brushed with the spirit of giving that compelled humankind to "remember and give."

Zaire stood in what seemed to be the hundredth store. He wanted to get Kim a gift. He couldn't seem to find the perfect gift that satisfied his instinct.

What do you give to someone who has basically everything? he thought. He wanted to let her know how he felt about her, as if she had no idea. His face lit up as he thought about her and how much she meant to him. She was his special lady. Brendan seemed to have uninvitingly popped into his mind. He suddenly became aware of his plight. He'd almost forgotten that Brendan was now in the picture. His countenance changed. He grimaced. His teeth clenched. He was subconsciously pounding his fist into the palm of his hand when a clerk, who was unnoticed, walked up to him.

"Can I help you with something?" Her voice startled him.

"Oh, I'm sorry. I'm in my own little world," he apologized. "I'm looking for a gift for a special girl."

A warm feeling came over him at the thought of his precious Kim Marie Futon.

As much as he was in love with her, it was a lonely, one-way relationship. He knew that for the present moment he was living in a fantasy world, but as he'd pledged to himself, he would go to great lengths to win her back.

He, Zaire Campbell, would have her back and their relationship would be even sweeter than before. It was odd, he thought, that he wasn't the least bit angry at Kim for dumping him for Brendan. He wondered what she saw in him anyways.

He vowed in his heart that Kim would one day be Mrs. Zaire Campbell. He knew that she cared about him, and that was enough.

The more he thought about Brendan, the more he loathed him. "He presumptuously came into the picture and stood between us," he muttered through clenched teeth.

"It's just not working out," she'd said one day. He had a hunch that Brendan was the "culprit." He knew that someone was trying to steal her away from him. She had changed. They were spending less time together. He had no idea at first who it might have been, but then it dawned on him. Through his ingenuity he found out. Certainly, it was a crime to steal someone's love. In that case, Brendan Clark was a criminal. *You're going to be sorry,* he thought.

He shook his head, as if to rid his mind of his thoughts.

"Can I ask your opinion on something?" he finally said to the store clerk.

"Sure can."

"Answer this: as a female, what gift from a guy would touch a girl's heart?"

"Uhum. Very general, but a good question, I must say, indeed. I'll narrow it down to this. Speaking for myself, real diamonds would make me flip! Like they say, 'Diamonds are a girl's best friend.'" Her eyes twinkled.

He stood staring at her, as if he was waiting for her to go on.

"A necklace with matching earrings and bracelets and a sentimental engravement would do me just fine," she added.

"Thank you. Sounds good to me. I hope it'll work for her."

"It'll work for any girl that's got good taste."

He laughed, trying to erase the pain he felt in his heart at the thought of not spending the rest of his life with her.

His whole intention was to win her back; therefore, he wanted to get her something that he knew would touch her heart in a special way.

Zaire was pleased with his accomplishment. He smiled as he walked out of the mall, carrying a tiny package in his hand. His Christmas shopping was done. The one person he had on his list was taken care of. He could hardly wait until Christmas Day.

How he was going to see her Christmas Day was something he needed to work out. Brendan was going to spend the day with her, for sure, the whole day, that was. He didn't care what happened, but he knew that he had to see her somehow.

The snow trickled down lightly. He pulled out of the parking lot and narrowly missed a young man who was skipping between cars.

"Oh, Zaire, keep your mind on the road," he scolded himself as he headed to his place.

He would have hated to know that Brendan was standing at Kim's door, waiting for her to let him in.

*****

The cold went right through his thin jacket and caused him to shudder a bit, but Brendan didn't mind braving the cold to see his precious Kim, his future bride.

Her father wasn't home, to his delight. He frowned as he noticed that Kim was taking a while to get to the door. He rang the bell again, and still there was no answer.

He began to worry. He could hear Roscoe scratching frantically at the door.

This time he kept his finger on the buzzer for a good fifteen seconds and waited yet a little while longer. There was still no answer.

Just as he was about to walk away, Kim opened the door. "What're you doing here?" She grinned cheerfully. "What a pleasant surprise! I could use some company. I really wasn't expecting you, Bren."

"You had me so worried just now. I've been waiting ten minutes for you to open the door."

"Oh, I'm sorry. I had my headset blasting." She laughed.

"Well…that's okay." He grinned as he stepped into the warm house. It was a vast contrast from the outside.

He climbed the stairs and pushed the door of Marshall's study. It opened slowly. One could almost walk past it and not notice that it was there. The same baby blue that was used to paint the surrounding walls was used to paint the door of the study. It sat meticulously on the east side of the house.

"I didn't even notice that it was open," said Kim as Brendan walked in. My father must have been in a hurry when he left. I couldn't tell you the last time I saw the inside, if I ever did, that is."

"You've never seen the inside of your father's study?" Brendan asked incredulously.

Kim shook her head. Brendan sat in Marshall's chair, and it rolled him smoothly to the desk.

"Boy, is this chair comfortable or what?" He ran his palm over the computer.

"This is a high-tech computer. He must have spent a fortune on it. You can tell he's rich."

Kim leaned her hip against the desk, folded her arms, threw her head back, and laughed so sweetly it sounded like music in Brendan's ears.

"My father is not rich. He's financially stable, but he is certainly not rich. He just looks like he is. He spends a lot because he likes high-quality *whatevers.* He always wanted nothing but the best. Years of hard work brought him financial stability, not by some other method. Sometimes I think he works too hard, though."

To Brendan, Marshall seemed like the perfect tutor for anything; if only he weren't so busy. He was a very smart man who knew a lot about computers.

Brendan glanced at the framed graduate certificate that Marshall had hanging on the wall.

"Computer programmer," he read out loud. "Now that's a great field to be in. That's big bucks."

Trying to get to know Marshall better wasn't a bad idea, he thought. On second thought, he was hardly ever around for anyone to hold a conversation with him.

The most that Brendan knew about him was that he was a white-collar worker, had a daughter by the name of Kim, and had a wife who passed away years ago. If he was going to be his son-in-law, which Brendan hoped one day would happen, then they'd need to get to know each other better.

"Oh, I wish I had one of these babies." He ran his palm enviously over the computer.

"If he ever catches us in here, he'd skin us alive. He doesn't even let me look at it."

"Aren't you the least bit curious as to what kind of programs he has on it?"

"Nah, I don't care. He's gotten me a computer of my own, so I don't need to bother his."

Brendan had almost forgotten the main reason he'd come to see her. "I was called in this morning to McDowell Computer Systems for my orientation," he said suddenly. "It only went for half a day. It's awesome, Kim. I like it a whole lot. It's a lot to learn, but I can do it. I know that I'm gonna do it. I've come over to ask you to celebrate with me."

"I am so happy for you, Bren!" she squealed.

"It's a well-paying job. I'm establishing our future that after we get married, we'll be financially stable." He watched her face for her reaction.

"Well, I think I might already be financially stable." She ignored the statement about marriage. "I don't think that my father would send me out empty-handed." She laughed.

"Well, that's his money. I've got to get rich for us," he said. "Grab your coat and let's go celebrate, baby!"

"Wait a minute. Jeannine promised me that as soon as she gets to Jamaica, she would call me. I'll leave a message on the answering machine to let her know about your job and that we've gone to celebrate. We'll be out for a while, won't we?"

Before he could answer, the door downstairs was slammed shut. It startled Brendan. Marshall? He was in his studio. He looked at Kim, who wasted no time in hauling him out the door. She looked over the banister and saw Meeghan, the housekeeper, juggling three paper bags of groceries in her arms. Kim sighed in relief.

"Hi, Meeghan. Need any help?"

"Oh," she cried and dropped one of the bags.

"I'm sorry, I didn't mean to startle you."

"It's all right. Everything seems to scare me out of my wits lately. Would you like some scrambled eggs?" she asked as she stared at the puddle of eggs at her feet.

"No, thanks, I'll pass." Kim laughed.

Brendan sided with Kim as she turned and locked her father's study behind her.

Chapter 5

Home Again!

"Ah, JAMAICA! Someone pinch me and wake me up!" said Jeannine. "I can't believe I'm home again! It's been too long. Home sweet home!"

At 1:40 in the afternoon, the jumbo airplane touched its wheels down in a smooth landing on the soils of Jamaica. A sigh of relief relaxed tense bodies. Lips curled into smiles as happy souls paid tribute to the god of the sky. Handclaps of cheers sent music in the air. Jubilant voices chitchatted as passengers pulled their belongings from the overhead compartment and said a quick goodbye to those nearby.

They anxiously headed for the exit. As they exited the aircraft, still cool inside, the familiar warm temperature and slight humidity lay beckoning, even inside the terminal.

Karen's true self appeared after the mask of fear from flying was lifted. She talked with Charles, who was busy pulling his and her belongings from the compartment.

"Thank you. I'm so glad we landed safely. I was so scared." She spoke more than three words this time.

"You have a pretty voice."

She blushed as she threw a hand luggage over her shoulder. "Thank you. It was nice meeting you," she said shyly.

Charles had no idea what type of effect the tract had on her, but he had a sense of peace within himself that through his journey on earth, he might never know all the lives that he had touched but he knew for sure that his God knew.

It was December 22, and the temperature was eighty-six degrees. "I've died and goooone to heaven," said Ben as he poked his way to the exit door. All the things he'd planned to do flooded his thoughts.

"Did you know," Washburn declared passionately, "that this beautiful island of Jamaica is located smack in the middle of the Caribbean Sea and is the third largest island in the Caribbean, which is, of course, the largest English-speaking island?"

"Well," he said calmly and laid a hand on his father's shoulder, "mi know sey some a we nuh know English at all." I know that some of us don't know English at all. "A pure Creole and patwah we chat." He meant *patois.*

"Washburn," his father rebutted, "no lectures, please."

He turned to his sister and grinned with pride in his knowledge. "Hey, J, did you know that Jamaica is located six hundred miles south of Florida, one hundred miles southwest of Haiti, and ninety miles south of Cuba? And oh, talk about the magnificent forests and mountains that dominate the island. The Blue Mountains is the chief range and runs east and west! Whew! My island home is a mixture of jungles, rivers, waterfalls, mountains, and great beaches!"

"Washburn," his sister replied calmly. She placed her hand at the back of his head and tilted his head toward her. She stood on her tiptoes, and with their faces inches apart, she declared, "Shut up!"

"Jeez, what's with these people?" He turned to his mother, and immediately she stuck a set of headphones into her ears and began to bop her head. Washburn picked up the end of the headset that was dangling at her side and held it before her eyes.

"Listening to music, ah?"

She smiled at him.

"I don't know about returning to the States. I think I'll just let you guys go back without me," he said gleefully.

A steady wind blew. From the top of the ladder they could see the surrounding trees that were rich in color. The passengers descended the twelve-step ladder onto the newly laid cement of the Jamaica Airport.

"So this is what Jamaica looks like?"

"You haven't seen anything yet," replied the hostess to the thrilled passenger as he exited the airplane.

An ongoing flow of people steadily flowed through the laborious necessity of customs.

Unclaimed luggage was pulled off the conveyer belt and placed on the side by attendants. Ben waited impatiently for their luggage to appear.

"We've been waiting half an hour for our luggage. We've only gotten one suitcase," said Washburn to an attendant.

"It's very busy during the Christmas season. Be patient, the rest will come," he said pleasantly.

Ida stood by the conveyer belt with her arms folded, watching ever piece of luggage as it carried them around and around. She tapped her foot and sang along to the Christmas carols that played over the airwaves of the RJR radio station. They played vibrantly one after the other, enhancing the spirit of the season.

Beyond the doors of custom, after all their belongings had been cleared, the Shrouders walked into the arms of welcoming friends and family members. Warm greetings from the anxiously exuberant crowd met them at the door.

Carlton and Mildred Shrouder didn't care how long they had had to wait for Flight 232 to come in. They had waited with great patience for the moment when they would see their son and his family, and it was a thrill to see them walking through the door.

Mildred turned to her husband and said, "As they say, absence makes the heart grow fonder."

A sense of freedom penetrated the very being of the visiting Jamaicans—freedom that saturated an inner strength and peace. Strength that was vital to the very sustenance of their personhood. Peace that rested the spirit and gave new hope.

Their spirits, dripping with the overflowing feeling of joy, revitalized their weary bodies with new strength.

Others alike basked in the dynamic experience of returning home or just from the fact that they'd gotten to visit a country that they'd heard so much about. Tourism was on the rise. What better place to be than in a country rich in a variety of tropical pleasures, a place where people of the world dream of vacationing?

There was a soft whistling of the wind among the trees. "It's always good to be somewhere else other than home, but home will always be home no matter where you go." Truer words had never been spoken.

Washburn dropped all that he had in his hands and did a dance in the middle of the parking lot.

"My grandson is as fit as a fiddle," declared Carlton with pride.

"Wherever your home is, that's where your heart is also. Talk about 'I Left My Heart in San Francisco,' well, my heart never left Jamaica," Ida said wholeheartedly.

Jeannine was fourteen when she left; therefore, she didn't have any trouble remembering her culture.

"Uncle Glen, it's nice to know that you haven't lost your charm. You're as handsome as you've always been," said Ida.

"Mi know." I know. He chuckled. "God nuh mek man no betta looking dan dis." God doesn't make man any better looking than this.

Carlton turned to Ida and said, "Please, nuh get him started, mi can't handle him any worst dan he his." He then turned to his sister-in-law and asked, "How anybody can live wid a perfectionist is beyond me."

"Love makes the world go around," replied Gwen. Her whole body shook as she laughed.

"This is my boyfriend, Henry."

Ben stared at Ingrid with open eyes. "Boyfriend? How old are you?"

"Eighteen."

"Time sure flies. You were only two inches tall when I left Jamaica."

"Are you going to be a grandfather anytime soon, Glen?" Ida asked.

Glen glanced at his daughter's stomach. "Nope! I'm too young to be a grandfather," he replied, shaking a finger at his daughter.

The crowded family minivan sat at the entrance of the building.

"There is hardly any room for us. Did you think that we were coming empty-handed?" Ida asked.

The thrill of seeing one another again brought overwhelming tears of joy.

The spirit of Christmas filled the hearts and homes of the inhabitants of Jamaica. The country's only two radio stations, RJR and JBC, were electrified with Christmas carols, sending the message of the birth of Jesus Christ, the messiah. They sent the magnetic sound of Christmas music to every home that had a radio.

Saint Elizabeth hadn't changed much since they'd left. As they bounced along the long and windy road, they moved their bodies to the cultural rhythm of the reggae music that played over the radio.

The air felt light and warm. The streets were busy with the noises of motor vehicles. There were people on bicycles, on motorbikes, in cars, in trucks, and whatever transportation that was available to take them from one point to another. Country buses were going in every direction. It was their daily routine.

"It looks so weird to see everybody driving on the left side of the street and the steering wheel on the left side of the van." Ben laughed. He grew up in Jamaica. He knew the culture, but now something that was routine in his life had suddenly became weird. Something that was once normal now had become abnormal.

Now that he had experienced another culture, the *old* way seemed abnormal. He was out of touch with his culture, and a reacquainting would bring him back to the regular routine of what he once thought was normality.

A rainbow of activities kept their thoughts and eyes busy. Higglers called out to passersby to stop and take opportunity of the bargains that they had to offer. Their arcades of products lined the street corners with hundreds of different items on display.

Ben and his family relived memories of their past life as they observed the sceneries that lay all around them.

"Everybody seems to be driving so fast. What happened to the speed limit signs?"

"The what, Ms. Foreigner?" asked Carlton. He cast his eyes in the rearview mirror and glanced at his granddaughter.

"You know, the huge two-digit number on the side of the road that tells drivers how fast they're allowed to go," she said with an attitude.

There was a burst of laughter that was as golden as the singing of the morning birds. A group of people in a minivan, so painstakingly free, were enjoying a moment in life that compelled them to lay aside every negativity of life and, for the moment at hand, give way to a common ground: joy.

"Speed limit? Child, you drive as fast as your vehicle can go," replied Carlton.

"Don't listen to him, Jeannine. There are speed limits, but nobody obeys them," Mildred corrected.

Everyone was drawn into the current of the chitchat that engulfed the minivan. Hearty laughter filled the air. As much as the sun was shining in all its strength, the people in this particular minivan bore resemblance of the nature of the day. Happy faces and shining white teeth were on display. They were happy, genuinely happy. If anyone had any problems, they had been forgotten. Something beautiful had taken place. Something had captivated their thoughts and emotion. The cycle of the everyday rhythm was broken. It was a change of scenery and a change of pace.

Everyone talked rapidly and excitedly about the past years that they'd missed together. They'd even gone as far back as their childhood. It was a reunion that was well appreciated.

"Alan Bamboo!" exclaimed Jeannine. "I remember the last time that we passed through here. We were on our way to Kingston to visit Aunt Millicent, and we begged Daddy to stop so we could walk through it and see the other side. Do you remember, Daddy?"

"Yes, indeed, I remember. I had no choice. I felt like if I didn't, I wouldn't be able to live to see the end of the day."

The bamboo was even more beautiful than they'd remembered it. On either side of the street, bamboo shot up high and curved toward the bamboo on the other side, forming a curved crossover arch, sometimes for miles, causing a tunnel effect. The sun's rays forced their way through each space between the bamboos, casting flickering inconsistencies.

As they sped past the Black River, Ida admired it once again. Jamaica's longest river, it had acquired its name from the darkness of the riverbed, which was lined with thick layers of decomposing vegetation.

The ride seemed to take only minutes, and time slipped by without being noticed.

More friends and relatives awaited them as they pulled up to the one family house.

It had started to rain.

Ida began to sniff like a dog. As suddenly as the rain had started, it came to a stop. The smell of dirt after a sprinkle made Ida remember the blissful days of her collection of dirt clumps. The tasty aroma of freshly sprinkled dirt would send her sniffing like a K-9 dog.

"Mmm…the fresh smell of dirt after the rain. In America, pregnant women normally crave for chocolate, but nothing satisfies more than a clump of dirt."

Ben frowned as he recalled the many trips he'd had to make to a special hill she'd picked out. He'd collected a few days' worth of dirt clumps only to learn that she'd run out of *supplies* in no time at all.

"Honey, doesn't the dirt smell really good after the rain?"

Ben looked at his wife and frowned again. "You can have clumps of dirt, I'll have what's in the kitchen," he said and headed inside.

A beautiful aroma of Caribbean food escaped the kitchen, highly inviting, and the Shrouders couldn't resist the temptation. The table was sumptuously decorated with mouthwatering dishes. Brown stew, oxtail, and rice and peas sat lavishly on the table. Everything looked picture perfect and tasted just as good.

Freshly made carrot juice chilled patiently in the refrigerator.

"Did any of you eat while you were in America?" Glen said.

Washburn kept his talking to a minimum while he concentrated on his meal. The visiting Shrouders savored the flavor of everything that went in their mouths. Jeannine licked her lips from one corner to the other and back again.

"I almost forgot what soursop juice tasted like."

"Save some for someone else," scolded Jeannine as Washburn gulped down two glasses.

An ongoing traffic of relatives and friends paraded the house. As they received visitors one after another, Ben and Ida generously handed out the things they'd brought from the States.

"Perfect fit," said Glen as he tried on a pair of sneakers.

Relatives and friends alike enjoyed the things that Ben and Ida had brought for them. It wasn't long before they were at the bottom of the barrels.

Carlton and Mildred couldn't have done anything more than what they'd done. They'd gone to the extreme to welcome their son and his family back home.

Carlton recalled the contact he had with the people of the district when he was a Home Guard. *Home Guard?* It lingered in his memory. There wasn't a time when he'd regretted being a Home Guard. A Home Guard aided the police department in the fight to keep the district safe. Carlton loved his district and would do just about anything to keep it safe.

Ben bit into an East Indies mango, and the juice dripped from the sides of his mouth.

He was halfway through his mango when he remembered that he hated to eat mangoes at night. Normally, he would eat a mango in the daytime so he could see any intruding worms wriggling their way about, but tonight he didn't care. He was raptured into the hall of memory, crystal clear memories that brought on pleasant feelings.

"Well, Dad?" Ben looked at his father and noticed the distant look in his eyes.

"He's not with us."

"What you say?" he finally asked.

"Where were you, Grandpa?" asked Jeannine.

"I was back in time during my Home Guard years."

Ben stared at his father. "You know how much I hated when you was a Home Guard."

Carlton nodded. "Yes, me know." He smiled in a teasing way.

"Kids laughed at me. 'Him father a home dog' was all I heard every time they saw me."

"I rememba. You did want to disown me."

"They laughed me to scorn," he defended.

Carlton's title as a Home Guard gave added meaning to his life. It made him feel important. People felt safe. As the Home Guards walked the streets of their districts, they were greeted and commended on their efforts in keeping them safe.

"Casey sure is missing out," said Jeannine.

"I know," replied her mother.

Ben had told his father that before he left Jamaica, he'd wanted to eat a bit of everything that was called food. Well, Carlton made his wish come true.

"I didn't say I wanted to eat everything in one day, though, Pop."

To Carlton, his son was the ideal son that any parent would want to have.

They sat on the huge rock that was in the front yard.

Ben looked up at the sky. Billions of stars stared back at him. "Nighttime is so fascinating, looking at God's creation." The moon was out, illuminating all around. They reminisced about everything they could think of from long ago.

*****

Brendan couldn't wait to figure out what Saint Paul had up his sleeves. So far, he was going by hunches, but he knew his hunches would prove right.

There wasn't anything tangible, nothing that gave clue. He assumed the disks would be the key to exposing him. Now that he was away for a while, he had his chance of sneaking back into the house to see what else he could find. He wanted to be able to explore every crevice. Maybe he could find something more concrete. This was his opportunity to do the big exploring that he'd planned. Hopefully, he'd be able to bypass the security alarm. If not, he'd think of another way. There was always another way.

How this man was able to fool even the people of his household was beyond him. As close as this man was to his daughter, or so his daughter thought, she had no idea.

He'd wanted to tell her, but then he thought it might backfire. What if he told her and she hated him for "accusing her precious father"? He couldn't take that risk. He just had to keep it from her, and someday, when the time was right, he'd tell her all there was to tell.

He hoped that she'd be able to handle something as heavy as her father's evil acts. His lifestyle was like night from day. He wanted to preserve their relationship, and he knew that *accusing* her father wouldn't be a way to do that.

He closed his notepad as he finished jotting down his plans for the time that he would be able to possibly access the house.

You're going to be surprised, he thought, *you're going to be surprised.* He didn't know how long it was going to take him, but he knew that Saint Paul, the big lawbreaker, was going to be truly surprised. Oh, yeah.

*****

While Ben, Jeannine, and the rest of the family celebrated their return to Jamaica, Brendan celebrated his good fortune of getting hired. He wished Jeannine were there to celebrate with them. For the few years he'd known her, it felt as if he'd known her all his life. She was his sister and no less.

The house was quiet when they returned. Kim walked over to the phone and checked the answering machine. There was no message from Jeannine.

"I guess Jeannine forgot about us. I'm going to get her for that. She promised me she would call."

Before the words were completely out of her mouth, the phone rang.

"Kim?"

"Yes? Oh, Jeannine! We were just talking about you! I thought you were never going to call. It's almost midnight, and we thought we wouldn't hear from you tonight."

"I'm sorry. I've just been so busy with everything and everyone that I hardly had time to get away and make a phone call."

Kim could almost hear the smile that bloomed on her face.

"Well, how's Jamaica?"

"Fantastic! I wish you were here."

"Promise me that you will bring me with you next time," she said gleefully. "Hey, Brendan got some great news. I'll let you talk to him. See you in three weeks."

"How's my girl?"

"Fine, Brendan. What're you doing there so late? Marshall might strangle you."

"I got great news. I got the job at McDowell Computer Systems! Yeah, I'm a computer programmer in the making!" he said with pride.

It was a good day. Brendan had almost forgotten about Saint Paul and the mysteries that surrounded him. He thought about the helicopter, the men in black, and the rectangular metal. He wished he had taken the metal. What would have happened? Maybe they wouldn't have been able to find the chest, he thought.

For three nights in a row, Brendan watched the area to see if anything else was going to happen, but nothing did. It was time for him to focus his attention in another direction. The house reentry and retrieval of the disk passwords were top priority while he had the opportunity to make it work.

*****

Carlton was full of stories, as he had always been. Jeannine was no longer afraid of his "duppy" stories that he claimed happened in real life.

"Grandpa, I know better now. Ghosts don't exist," she defended.

"Who said anything about ghosts?" he replied.

"Ghosts, duppies, same thing. They don't exist. There is no such thing as a 'rolling calf,' Grandpa. Those scary days are done. I'm not afraid of ghosts anymore."

Ben laughed as he listened to his father and daughter battle out their opinion differences.

"Duppy real and you know it, chil'."

"Grandpapa, they are a figment of one's imagination," Washburn added.

"They brainwash you in America too, Washburn?"

"I think I might have to change my strategies." He laughed.

No one around could tell stories like Carlton. True or made-up stories, he was the greatest storyteller they'd ever known. Neighboring children would huddle together on his veranda and listen to him tell stories one after another, and he seldom read a book to them. Stories from experiences and heresies were mostly what he was interested in telling, and they were all eager to listen to him. They couldn't tell what was real and what wasn't, but it didn't matter. He was very articulate. He was like a walking library. He knew almost everything about what happened before his time, what was happening during his time, and what would take place after his time. He was their idol.

He often talked about the great people who had made Jamaica what it was. Marcus Garvey, Bustamante, Paul Bogle, and Nanny were among the heroes of Jamaica he talked highly about.

Indeed, they were happy to be home. The awesome feeling that they felt was hard to explain. Ida put it in a simple term: Nuh wey nuh betta dan yard. Nowhere is better than home.

They enjoyed every tasty food and all the visitors that came to see them. It was about 2:30 a.m. when they finally went to bed. They hit the pillow like a dead man's fall and fell into slumber until the cock crowed.

*****

Benjamin Shrouder stood on the veranda and took a deep breath, then let it out slowly. The crowing of the roosters brought back fresh memories. The early-morning breeze whistled among the trees, and it gave him a sense of peace.

Their chauffeured trip to Kingston would start out early, and he couldn't wait.

He packed his laptop in his black traveling bag. He hated that he had to bring his work all the way from the United States, but he had no choice. He still had had no luck in finding his disks, and every now and then, his mind flashed back to them in an utter torment. He grimaced at the thought of them falling into the wrong hands. The disks were confidential and would cost him a lot if discovered.

He subconsciously crossed his fingers in the hope of finding them hidden in some corner of his house.

*****

Downtown Kingston was busy, as always. It was about ten thirty when they got to the heart of town. The streets were busy with city buses, country buses, and every type of transportation imaginable. Things were alive with the everyday activities of routine lives.

"Fresh roasted peanuts! Get your fresh roasted peanuts."

Jeannine turned around and watched the handcart whistle by as the man called out for customers of his hot, tasty peanuts.

"Mmm, they smell so good," she announced. Washburn agreed and chased the cart across the street and bought a bag for everyone. Jeannine sniffed the bag, and her mouth watered.

Moving carts of all kinds, shapes, and sizes, sidewalk salespersons, department stores, and people of all nationalities added accent to its beauty.

"What do you think, dear?" Ida asked her husband in a girlish tone as she modeled a straw hat.

"That one was made just for you. You look gorgeous," responded the salesman in his deep Jamaican accent.

"Yeah, he'll say anything to get me to buy his hat," she whispered to Ben.

"It does look nice on you, Ida," Ben replied with sincerity.

"You're right. Anything looks good on me," she bragged as she stared at herself in the mirror. "I've got to buy something for so many people. I wouldn't hear the end of it if I were to go back to the States empty-handed. I think these would be great to bring back as souvenirs," she said as she picked up a handful of handmade embroidered straw fans.

It was hot. The air was still. Washburn adjusted his shades a bit to cover his eyes completely from the sun but suddenly pulled them down a little and peered over the top. He turned in a trancelike way and watched a young girl walk by until she disappeared into the crowd.

"Ooh, Jamaican girls are the bomb!" he exclaimed.

It was in Kingston that Ben had met Ida. He'd gone to Kingston to visit his mother's brother, as he had always done on occasion. It wasn't very often that he'd gotten to see his cousins, and paying them a visit periodically was always a pleasure.

He was eighteen when he met the pretty seventeen-year-old Ida Charette, and he knew that he had to move to Kingston permanently.

"I just want to live with Uncle Joe a while," he'd told his parents.

"Why all of a sudden?" asked his father.

Ben didn't want to reveal that he had met a girl that he couldn't get out of his mind. Ida was having the same trouble keeping Ben out of her mind.

Hyacinth and Eunice took them to almost every part of Kingston in one day.

Washburn bought two strawberry snow cones just for himself. "I haven't tasted Kool-Aid this good in years."

"It's syrup, to be most correct," corrected Hyacinth.

Ben couldn't resist coming to Kingston and not getting any of Tastee's patties. They could smell the aroma of the patties even before they got to the building.

"Mmm, this is too good to be true," he said as he took a huge bite into one of the beef patties.

From Kingston they headed to Saint Thomas. "Donald Quarrie Secondary School!" exclaimed Jeannine.

"I remember when they built it," said Ida as they sped by the secondary school.

"Wow, it's so good to see these places again." The familiar places of Saint Andrews brought on a delightsome mood.

Jeannine compelled her father to stop and spend the night at the Nine Miles District in Bull Bay.

"I don't see why not," said her mother. "I'd like to visit a few old friends."

"I remember the good old days when we used to get together and play all kinds of games. I was the best in all the games," she bragged. "Dandy shandy, net ball, cricket, soccer, loudie—you name it, I played it. Loudie was one of my favorite pastimes. I'd spend hours playing one game after another until well past dark on many occasions," bragged Jeannine.

"How could you be working at a time like this?" asked Ida. Ben ignored her, keeping busy punching keys on his laptop.

He paused for a moment. His eyes stared blankly at the passing scenes as a puzzled look covered his face. He raised his hand to his chin and rubbed it gently. Every now and then, his mind wandered back to the missing disks.

He shrugged his shoulders and proceeded to punch the keys on the keypad. He stopped suddenly and stared at the screen. He pointed his pen at an area on the screen and grunted.

"Look!" Jeannine pointed across the street at a fisherman who was unloading a truckful of fish. "I haven't seen that many fish since I left Jamaica."

The rumbling of the sea could be heard from the bottom of Greenvale Road. They could almost see it from where they were. It was the same beach that Washburn and his sisters would visit every Sunday when they were kids.

Ida turned and looked behind her at Ms. Jones's shop. The line was out the door. Everything to prepare for Christmas was being looked over and purchased, crates of sodas, flour, and seasonings. The Christmas spirit in Bull Bay was as jubilant as always.

Children frolicked through the neighborhood, singing Christmas carols and tossing star-lights in the air.

The district was alive, alive like nowhere else on Earth. As dark as the night was, people went back and forth, preparing for Christmas.

Beatrice Dobson was her witty old self. She did everything she'd always done. Even though she'd lost one of her eyes to cataract, she still cooked the greatest meals, threaded needles, and sewed by hand.

"You haven't lost a thing, Mama," said Ida. Pops was no less witty than his wife. They were overjoyed to see their daughter and her family again.

Chapter 6

Merry Christmas!

The night was busy with the excitement of the big day. Crates of sodas were neatly stashed away for the annual event. Pigs, goats, chickens, cows, and all kinds of livestock were being slaughtered. Sorrel juice, soursop juice, and carrot juice lined refrigerators in bottles of all sizes. It was Christmas Eve, and everyone was busy preparing for the big tomorrow.

The moon was out. The sky glittered with billions of stars, and the air felt warm and comfortable. Children and adults alike were out late, throwing star-lights and playing games or just being silly. Children lay in the streets and drew outlines of one another. Ida and Jeannine were busy helping in the kitchen with the last-minute preparation. Christmas was only a few hours away, and the excitement exhilarated.

*****

A white Christmas, indeed! It looked as if it would snow all day long. Milolta glistened as the fresh snowflakes twirled their way to the ground. Eighteen inches of snow masked the town in a happiness not seen in a number of years. Little children were seen on tiny slopes as they slid back and forth.

Kim awoke to the ringing of the telephone. She looked at her clock through sleepy eyes, 6:02 a.m. She fumbled for the telephone. A cherry voice at the other end greeted her.

"Merry Christmas, gorgeous!"

"Merry Christmas. Who's this?"

"You don't know who this is?"

She paused a moment and then murmured, half-asleep, "Oh, Zaire, you called kinda early."

"Yeah, but I waited as long as I could," he responded. "I'd like to see you today. What time do you want me to come and see you?"

She sat upright abruptly and pondered his question. "You can't. I'm going to be real busy."

"Well, now that you've got an early start, you should be able to fit me into your busy schedule right about now. I'll see you in half an hour."

She began to protest, but then she heard a click, then the dial tone.

She placed the receiver on the hook and fell back on the bed.

Minutes later, Zaire stood at the door and rang the doorbell. Kim didn't wonder who it was. As she opened the door, he handed her a tiny gold box. He watched her face as she opened it. Her eyes sparkled as she pulled out a glittering diamond necklace and a pair of matching earrings. *To Kim with love, Zaire.*

"Oh, Zaire, you must have paid a fortune for these! You shouldn't have, but thank you."

"Anything for a beautiful lady," he replied as he pulled back her hair and hooked the necklace around her neck.

"Won't you put the earrings on and see how they look together?"

"Perfect," she said as she stared at them in the mirror.

Zaire didn't think he needed to stay but for a few minutes. His gift was enough to cause her to keep her mind on him all day. He felt good within himself as he walked out the door.

Kim waved goodbye as he drove away. She closed the door and walked over to the mirror and took a peek at her new adornment.

Moments later, the doorbell rang and she hurried to answer it. Standing with his back turned toward the door was Brendan. He'd just missed Zaire by a couple of minutes. She pulled up her collar to hide the necklace and covered her ears with her hair.

"Merry Christmas! You look surprised," he said as he watched her face.

"Oh, I wasn't expecting you so early, that's all," she replied as she tried to keep Zaire's present concealed. "I'll be right back. I'm going to get your present."

She hurried up the stairs. She took off the necklace and earrings and put them back in their gold case. The new jewelry dazzled in the light when she placed them on her dresser. She picked up the package that she had for Brendan off the chair. All that day, Kim couldn't shake the thought of how much Zaire cared about her. It was a good feeling to know that men found her attractive. She and Brendan were honest and open with each other, but regarding the current matter, as she thought about the necklace, no, not quite.

*****

Merry Christmas! The day had finally arrived. Sleepy eyes fluttered open as the country awoke to a very special day of the year, December 25, the celebration of Jesus's birthday. They celebrated happily the once-a-year event that brought joy to people of all ages in all countries. The eighty-five-degree weather with a mild southwest wind was just right.

The rustling of the wind among the trees early Christmas morning brought on a delightsome mood. The spirit of Christmas was intensified in the hearts of the people, and it was easy to see.

The day was busy with the ups and downs of the people. People were coming and going from the Shrouders'.

It wasn't anything new. Every Christmas people normally visited friends and neighbors and shared in the great spirit of giving. Kitchens all over the island were filled with the blended aroma of Jamaican cuisine, some of the greatest food on the planet.

Tables decorated with a variety of flavorful foods and deserts accented the mood of Christmas Day. Chitchats, exchanging of gifts, laughter, and smiles were weaved into the fabric of a merry Christmas Day. They talked about everything and anything as they basked in the bliss of happiness. Even well after Christmas, the spirit lingered on.

"Good day and Merry Christmas!" said Ms. Dorcas. "Mi bring yu something." I brought you something. She handed Ida a basket.

"Blue drawers—oh my goodness, it's been too long since I've had blue drawers!" She unwrapped one of them and sank her teeth right into it.

"I made plenty of these buoyos, Ida. If you want more, just let me know."

"Buoyo, blue drawers…whatever you call them, it doesn't matter. It's the taste that counts."

Ida poured her a glass of sorrel juice.

"This is delicious," she said as she sipped it, savoring every sip.

There was plenty of food at the Shrouders' for the whole district. Stewed peas made with salt beef and pig's tail, rice, and peas—with gungo peas, that is. Red peas were on vacation for the season; white rice, curry goat, curry chicken, cow foot, bully beef, escovitch fish, fried sprat, jerk pork, jerk chicken, carrot juice, rum punch, soursop juice, cherry drink, and plenty of water. To top it off with a mouthwatering desert was sweet potato pudding, carrot cake, cornmeal pudding, and some famous blue drawers.

Washburn had two plates—one couldn't hold all the food. He indulged in everything that was prepared. Ida shook her finger at him and told him that he was bound to get sick.

"I'll worry about that later, Mama," he said without looking up.

Ida and Jeannine walked through the district and visited friends and relatives. It had been a long time since they had Christmas without snow. They trod the roads of Jamaica until they became weary.

*****

"Cock-a-doodle-doo!" Jeannine was awakened by a familiar sound just outside her window. It sounded good. The crowing of roosters early in the morning was a signal that day was breaking.

She was up before anyone else. It was semidark when she opened the doors of the house. The air felt cool and clean.

A gentle breeze from the seventy-eight-degree weather tickled her face. It carried the fresh smell of the flowers that lined the front yard. Beads of dew sat undisturbed on each leaf.

It was a pretty quiet morning. The sound of a distant vehicle every now and then broke the stillness. Fee-Fee and Cottie must have heard her footsteps, because they came running from the back of the house. They wagged their tails friskily and licked her legs.

"Ooh, that tickles. Well, it's good to see you too." They cherished her. They were good dogs. They weren't guard dogs, though, because they would lick the hands of a burglar.

She walked around to the back of the house. Cottie wagged her tail frantically and ran behind a barrel filled with water.

Ruff ruff. She barked friskily and ran back and forth to the barrel.

"All right, what are you hiding?" she asked as she trailed behind him.

She dug her feet into the ground, and Jeannine giggled as she dug with her. Fee-Fee felt left out, so he started to dig along with them.

"A bone!" she exclaimed. "I thought you were leading me to buried treasure." She rose to her feet and brushed the dirt from her hands and knees. "You're more fun than some people I know," she said as she stroked their backs.

She walked back to the front of the house and sat on the veranda. She closed her eyes and took deep breaths and then let them out slowly. "Ah, Jamaica!" she breathed out. It felt really good to be home. She felt a surge of peace long forgotten.

She scanned the surrounding area with her eyes, as if she were seeing it for the first time. What a beauty.

A sheet of orange paper caught her eye. It was wedged in a crevice at the bottom of the fence. With curiosity, she walked over and pulled it out.

It was a hand-scribbled note in sloppy handwriting:

Jeannine, for your eyes only:
A mystery you must solve.
Riddle me this,
Riddle me that.
Guess me this riddle or perhaps not.
On it the sun sets and rises,
It comes in all shapes and sizes,
It's as old as Moses,
Outside your door it poses.
A clue to this riddle
Sits in the middle.

"Huh?" She frowned and posed a puzzled look. "Who wrote this?" she demanded.

Cottie and Fee-Fee looked at her questioningly.

She walked back to the veranda and sat down to study the note carefully.

She didn't recognize the handwriting. "Or..." She paused and bit her nail. "Unless someone wrote it with his or her opposite hand so I wouldn't recognize the handwriting."

She alighted off the veranda and walked back to the gate and opened it. She took a few steps onto the sidewalk. There was no one in sight.

Had someone been watching the house to see when she was out and had meticulously placed the note there?

Maybe one of her cousins was playing some kind of joke on her, she mused. Whatever it was sounded interesting, and she wanted to play the game.

She held up the paper to the sky as if to uncover some invisible clue. There was nothing but the pencil marks against the orange background.

She slowly turned about completely and scrutinized everything in sight—nothing seen. She closed her eyes and thought hard. But nothing popped in her head. She looked at the note again. She puckered her lips and shook her head.

It was outside for sure. It was a wide-ranged riddle, she thought.

There were too many things that were outside her door that came in all shapes and sizes and that were older than Moses. The sky for one. Trees, mountains, and rocks. She paused abruptly.

"Washburn did this," she said matter-of-factly. "He's trying to trick me. But then again, what if he has nothing to do with it? Should I try to find out if he wrote it, or should I just play the game?"

Back to the riddle. It was hard to guess at something that was so broad in scope. She didn't mind anyways. She liked challenges and figured whoever wrote the riddle would finally reveal what it was and then they would have a good laugh.

She shrugged her shoulders and tucked the note in her pocket, having no trouble dropping it from her thoughts, at least for the moment. She'd decided to deal with it another day because she had other things to tend to.

*****

It didn't take her long to fall back into the rhythm of things and become reacquainted with the ritualistic lifestyle of Jamaica. She was her old self again, and she felt good about it.

Cornmeal porridge with fried dumplings was one of her all-time favorite breakfast food. The hard crust at the bottom of the pot was always reason for a quarrel with her brother and sister. They argued endlessly about who would get the pot. Scraping the porridge from the bottom of the pot with a spoon sent a twirling of hardened cornmeal that was too delicious to give up easily—even if it meant she had to wash the pot.

"Child, you make porridge as good as your grandmother," said Mildred as she rolled another dumpling and popped it into the frying pan. A bowl of golden fried dumplings sat on the kitchen counter.

"With real homegrown cinnamon, vanilla, and nutmeg and freshly squeezed coconut milk, plus sweetened condensed milk, you can't go wrong, Grandma," she replied with a smile that was so gentle.

"Oh, you have a picture-perfect smile."

"Thank you, Grandma."

"When yu check it out lawd, nuh weh nuh betta dan yard," she sang.

"You remember that song from so long ago?" Mildred asked surprisingly.

"Yeah, I remember watching it on television. I remember it so well as if it happened just yesterday. The guy who sang it at the festival had a crockos bag filled with all kinds of produce. He poured them all out onstage as he sang the song. It won the festival. I remember clearly."

Breakfast was tantalizingly good. Cornmeal porridge and fried dumplings just weren't enough, though. Ackee and salt fish, roasted breadfruit fried to a golden crisp, and steamed callaloo crowned the table.

Ben took a sip of the cerasee tea and frowned. "I know that cerasee tea is good for me, but I can't handle any bitter herbs at this point in my life. Blue mountain coffee or hot chocolate will do just fine."

"Herbal tea is de best ting for you, boy. Cerasee clean your blood and make you healthy. You know that?" Carlton said, scolding his son.

After breakfast, Ben sat on the veranda and opened up his laptop. He planned to enjoy his vacation with his family despite the fact that he might never see those disks again.

"I'll take care of business when I get back," he consoled himself. He shoved the thought aside. His cell phone rang, and he glanced at the screen to see who was calling. It was from Milolta. He didn't recognize the number. *Maybe they're calling from a payphone,* he told himself. He answered it.

"Hello," he repeated. He didn't recognize the person's voice due to the breakup in the line. He stood up and moved around to get a better reception.

"Can you hear me?" the voice echoed into his ears.

"Yes, I can hear you a little better now." He walked to the back of the house. "It's got to be important, since you called me on my vacation."

"Indeed, it is."

His conversation lasted about ten minutes. His whole countenance had changed. He closed his laptop and stared at nothing, but he tried to brush the conversation aside so he could keep the promise he'd made to himself to enjoy his vacation. He managed a smile.

"What's the matter, Jeannine?" he asked his daughter. "You look like a mannequin?"

"Oh, nothing. Just thinking about something." The puzzle was getting the best of her.

She tried again to dismiss it from her thoughts, but this time it was harder. She told herself later that night she would spend more time trying to figure it out.

*****

Early Saturday morning, Ben pulled out for Dunn's River Falls. The temperature was comfortable. They weren't the first ones to arrive.

Ben unloaded the van all by himself. Everyone else was too busy talking about how beautiful the place was and how much fun they were going to have.

"I won't have any if someone doesn't help me," he complained.

"Oh, what a sight!" said Jeannine.

"I've stayed away too long!" Washburn was as equally fascinated and enthused about the Dunn's River Falls. "I almost forgot about its beauty." It had been years since they'd visited the site and were as equally thrilled to be there as the tourists were. They stood in awe.

"We come here almost every year," said a tourist as she locked arms with her husband. "This place is too good to be true, isn't it?" Without waiting for an answer, she rambled on. "Did you know that it's only two miles west of Ocho Rios?"

"Kinda, sorta," replied Jeannine, feeling a little flushed at the fact that foreigners knew more about her country than she did.

At six hundred feet high, the Dunn's River Falls cascade gushed from one emerald body of water to another, twirling noisily down the rocks and through each crevice as it gushed into a sparkling beach.

Jeannine lay on a rock and closed her eyes. The rough-flowing water massaged her body while the cascading beauty of the waterfall captivated her spirit and seemed to revive it.

A Jacuzzi doesn't come close to this, she thought as her body welcomed the cool massaging water.

"Come on, Jeannine," called her mother from above.

She raised her head and looked up. Ida stood with her hands on her hips.

"Don't you want to get to the top?" she called.

"Where are the others?" replied Jeannine.

She didn't know how long she'd been lying on the rocks, but she didn't care. Time was of no essence then. She had all day—and all night—if she so desired.

"Way ahead of us," her mother responded.

Jeannine climbed the slippery rocks cautiously, placing her feet firmly in the crevice of the rocks as she held on to each ledge, making her way to the top. Beautiful shrubs framed the waterfall as they lined the sides, getting their abundant nourishment from the flowing water. It was like a beauty that could only be imagined—a dreamland.

Jeannine climbed gracefully, sure-footed and calculating. Memories of her childhood swept through her thoughts. She had been the tomboy of the neighborhood and could climb rocks and trees just like any boy, better than most.

She beat them all in soccer and even in marbles. Her left hand and her sharp eye knew just where to flick the marble that she held tightly between her thumb and index fingers.

She made her way to the top and looked over toward the beach. It looked still. The people were far away and looked small and insignificant. What a great day, she told herself. Every day should be like this.

They spent the entire day at Dunn's River Falls. As beautiful as the day had been, the night was no less beautiful.

"Nature looked good night and day," said Jeannine as she enjoyed the night air. Night bugs lit up the neighborhood as they floated in the air. Little children caught them and put them in bottles until the morning, when they would let them go.

Everyone complained of aches and exhaustion from their trip, all but Washburn, of course. The mannish water soup was a comfort. Saturday and soup went hand in hand. A lot of Jamaicans couldn't even imagine a Saturday without some kind of soup. From mannish water, pepper pot soup, beef soup, fish tea soup, and cow cod soup to gungo peas soup, and the list went on.

Ida always enjoyed Mildred's poon tan up (spoon stand-up) soup. It was soup that was so thick she could easily plant her spoon in the bowl and it would stay standing up without falling over.

Jeannine sat on the huge rock that was in the front of the yard. She stared up at the black sky, which was partially illuminated by the countless stars that sprinkled its way across it.

She cupped her hands to form a pair of binoculars. She wanted to see nothing but the dark sky with its tiny dots of light.

She picked out a star and pictured herself floating into space to sit on it. "The stars are billions of years old," she reminded herself. Speaking of old made her remember the note. She rehearsed the words over and over in her mind. It wasn't hard to remember it since she'd read it so many times. Something very old was outside her door. If it was beyond the fence or in the yard was a question that was unanswered.

The moon was beginning to rise, and it gradually transformed the dark sky into a radiant beauty. She stared at the tiny circle that sat at the center of the sky, or so it seemed. *Who knows where the center is?* she thought. She called out everything that sat in front of the house.

"Now what?" she asked herself. "How will I know if I've got the right answer? Whom do I tell? What's next?" So far, no one had mentioned the riddle or even peculiarly asked her any question as if to find out if she'd solved it.

She jumped off the rock and danced in the moonlight. Her shadow mimicked her. "What sits in front of me but this huge rock," she said all of a sudden. She thought for a moment. *Could it be the rock that sat in the yard, or did they mean something else that sat beyond the yard?*

She walked around the rock. There was nothing unusual about it. Nothing different from what she'd already seen.

"I hope they don't expect me to move this rock!"

She stooped to the ground and peered underneath, but nothing out of the ordinary struck her. She got down on her knees and dug around it with a piece of stick.

"Gotcha!" she exclaimed with delight when a piece of orange paper rose to the surface.

"What?" asked her mother, who'd just walked out of the house. She sat on the veranda with a novel in her hand, but then suddenly she rose to her feet.

"I almost forgot about those coconut drops I got from Ms. Ella. Would you like some, Jeannine?"

"Oh, no, thank you," she replied.

She stared at the paper. Suddenly a shuffling noise caught her off guard. She let out a yelp and dashed toward the house. She bumped into her mother and knocked the book out of her hands.

"What's the matter with you?" asked Washburn, who was walking behind his mother.

"Nothing," she replied and headed in the kitchen.

"You're too old to be afraid of ghosts, Jeannine," called her mother after her. Washburn dropped to the floor and laughed hysterically.

"Are you all right?" asked Ida.

"Yeah, something moved in the bushes behind me and…" She paused as she stifled a grin. "It scared me out of my mind."

She laughed softly.

She read the piece of paper:

The answer to the previous
That was not too obvious
In disintegrated particles
You sure can guess these articles

It roars and rumbles
On particles it tumbles
The sound of its might
At the end of its flight

In color, shapes, and sizes
These might have surprises
Dwelling among particles, maybe under or above
To collect them some do love number 15

"Mmm, sounds like a real brain-teasing mystery to me. Just the kind I like."

Washburn hadn't looked suspicious in any way for her to believe that he'd scribbled the notes.

Her breathing became rapid at the thought of the challenge. She stared blankly at the words on the paper as her mind searched for possible answers, but she had no clue as to its meaning. But as she studied harder, possibilities arose.

Word by word, line by line, she studied it. "The answer to the previous clue was *rock.* Disintegrated rock becomes particles of either *dirt* or *sand.*"

She pulled out a notebook from her purse and wrote, "Dirt/ sand." Something tumbled on the dirt or sand.

Feet. Rain. She was stumped. The third clue seemed even more difficult.

As hard as she'd tried, nothing more came to her. She pulled out a pocket dictionary and looked up almost every word that was on the paper. Still, no luck.

I'll never get this one for sure, she thought in disappointment and tucked the note in her purse.

Mildred was never one to sleep late. Every morning the alluring smell from the kitchen aroused her household. For this particular morning, breakfast was salt mackerel with boiled dumplings and banana and sweet yam with piping-hot, strong black tea.

Just around midday, Ben gulped down the water from the little hole in the coconut jelly, then chopped them open with a machete and ate the jelly inside.

His father was in no less a talkative mood than he was any other day. It didn't matter if his audience was familiar with the information he issued or not; he just conversed. Ben told him he should have been a teacher because he knew so much. He kept up with the world and its affairs. For every world issue that was made public by way of the news, whether it was by television, radio, or through the newspapers, Carlton Shrouder was in tune with every piece of information. He could tell you how many people were in China or even tell you the square mile of a country. Encyclopedia was his nickname that they would use fondly at times.

"Did you know that the Jamaican bauxite puts us as the third largest bauxite producer? Our bauxite mining began in 1952 and is still going strong. With the production of bauxite, from which comes aluminum, we play a key role in the production of many household items, such as pots, pans, foils, and dishes. And large amounts of aluminum are used in materials used for transportations, such as cars, boats, trucks, aircraft, and aircraft engines. We also produce gypsum, marble, limestone, and other valuable minerals."

"Me want to hear 'bout the heroes again, Mr. Shrouder," said Fabian rather impatiently. There was nothing appealing to him about any minerals found in Jamaica, or anywhere else, for that matter. What intrigued him most was the unique lifestyle of the national heroes.

"Again?" Mr. Shrouder retaliated. "You've heard it so many times you ought to be telling it to me by now. With your twelve years of life and of all I've taught you, you should be able to run the country."

"I can," he said with confidence. He cleared his throat. "Well, students, our lesson today is about the Jamaican national heroes," he began in a deep, manly voice with his hand on his chin.

"The first one we'll talk about today is Paul Bogle." He raised his head and looked into the eyes of his students, Ben, Ida, Jeannine, Washburn, Mrs. Shrouder, and Mr. Shrouder.

"He was a Baptist leader in Stony…somewhere."

"Stony Gut," Mr. Shrouder added.

"Yes, yes. Stony Gut. I remember clearly now," he said like a confident professor. "He fought against poverty and injustice, and they hung him sometime in the 1800s. Alexander Bustamante was the first prime minister of Jamaica. He started the Jamaican Labor Party, known as the JLP, and Norman Washington Manley started the People's National Party, known as the PNP."

"You're the smartest kid I know, Fabian," said Jeannine. "All I can remember are their names and a little bit of what some of them did. You know more than I do, kid."

"Well, I don't know *everything*," he said in his normal childish voice. He turned to Carlton and said, "What did Marcus Garvey do?"

"I know," said Washburn. "He sought the unification of all black people. He was committed to the concept of emancipation of the mind."

"All our heroes, including Nanny, George William Gordon, and Sam Sharp, all worked to improve the lives of black people in society. We are reaping the benefit of their sacrifice."

*****

Jeannine walked barefoot on the shore of the hot, sandy beach. The white sand crunched under her weight with each step she took. The crystal clear sea lay still and inviting, glistening like a rear diamond in the bright sunlight.

The intensity of the sun interrupted the royal-blue sea, creating tiny diamond-like specks, specks that created awes in onlookers.

The awesome beauty of the beach kept its visitors coming back and spending long hours as their bodies soaked in the goodness of the cool, salty water. Vibrant waves roared and rolled to shore with a splash that was teasing.

Washburn threw his hands up in the air, tilted his head back, and hollered, "Hallelujah, free at last, free at last, thank God almighty, I'm free at last!"

Jeannine laughed so hard her stomach ached. "Okay, Dr. Martin Luther King Jr. III, what're you free from?"

"I don't know, but I'm free." He chuckled.

The air was fresh and clean, captivating their mood and framing it with an aroma of peace. The scenery saturated their spirit and unfolded them from the cares of an everyday life to one that was filled with bliss.

Fluffy white clouds hung below the dark-blue sky. Birds were busy going back and forth. Some were fishing for food; others just lazily floated around, giving nature a supernatural accent. Little children ran around, tossing sand or just giggling in a carefree way, catching butterflies and putting them in cans—treasures for life.

"Mine's the prettiest," said one little boy.

"Mine's bigger," replied his sibling. She pouted and walked away.

"One thing I like about walking on the beach is that the sand makes the bottom of my feet clean and pretty because it scrubs your feet as you walk," said Washburn.

"Sand! Sand, sand, sand! The answer to a disintegrated rock is sand, not dirt, because waves tumble on sand!"

"What are you talking about, Jeannine? You've lost us."

"Oh, nothing," she said excitedly to her father. "The clue is *sand* and *waves*."

She was halfway through figuring out the whole clue, and she was thrilled.

Wave sand. Wavy sand. Sand wave. Sandy wavy. "Nah," she said out loud. "Just doesn't make sense."

"Talking to yourself again, Jeannine?" asked her mother. Later that afternoon, Jeannine resigned to her room to spend time on the brain-teasing riddle.

"What if I'm doing this in vain? What if I'll never find out who wrote it or what it means?" Even those thoughts didn't stop her from working on the riddle.

With a thesaurus and dictionary and the two sheets of orange paper sprawled out on the table before her, Jeannine indulged in the mystery.

She rubbed her burning eyes but was nowhere near ready to give up for the night. She repeated the words of the clue over and over. "The sound of its might at the end," she mused out loud. "It must be talking about the waves."

Splash? Yes, splash! The wave makes a splash at the shore. The shore is where it ends. It splashes on the sand. Sand and splash. Sandy splash, she mulled over in her mind as she took out her notebook and added the words *splash on sand.*

After a few days of brainstorming, a glimmer of light was shed on the third paragraph. She had finally figured out that it probably all had something to do with the beach.

Seashells were all she could think of that dwelled among the sand. It was normal to see people collecting seashells.

"Why couldn't I have guessed that before?" Seashells, splash, sand. She had no idea what she needed to do with them. Neither did she know what to do with the "number 15."

Ben and his family made endless visits to the beach, and Jeannine used every trip to work on the puzzle. Canoeing and river rafting brought out the kid in Ben and Ida. Almost every waking day of their stay was spent doing something exciting.

How could they resist going to the beach when it was so close? Besides, they'd better make the best of it, because there was no telling when they would have the opportunity to visit again.

*****

Rain dropped from the sky like bullets from an automatic gun, giving rise to the old adage "When it rains in Jamaica, it pours." Jeannine and Washburn sat on the veranda and watched as little puddles formed and then turned into streams. Heavy rain gushed from the sky as if God had opened up the windows of heaven and had let loose the fountain of water. It dropped noisily on housetops, creating the mood to pull the covers and slumber in dreamland.

"It's been raining for hours. This is sleeping weather," said Ben as he snuggled in bed.

Ida threw the covers over her head, declaring in a muffled voice, "Don't ever wake me up!"

A smile lingered on Jeannine's face as she listened to the raindrops on the roof of the house. It reminded her of childhood and how much fun it was to play in the rain. Her thoughts shifted to the riddle. She couldn't wait to see what the end of the riddle would be. She still had no clue as to who wrote it. It was specifically written to her, and seemingly, no one else should see it. It was her secret riddle.

She mused on the three words that she'd figured out. She rehearsed them over and over in her head and tried to make sense with them.

Splash, seashells, and sand—all associated with the beach. But how did they tie in? What if that was all she needed to figure out? What then? Who would she tell? Maybe she ought to just wait and see what happened in the next few days.

She thought about the number and how much of a misfit it was in her solution. She sat upright in the bed. Seashore. Sand, seashells, waves were all at the shore of the sea. Seashore Place. *Fifteen Seashore Place? Mmm.* Her heart raced. Seashore Place, at least an address with that name, was just a mile from the house. Could it be that? she wondered.

She shook her head. *What would that have to do with anything, anyways? A wild-goose chase,* she thought.

The more she thought about it, however, the more it appealed to her.

She'd figured more or less that it was a possibility that she had finally figured out the clue, but then what should she do about it? She had an idea. She would go to 15 Seashore Place tomorrow and see what was there. She could hardly wait until then.

She trailed off to sleep with 15 Seashore Place on her mind.

*****

"So this is what Fern Gully looks like," said Washburn. "I've never seen this before, and to think I was born here. It really is a shame that tourists enjoy my country more than me. There are places in Jamaica that I've never gone to."

"Well, there is no Jamaican that can say they know every nook and cranny of Jamaica," said Ida. "Plus, it depends on where you live. Those who live close by and have to use this road to travel see it more often than those who live at the other end of Jamaica."

"We passed through here once before when we were visiting your uncle. You were just a baby then."

The three-mile-long gully was draped with ferns on either side of its zigzagging path in Ocho Rios. The trees on either side bent to one another and sheltered the road, giving an awestruck mood.

Ben took snapshots and hoped that the pictures would come out perfect. "I can't wait to see them."

All the while, Jeannine kept her thoughts on the riddle to herself. As soon as she got back, she would go to 15 Seashore Place.

They didn't return home until late afternoon, but Jeannine wasn't too tired to take a walk to Seashore Place.

As she stood in front of the abandoned building that had *15* in bold italic letters, she shrugged her shoulders in disappointment and turned to walk back home.

That building couldn't have anything to do with the riddle, she thought. She was hoping that someone would grin at her and congratulate her on being so good in figuring out the riddle.

She took a few steps but then stopped in her track. Maybe she'd better take a look inside to see if a clue was there. About a quarter of a mile down the road was the house she lived in before they'd moved to Bull Bay in Saint Andrews.

She purposed to pay a visit to the neighbors after she'd searched the abandoned building. When she entered the dusty house, she had to peel her way through the cobwebs. She searched for anything that might look like a clue.

She spotted something orange halfway buried under a piece of board.

"There!" she exclaimed with excitement. By now she'd gotten the idea that the clue would be on an orange piece of paper.

She brushed the dust off and read the pencil-scribbled note out loud:

So far you've come the riddle to complete
A few more clues and the giant you'll defeat
The house before you holds the key
At the side of the house the clue you'll see
Add that to scarlet, a color so bright
The color of richness, the color of life

She jumped up and squealed a controlled holler as she rejoiced at finding another clue. *So this is a real mystery.* "This is getting good," she said. "What'll be my reward?" she wondered out loud as she smiled from ear to ear.

She looked out the paneless window at the house that sat directly across the street. A small three-bedroom house with a shed on the side, it looked unoccupied—no curtains in the window or any chairs on the veranda. There was not an animal or a person around.

The shed was the only thing at the side of the house. Her adrenaline began to pump even faster. So far, it had been interesting, but she was beginning to worry. She didn't know why, but all of a sudden, she felt uncomfortable about the whole thing. She fiddled with her hands nervously. Well, she was only there for a few minutes and couldn't draw any conclusions just yet.

She stared across the street at the house that occupied a spot that was vacant only a few years ago. While she was away in the States, someone had purchased the lot and had built a house. She had no idea who lived there.

She exited the abandoned building, made a left, and held her head straight as she headed back to the house. She didn't feel like visiting anyone anymore.

She took out her notepad and jotted down her discoveries of the day.

Wherever this riddle was leading her, she was going to follow it all the way. After all, she'd come this far; she might as well continue.

"The color of scarlet is red. What gives life but God? Red? God? Nah. What is the color of life? Scarlet is red. The color of life is...blood. Blood is red. Blood red. Red blood. Add that to *scarlet*." She stared at the note until her eyes crossed. Shed red. Shed scarlet. Shed blood. Bloodshed. The words fell from her lips almost subconsciously, but in a few seconds it dawned on her like a rude awakening. "Bloodshed!"

"Ah!" Goose bumps covered her body. "That can't be the answer. Did someone die?"

Why did they pick that house? It wasn't the only one with a shed. There were three other houses with sheds that she'd passed to get to the one that the clue referred to.

She didn't know what to do next. She almost didn't want to know. She was curious on one hand, and on the other hand, she wanted to forget about the whole thing.

What if the riddle led her to something horrible? She swallowed hard. She wanted to give up. She could quit right then and probably save herself from a traumatic experience. *Sometimes it's better not knowing,* she thought.

Bloodshed. A chill ran up her spine. The more she thought about it, the more she didn't want to be involved. She came for a vacation and wasn't about to let anything ruin it. Bloodshed didn't make a vacation a thrilling one. A chilling one was more like it. She groaned.

A gruesome thought filled her thoughts. She tried to shake it from her mind. She was having a good time, enjoying herself in her country, until someone singled her out and pulled her into a mystery. What if it was a clue to unfold a murder plot? On that thought her curiosity was renewed. If she could help save someone's life, then she was all for doing whatever it took to solve the puzzle.

She still hadn't told anyone about the riddle. For days she kept looking for a clue, but none came. She wanted to know who was living in the house that the clue referred to. If the riddle was indeed legitimate and the people who lived there were in danger, how would she warn them? If the riddle turned out to be a hoax, then she would look like a fool if she ever mentioned it to anyone.

It'd been a few days, and she hadn't gotten any more information other that what she found in the abandoned building. She'd decided to walk by the house and take a good look at it again.

She wasn't quite sure concerning the significance of the number of the house but guessed it to be 17 since it was directly across from 15.

Later that night, she pondered the mystery. She knew that she had to find the answers or it would haunt her for years to come. She braced her mind and prepared herself for the worst. She was going to go through with it no matter what. Who knew, she might save someone who would be eternally grateful to her.

Early one morning she saw the orange sheet of paper that she'd been looking for. It was stuck at the bottom of the fence in the same spot she'd found the first one.

The numbers you see
Hold the victory to be
ABCs and 123s
5-13-13-5-20-20 number 42

If at all you will
The riddle you won't spill
The paper you are holding
Riddle is close to unfolding

The answer to the first added to the numbers
3-12-1-18-11-9-5

With gratitude in my heart
I thank you for playing a part
The solution of the riddle
Still won't bring him to prison

"Someone was murdered!" She felt faint. Her hands shook as she stared at the paper anxiously.

"Who lives at 17 Seashore Place?" she asked her grandfather when they were alone.

"Nobody." He looked at her questioningly. "Why do you want to know?"

"Just wondering. It's a nice house. It was an open lot before we moved to the States."

"Mr. Bob bought the lot and built a house on it." He sighed and shook his head regretfully. "He was murdered right there a week before you came."

She choked. She'd thought that maybe the riddle was a fluke, but now she knew beyond the shadow of a doubt that someone was trying to tell her something.

Carlton rubbed her back to appease her cough. "Are you all right?"

She nodded. "Did they catch the person who did it?"

"No one heard or saw anything."

She almost dropped the plate she had in her hands. Now more than ever, she wanted to solve the riddle.

She rehearsed the words of the puzzle over and over. *I just have to figure it out,* she thought.

*****

Day in and day out, Jeannine worked hard on the riddle, finding no other way to use the numbers but in the letters of the alphabet. The numbers spelled a word, *Emmett*. She assumed that number 42 was the number of a building on an Emmett Street. But on second thought, she wondered if number 42 was the age of someone whose last or first name was Emmett. Who was Emmett, or where was Emmett Street? She knew of neither one.

"We're leaving now, Jeannine. Are you sure you don't want to come along?" asked her mother for the tenth time.

"I'm sure. Take your time, please."

She was finally alone. She could ponder the riddle undisturbed.

Sitting in a chair on the veranda, she saw a middle-aged man pass by the house and said, "Excuse me, sir, but do you happen to know of an Emmett Street?"

"Yes, there is an Emmett Street up by Tawna Hill."

That was it. One way or another, she had to get to Emmett Street. She didn't know what she needed to look for, but she had to go and view it from a distance and maybe ask the neighbors a few questions. If it yielded nothing, then her next game plan would be to treat it as a name rather than a location.

The next step of the riddle was simple. Since she'd used the alphabet to figure out Emmett Street, she knew that the other numbers were fashioned the same. *Clarkie.*

"Ah, a name! Oh my goodness!" She could hardly contain herself. "Clarkie Stone. Clarkie Rock. Clarkie Emmet. I bet he's the murderer!"

"Wait a minute. Clarkie Rock." She scratched her head. "This can't have anything to do with the Clarkie I know. His real name is Clarence Rock. The riddle probably would have said *Clarence* if it meant Clarence Rock." Goose pimples covered her body. "What if it's about Clarkie? Was he the murderer or the riddle writer? Clarkie wouldn't hurt a fly," she assured herself. "He's always been a good person, friendly, kind, considerate." She couldn't remember to what street Clarkie had moved.

She hoped and watched for someone to come and tell her that they'd written the riddle. At the end of the day, she found another sheet of paper.

"Two riddles in one day. This better be the last one."

A girl I've known
Before she was grown
She's stolen my heart
We can't be apart

A ball of light
That breaks through the night
Behold its peek
At Wellington's Creek

Jeannine, sweet little dove
He's stolen you, my sweet love
Clarkie shall die
In the twinkling of an eye

"Someone is going to murder Clarkie? Now this is way over my head." She gulped. "Who in the world are you?" she yelled in despair. It was someone she knew, based on the note, but she just couldn't figure out who it might be. She figured the second verse to be full moon, and she dropped the paper as if it were on fire when she learned that there was a full moon that night. She glanced at the clock on the wall, and it read eleven thirty. Scribbling a note to her family, she taped it over the keyhole of the door. They'd see it as soon as they got ready to unlock the door. "I'm at Wellington's Creek. Call the police—Jeannine," it read.

*****

Not knowing if Clarkie would be there, she had to take the chance. She walked through the bushes instead of taking the tracks that led to the creek. By the time she got to the spot, it was eleven forty-five. She sat breathlessly on a rock in the bushes and waited.

Ms. Joycie was there with a wash pan full of clothes. *Go home, Ms. Joycie,* Jeannine pleaded silently. She breathed a sigh of relief when Ms. Joycie rinsed the last of her clothes in the running water, put the wash pan on her head, and walked up the hill to her house.

She heard a noise and peeked through the bushes. "Kincaid," she whispered, trying to get his attention. "Please call the police. Something terrible might take place tonight."

Kincaid turned his head slowly toward her.

"Kincaid! Don't just stand there. Go and call the police, please," she pleaded.

Kincaid pulled an orange sheet of paper from his pocket and held it high over his head. Jeannine stared at him silently.

A girl I've known
Before she was grown
She's stolen my heart
We can't be apart

A ball of light
That breaks through the night
Behold its peek
At Wellington's Creek

Jeannine, sweet little dove
He's stolen you, my sweet love
Clarkie shall die
In the twinkling of an eye

"Where'd you get that?" she stuttered.

He read another riddle.

"Jeannine," a voice called her.

"Clarkie!" she bellowed. "Run!"

Clarkie laughed. "First you sent me a note inviting me to meet you here, and now you're telling me to run?" he said, a bit bewildered.

"I didn't send you any note. Kincaid did." She pointed over at Kincaid, whom Clarkie hadn't noticed. "He wants to kill you," she added with emphasis.

Kincaid let out a slight laugh. "She's right," he said and pulled a handgun from his waist. Clarkie stepped back a bit. His face became suddenly serious.

"Me neva like yu from mawning." I never liked you from the beginning. Kincaid pointed the gun in Clarkie's direction. "I've always liked Jeannine, but you, you dirty dog, you're trying to steal her heart. Well, this is your last night. Mi wi have har and you won't." I'll have her and you won't.

"Kincaid," she called softly, "you never told me you liked me. And besides, Clarkie and I are just friends. Whatever made you think—"

"Don't say it!" he hollered.

"So, Kincaid," she said, trying to prolong the conversation in hopes that her family had seen the note and alerted the police. She also hoped that his attention would shift from Clarkie. "You wrote all those riddles?"

"Yep." He smiled. "I'm good, right?"

"Why didn't you just come out and tell me?"

"I wanted to know how smart you were. You're very smart. You passed the test. It made me love you even more. I have a smart girlfriend."

"Do you know who killed Mr. Bob?" she asked.

"You don't know? I thought you'd guess that. You're looking at him," he said with his chest held high in pride.

"You?" she asked incredulously. "But why, Kincaid?"

"It was that blasted glassy eye of his." He chuckled. "Stand over there where I can see you better while I satisfy Ms. J's curiosity before I kill you," he ordered.

"What about his eye, Kincaid?"

"I hated his eye. There was something about that dumb glass eye of his. Every time he looked at me, it seemed as if he was looking into my soul. I didn't trust him. His expression told me he knew things about me I didn't even want to face. Even in my sleep, I would see that eye just looking at me. I had nightmares over that eye. I had to get rid of him and his glass eye."

"Jeannine," he said in a more solemn tone. "I've always loved you but never had the courage to tell you."

"You have more courage than most people I know," she snapped and regretted her tone. He seemed not to have noticed her anger.

"When you're gone, Clarkie, you'll be out of the picture and she'll focus on me."

Clarkie closed his eyes and pleaded for his life. Jeannine ran and stood in front of him.

"You wouldn't shoot me, would you, Kincaid?"

"Well…" He paused. "If I had no choice, yes."

She gulped hard and fast.

"Move!" he commanded. She stood firm. He walked toward Clarkie and gently shoved Jeannine out of the way with his free hand. He pointed the gun at the back of Clarkie's head. Clarkie fell to the ground and pleaded again for mercy.

"You know what? I killed Cyclops too."

"What?"

"You didn't figure that one? Hello, 42 Emmett Street. That was where he lived. Well, him did just a tek up space in this world!" He was just taking up space in this world. With his heavy Jamaican accent, Kincaid switched back and forth from the Jamaican patois to English.

"Jeannine," he continued, "the man was totally useless. You can't feed yourself, you can't bathe yourself, you can't use the toilet by yourself—you just lie there all day, depending on somebody for everything. Well, you got to go. I helped him, that's all. He was the first person I ever killed. I didn't plan on killing anybody else, but Bob thought I was a bad person. He made me feel funny, so I got rid of him. You know what, Jeannine? After I get rid of this one, then we'll live happily ever after. I promise I'll never kill another person. Say goodbye and tell the Lord I say hello."

Clarkie heard a click and knew that his life was over. Kincaid then felt a firm hand grab him by the back of his neck and a hand at his wrist simultaneously. In a moment he found himself on his face with his nose pressed hard against Jamaican soil.

"Got you right here on tape, Kincaid," said Washburn as he held up the tape recorder.

"Bring me the rope," said Ben to his son as he pressed his knee hard into Kincaid's back. "Are you all right, J?"

"Yes, Daddy. I thought you'd never get here."

"I'm glad you're all right," said her brother with a smile.

"The police are on the way."

Kincaid struggled to keep his nose clear. Ben and Washburn tied him into a bundle and waited for the police to arrive.

*****

It was time to go, time to say goodbye again. It was a day like any other day, but the sadness Jeannine felt in her heart set that particular day apart from all others.

"I think we have everything." Ben was happy. He had a wonderful time. He was looking forward to going back to the US in no uncertain terms.

The weather was indeed gorgeous. The temperature was warm and pleasant, and she welcomed the soft feel of the wind on her body. The sun peeked out of the gray clouds every now and then, but Jeannine's spirit slumped under the fact that she was leaving, again. She hated goodbyes.

A lot of good things happened while they were there: the pleasures that they'd indulged in and the fact that Jeannine was of vital assistance in the community. *Oh, Kincaid,* she thought. Whatever brought him to the brink to do such awful things? He wasn't the same Kincaid that she'd grown up with. Something happened that had caused him to lose all rational thinking. And Clarkie. He was a lucky guy, she knew. On second thought, she thought if she hadn't come back to Jamaica, he wouldn't have been in that predicament. She'd only seen Clarkie a few times only to catch up on old times. Whatever caused Kincaid to think that she and Clarkie were dating? Well, he wasn't rational, anyway. She dismissed her thoughts. *I've got to let go of all that,* she told herself.

"Don't you even desire to stay longer?" she asked her father. Ben looked too happy, if one could put it that way. She was offended and thought, *He had been born here. Why would he act as if he couldn't wait to leave? It didn't add up.*

"I love Jamaica, but right now I live in the United States. I love both countries. I'm happy for the great opportunity to enjoy my country again, but there's nothing wrong with wanting to go back to the States."

She didn't care for his answers even though she knew it made sense. She liked America a lot. It was the "Goodbye" and the "I won't see you for a while" that she hated.

*****

Bags and suitcases stuffed to capacity were stashed in the van, and all were ready to go. Ackee, puddings, jerk chicken, coconut drops, whatever they could fit in their luggage, were shoved in.

Truth was, the ride to the airport was like a funeral service. Jeannine didn't say much. She rehearsed the goodbyes that had transpired the day before and went over the ones that took place before they set out for the airport.

All the places that they'd passed on their first day back in Jamaica seemed to fly by in the opposite direction as they headed toward the airport. A tear escaped her eye. She quickly brushed it away before someone noticed it.

The visit was extravagant. It was one that no one would ever forget. Suddenly, she scolded herself for feeling gloomy. She held her chin high and relaxed her tense body. A smile broke through. She counted it a privilege to have gotten to see her blessed country.

Jamaica, their island home, would always be there, and they would never deny their heritage. Who knew? Maybe in the future they would return home for good, but now, destiny demanded that they return to the country that they had lived in for so long. Maybe destiny might bring them back home to live in the land of their birth. It was in God's hands.

They waved goodbye as they entered customs and waved again as they walked out the building toward the airplane.

Jeannine paused and looked around at the country she knew she might never see again for a long time.

"Nah, I'll be back again soon, I think."

She looked at the ground again. In her heart she blessed her country, such a beautiful place. "I love you, Jamaica. Always."

Beaches clear as crystals, sceneries of great ecstasy, great tropical dishes, and all the other things that they'd enjoyed did not come close to the feeling of pride wedged in their hearts from the fact that they were a part of the country that produced such beauty and life.

"I will always love America because I have chosen it to be my country of residence, but nothing can take the place of Jamaica—always number one in my heart. Jamaica, my island home."

Jeannine sat perfectly still and took long, deep breaths. She purposed not to shed another tear. She leaned her head against the aircraft window. The fresh, clean smell of the aircraft reminded her of spring—new birth, new life, new hope. Who knew what the future held. Maybe, she thought, after finding Mr. Right she would return to Jamaica permanently. She wanted her children to learn about her heritage through experience. Maybe then she'd move back to the States.

Whatever, she thought to herself. *Too far into the future to think about.*

*****

Casey prayed that her family would have a safe flight. She was a little nervous, but she knew that they would be all right. She couldn't help but think about how much she'd missed and needed them, even Washburn. Wow, what a revelation. She smiled.

She was glad that Barry was in town that week. He was still stationed in Saviannia but was able to come home for about a week or so. He'd been waiting for a year to be transferred to Milolta so that he could be with his wife, but it just hadn't happened yet.

He would have loved for her to live in Saviannia, but she just couldn't leave her family. She hated the thought of not seeing them for any length of time.

He hoped that it wouldn't be long when he and his wife would be able to live together.

*****

It was 8:30 p.m. when the Air Jamaica flight arrived at the Milolta International Airport.

The Christmas rush had passed. The intensity that was felt in the air had lessened.

A few weeks ago, they were in a frantic mood, rushing to catch their flight. Now they were in no kind of hurry. With darker complexion and a calmer mood, they walked slowly to the waiting area, tugging on their luggage.

Exhaustion was setting in. "Hopefully, Casey and Barry are already here. I just want to get home." Ben yawned. Constant late nights and vigorous activities had taken a toll on them.

As they walked down the long hall, they reminisced about the country they had just left a few hours ago. "Eventually, I want to go back to Jamaica. Maybe after I've retired," said Ben.

"How about we go back right now?" Washburn said.

Ida looked at him and smiled faintly. "Someday we will. Someday," she replied.

"Welcome home," said Barry as he handed them their coats. A broad smile covered his face.

It was cold. It was a vast contrast between the ninety-degree weather they'd left not too long ago.

It felt good to be back.

"It's good to see you guys again," said Ben.

"I hope you brought me back a piece of the island," declared Casey.

"We've brought back more than the island." Ida laughed as she pointed to the numerous pieces of belongings.

"Nice tan," teased Casey.

"I got something special for both of you. I know you'll like them," said Jeannine to her only sister.

They stepped out of the airport building and into a blizzard. The bone-chilling wind cut through their coats as if they were made of strings. The ground was covered with twelve inches of snow.

"What a day to choose to come back from the island," said Ben as he wrapped his long down coat around him.

"I'm freezing," complained Jeannine through chattering teeth.

Chapter 7

Snow, Sleet, and Chills!

"What's up, tan girl?" Jeannine had come back a little darker than she'd left—not that she'd intentionally caused her skin to get darker by lying out in the sun, but because Jamaica was basically hot all year-round. Thus, the tan was unavoidable.

She looked at the back of her hand and replied, "It's only temporary. It'll wash off." She laughed. "Gosh, I miss you guys. You really missed out on a mystery. I wish you were there to solve it with me."

"You solved a mystery while you were in Jamaica? What was it, the mystery of the mind?" Jealissa teased.

"It was far better than that."

"Tell us all about it, Jeannine. We're all ears."

"One morning, I was sitting on the veranda and my eye suddenly caught sight of a piece of orange paper that was stuck to the bottom of the fence. As curious as I've always been, I went over and pulled it out and opened it to see what it was. What I found was a riddle."

She walked over to her dresser and pulled out a few sheets of orange papers. She handed the one on top to Jealissa. Kim walked over and peered over her shoulder. "Interesting," said Kim. "I like challenges. The mystery of the orange paper."

"I'm not sure you'd like this one, Kim, but hold on to your seat. The best, or should I say the worst, is yet to come. After reading the riddle, I thought, surely, someone like Washburn had something to do with this. Someone I knew was trying to play with my head, but as I like challenges, I tried to figure it out."

"This person probably had a crush on you, Jeannine. I can tell by his first line. *For your eyes only*. Oh, the James Bond thing."

Jeannine challenged the girls with each sheet of the riddle, and it was like a brain-teasing game to them.

"I don't know how you figured out all that, Jeannine. I feel like my brain is about to explode. I like challenges, but not when they're this deep. Thinking too hard gives me a headache," Kim told her.

After hearing about Jeannine's ingenuity in translating the riddle, they commended her. "Jeannine, I must say that you're very brave," said Jealissa with pride.

"You're very resourceful too," added Kim. "I don't think I could have handled it the way you did. Just hearing about it gives me the creeps too."

"The first note would have freaked me out. I hate mysteries and always think the worst," said Jealissa.

"Some vacation," Kim added, "but as long as the ending was good, then it's all right."

"You know what, girls? I always thought that fate has a lot to play in everybody's lives. It was just my fate to be there to experience all that. I don't think I could have avoided it. We're all driven by some unknown force, and our steps are ordered by some greater power."

They nodded in agreement.

*****

Saint Paul caught a glimpse of Brendan in the parking lot of the Brennan's Supermarket. Brendan had just gotten out of his car and was about four car lengths from his car when he sneaked up behind him and said very calmly but firmly, "Brendan Clark, you walk casually over there and get into my car. I have a gun, and I don't want to use it."

Had he met his doom? Brendan wondered. *Certainly, on a busy Saturday morning in the parking lot of a major supermarket, someone would notice and come to my rescue.*

He turned around slowly and faced Saint Paul. "Why?" Brendan asked innocently.

Saint Paul was annoyed. "You know why," he said between clenched teeth. "You're going to bring me to your house, and you're going to hand me my disks."

Brendan opened his mouth to speak, but Saint Paul interrupted him.

"Don't even think about trying to deny it."

He's bluffing, Brendan thought. *There is no way he could have found out that I took his disks. I locked the door behind me. And besides…*

"Now!" Saint Paul ordered.

"Excuse me. Excuse me," Brendan called to a woman with a little boy about five years old.

She turned and looked at him.

"This gentleman would like to know what time it is, and by golly, I've forgotten my watch."

She looked at her watch and replied, "It's 10:35."

He turned to Saint Paul and said loudly, "It's 10:35, sir. Have a great day!" Then he turned and walked back toward his car with a high-pitched whistling. He called to the woman and said, "You have a beautiful child."

"Thank you," she called back with a smile.

Saint Paul stood there helplessly, with a grim look on his face.

What if I'm mistaken? What if Saint Paul isn't into anything illegal? I could be charged with stealing, not to mention trespassing, nuisance, and a string of other things. But that was far from Brendan's mind, because he had no doubt Saint Paul was up to something. The aura about him was too strong to just be nothing.

Brendan wanted to find some kind of avenue that would lead him to some tangible evidence.

The next morning broke fine and lovely, and Brendan awoke in good spirits. He wondered about his day and what he could accomplish to satisfy his human heart. He hadn't been able to get anywhere with his investigating.

"Following him to work today isn't such a bad idea," Brendan thought out loud. On second thought, he'd decided to go directly to his job and watch secretly for his arrival. He knew Saint Paul would recognize his car, and didn't want to risk being spotted as he followed him. He congratulated himself that he'd done a great job when he'd followed Saint Paul from the DMV, and knew he might not be as lucky this time. He glanced at his watch.

He should still be in bed. If' he's working today, we'll see what he's up to now, won't we? Brendan thought seriously.

Dimension Computer Galaxy Corporation (DCGC) was directly across from the Milolta Diner. Brendan parked at the back of the diner and acquired a seat facing his job.

He ordered a Western omelet, wheat toast, sausages, and a cup of hot chocolate. He ate slowly and sipped his hot chocolate carefully as he watched the road for his car.

At 8:33 a.m., he spotted it a block away. Brendan's lips stayed firm on his cup as he eyed the car. Saint Paul pulled up to the side of the diner, and Brendan gulped his hot chocolate. It sent a stream of lavalike sensation down his throat.

There's plenty of parking space left at his building. I hope he's not coming here to eat, he thought. He knew that Saint Paul hadn't pulled up to the building because he'd spotted Brendan. The diner's windows were dark, and no one could see anyone from the outside.

Saint Paul got out of his car and walked to the front of the diner. Brendan's table was located in the left-hand corner, just a few tables from the front door, and he sat immobile as his brain froze and refused to give information. Just as Saint Paul opened the door, he dropped his fork and stuck his head under the table to pick it up. There was no way Saint Paul would have missed him unless he'd walked in with his face buried in the morning paper. He walked to the cashier, and she took him to a seat in the back, where a wall separated the two men from viewing each other.

Brendan pulled his head from under the table and breathed a sigh of relief. Now he had to decide if he should leave or just sit there. If he got up, Saint Paul might somehow see him, so he decided to take his chance and just stay sitting at his table. His mind was frantically thinking, *How can I prevent Saint Paul from noticing me? Even if he saw me from behind, he probably would recognize me. If he left, it would be even easier for him to spot me.*

He decided to risk his chance. *Even if he saw me, what could he do in broad daylight* in *a diner?* Brendan didn't want to chance getting detected, so he stayed put.

Today is my lucky day, he thought as he picked up the huge book-like menu that the waitress had forgotten to take. He turned his chair so that he would be facing Saint Paul as he walked down the aisle to the exit, knowing he could hide his face behind the menu.

He eyed the aisle cautiously. He'd hate to think that the moment he shifted the menu a bit past his eyes could be when Saint Paul might come down the aisle and meet his gaze.

Brendan kept his cool and stayed until Saint Paul walked out the door twenty minutes later. *Must have had a light breakfast or had called in his order,* Brendan thought, knowing how long it usually took for one to get their orders at the diner.

He got in his car and drove to the parking lot across the street.

Well, he thought, *he didn't wear a disguise to work. When and where does he wear a disguise?* He wondered, *Was that the only time he'd worn it at the motor vehicle's office?*

No need to stay here and muse, he thought. He rose from his chair and proceeded to go out the door, but then Saint Paul came out the front door of his building and headed straight to his car.

Where is he going now? Brendan watched as he drove out of the parking lot. He ran to the back of the building and jumped into his car and took off, but by the time he got on the road, Saint Paul was nowhere in sight.

Well, so much for that, he thought and headed downtown to see what Charles was up to.

Charles wasn't home, but he'd decided to hang around a bit. After all, his two favorite girls were there.

"Get your skiing gears on, everybody, because we are heading for the mountains, Snowy Mountain, that is," Charles said as he pushed open the door.

"Take off your boots on the mat," Charles's mother reminded him before he took another step.

"Brrr!" His hair dripped with snow. "I was just sledding with a bunch of kids on the slope in front of the corner store. I'd forgotten how much fun it was to slide down those slopes.

"Let's go skiing this weekend. Who's with me?"

"I have never gone skiing, and I don't think I want to start now," Jeannine said firmly. "It's too dangerous. I've heard of too many accidents like avalanches or someone hitting a tree"

"They do have an area for dummies," Charles interrupted.

Jeannine threw a cushion at him, but with swiftness, he ducked out of its way.

"Cunning, aren't you?" She laughed.

"It'll be fun, J. I've gone, and this place is really nice," Kim added. Brendan agreed. "Besides, I'll be there, J. Nothing will happen to you."

"I think it's a great idea that we all go!" said Jealissa feverishly. "We really haven't done anything together lately."

They compelled Jeannine, and she gave in.

She watched as skiers skied down long and windy slopes. She envied their ability to ski with such professionalism. It looked like too much fun for anyone to just be a spectator. She couldn't help but want to give it a try.

First-time skiers tumbled their way on the slopes, trying to get the feel of it. Their inability and clumsiness didn't stop Jeannine from getting on her skiing gear. Even the falls looked like a lot of fun.

She plopped down on the snow and, with Kim's help, geared up.

The snow sparkled from the glare of the sun. The air was crisp and cold. Jeannine took a deep breath and filled her lungs and then ventured out to ski.

She stood firm and refused to move. "Push yourself forward just a little bit, Jeannine," begged the girls.

"I will. Just give me a moment to think about how I'm going to do it."

"Okay, one, two, three," she counted to prepare herself for takeoff, but then she just stood there. She took another breath.

"I'll help you," said Kim, and she gave her a shove.

Jeannine screamed her way down the amateur slope. "Stop, stop!" she hollered, but her skis kept on going. *Plop.* She came to a sudden stop in a pile of snow that was way off course. Kim and Jealissa were at her side in seconds.

"Are you hurt?"

Jeannine laughed hysterically. The girls burst into nonstop laughter.

"That was fun," she said between giggles.

"How's it going, girls?" both Charles and Brendan yelled from way above them.

"Just peachy!" Jeannine hollered back.

She finally made it back to the top of the slope. She poised herself again for takeoff.

"Stand back," she commanded. "I'll do this myself, thank you very much!" She tilted her body forward and gently started her way down the slope. The wind tickled her face as she glided slowly.

Her first time skiing was more fun than she'd thought it would be. She was glad she had decided to spend the day at Snowy Mountain.

"That was fun, guys," she said as she sipped her hot chocolate. "I am looking forward to going again with you. I was really getting the hang of it close to the end of the day. If I keep this up, I'll be a pro in no time."

"I'm glad you had fun, J," said Brendan.

Even though Jeannine didn't like the cold weather, there were beauties in winter that she admired. Freshly fallen snow was beautiful. It was white and pure, soft and fluffy. It beautified trees and mountains and rocky hillsides. Snow falling from the sky seemed to fall in slow motion as they twirled their way to the ground. It fascinated her. Winter wasn't so bad, after all.

Brendan went home to find that he had had an unexpected visitor. He stood inside the door with his mouth wide-open. Everything had been turned upside down. When he walked through his rooms, he found a note taped to the bathroom mirror:

> *The disks. Give them up. Keep your mouth shut or you will die!*

Yeah, right, he thought. For some reason, Brendan wasn't afraid. The lock on his apartment door wasn't broken, and he knew very well how he'd accessed the apartment. Somehow, he must have swiped the key from his daughter. Not wanting the police to get involved yet, Brendan purposely broke his lock so that his landlord would have to change the lock. "I will not give up those disks. I won't stop until your dirty secrets are out in the open!" he growled in finality.

*****

It was cold outside, but inside Charlie's Pub, the heat was exhilarating from the bodies of the few men and women who had come out for a good time.

"Hey, Charlie, another one for the lady. It's on me."

"What're you trying to do, get me drunk, Petie boy?"

"I wouldn't do such a thing, Ms. Esther Sue, and besides, I'm not drunk. Just feeling good, that's all."

"You sure know how to get them ladies, Pete," said Charlie with a grin.

"When you're as charming as I am, you can get any woman you want," he bragged in a whisper.

Just then, someone tapped him on the shoulder.

"You been messing with my girl, boy?"

Before Pete could answer, he found himself flat on his face at the feet of a stranger.

"Hey, break it up or I'll call the police!" shouted Charlie.

"I didn't know that was your girl, man. I'm cool with that." He walked out the door, feeling a bit embarrassed.

Danny shook his hand in pain. "He's got a face as hard as a block of iron."

He turned to the young lady and snorted, "Must you flirt with every man that walks on the face of the earth? Come here." He yanked her by the arm and pulled her closer to him. "I'm telling you straight, Esther Sue, if you don't quit flirting, it's going to be over between us, you hear? How can I trust you when you act like that?"

"You're the only one for me, baby. All them other guys don't mean nothing to me," she said.

"All women are the same."

Nobody ever cared about what Simon had to say. Normally, they would argue over opinions and then it would turn into a brawl, but not when Simon spoke. He carried on a conversation all by himself.

"All they want is your money. Every woman loves money. That's why a man has to drink. Ninety-nine percent of all broken homes are due to women who love money just too much."

"Hey, you, stop droolin' on my counter," fussed Charlie. "I think you've had enough to drink. Thy speech betrayeth thee."

Yes, two-timing Simon was drunk again. He made a fool of himself every night, and tonight was no exception. How his wife put up with him, one would wonder. He spent his money on liquor and then blamed his wife for stealing his money from his pockets. He never knew what was going on. If you asked Simon what he did yesterday, he wouldn't be able to tell you for a million dollars.

"Go home, Simon," a voice from behind him echoed in his ears. "You've had enough to drink."

"Who're you?"

"Open your eyes wider. It's your mother's son. Ring a bell?"

"Oh, just kidding. So how is the old lady?"

"Dead!" said Marshall crossly. "Twenty-five years now, Simon! I'm going to tie you down in your house and leave you for the rats to eat. You're not worth anything, Simon, not even a nickel."

Marshall took him by the arm and pulled him off the barstool.

"Okay, okay," Simon complained.

"The door is this way," said his older brother as he led him out the door. "If it weren't for Bea, I wouldn't care if you rot in here. Where's your car?"

"It was right here…"

"It *was* here? I suppose *it* couldn't wait any longer, so *it* went home without you?" Marshall snapped.

"I suppose," Simon slurred.

"You're a piece of…" He didn't finish his sentence because he figured, more or less, that Simon wasn't worth the breath of air it took to speak, so he drove him home in silence. Simon rambled on endlessly with no response from Marshall. Minutes later, Marshall pulled his car up in front of Simon's apartment building.

"You live right there. You remember, right?" Marshall asked.

Simon didn't answer. Marshall hauled him out of the car and helped him to the door, and after he rang the bell, Beatrice answered. It was two thirty in the morning.

"Here is your *thing*, Bea. More power to you," Marshall said as he shoved Simon through the door, then turned and walked away. Beatrice frowned and moved back in order to make room for Simon to stumble in.

"Thanks, Marshall," she said.

"Out of the four of us, he had to turn out to be a no-good drunk," Marshall muttered as he thought of his mother and how his younger brother's lifestyle would have made her feel. Florence Futon had died when Marshall was only twelve years old. Marshall blamed his abusive father and hated him.

His thoughts drifted back to Simon. "Only a mother could love that," he muttered. He felt sick to his stomach as he climbed into his car. The smell of alcohol lingered.

I hate that smell more than anything, he thought. *Why do I even bother?* As much as he hated his brother's lifestyle, he felt a compelling force to keep an eye on him. Maybe, psychologically, he felt his mother was watching, and he wanted to make her happy.

He coldly shoved his brother to the back of his mind and thought of his life. He didn't have a lot of family members around, but he did have a lot of material possessions, even though he hadn't grown up in a wealthy family.

Whatever it takes to be financially stable, I will do it, he had promised himself when he was just a boy. That thought had never left his mind, because he hated being poor. His father hadn't helped much because he had seldom been around.

"Mommy, where is Daddy?" he remembered asking.

"He's at work, pumpkin" was always her reply. It wasn't until he'd become of age that he'd learned his father had spent most of his time in bars.

Marshall pulled up into his driveway and noticed Kim's car wasn't there. It was late, and naturally he wondered where she was.

He remembered the day that she was born, nineteen years ago. She was a young lady now and no longer his little girl. Inside the house he found a note taped to the telephone:

Daddy, I'm spending the night at Jeannine's.

Relieved, Marshall turned off the lights and climbed the stairs to his bedroom. It had been a long day. He got into his bed and picked up the TV remote, and before Marshall's head hit the pillow, he was sound asleep.

*****

Juan Riversa was dead. "He had to go," said Saint Paul, "because he knew too much and was a smart man. He had to be taken out before he could blow my cover." The man in the mirror didn't respond, and Saint Paul just stared back at his reflection, as if it were telling him all he wanted to hear. It was six o'clock. Then he flicked on the television set because he knew Juan's story would be on. He had nothing to worry about, though; they'd never find his fingerprints at the crime scene, or on Juan, for that matter.

Juan had always worked dirty, and working for Saint Paul had been nothing new to him. Saint Paul adjusted his tie while his eyes stayed focused on the TV set. There it was, the top story:

> *Juan Rivera, forty-four, of 10 Summerset Drive, died from a single gunshot wound to the head. The police don't know the motive behind his murder or who might have done it...*

Saint Paul smiled. "And they'll never know," he gloated as he switched off the television and carefully sipped his coffee.

He thought about why he had had to order Juan's death. He'd walked up behind him a couple of days ago and overheard a portion of his cell phone conversation. "He's into it, and we've gotta let them know." Juan had swiftly turned around when he had seen Saint Paul and had abruptly ended the conversation. Saint Paul thought he'd acted guilty and strange, because he'd started to stutter and not been able to speak a clear sentence.

Saint Paul hadn't said anything about the conversation, but after that, he knew Juan had to go. *Possibly, the conversation was innocent, but why take the chance? Better be safe than sorry,* he had thought.

*****

Brendan had intended on pulling down Saint Paul. He went to his house and was relieved to see that it was dark inside. That was a sure sign there was no one home, added to that fact that there were no cars in the driveway. He was convinced it was safe to enter the house.

Casually looking around, he saw that no one was in sight—not even neighbors. His chance was at hand, and he was taking it.

He pushed the key into the keyhole, turned it, and gently turned the knob as he entered the house. Quickly but quietly, he closed the door behind him, reached for the alarm, and punched in the code that turned it off. Even though it was equipped with a silent alarm, he had confidence that it hadn't gone off. Months ago, he'd found out the code and memorized it until he could say it backward with ease. It was a complicated one made up of letters, numbers, pounds, and asterisks.

Don't forget to set it back when you're done, he reminded himself. He had to get to the safe. It was dead quiet. He climbed the stairs gracefully. Even though he knew that everyone was away, his nerves were on edge.

He moved about cautiously. The safe was in the same spot where he'd seen it the last time. A slot, about an inch long, was almost at the bottom of the safe. The coin was still in the top drawer. He took it out and slipped it into the slot. He pulled the lever and heard a click. His eyes widened as the door glided opened.

Then he heard another soft click and knew it hadn't come from the safe. Turning around, he faced a pair of size 12 shiny black shoes and the six-plus-foot figure of Saint Paul hovering over him with a .38 revolver inches from his face. He knew he was a dead man.

Brendan knitted his brow as his eyes caught the white name tag on his jacket. *Ed Coons? He's got an alias?*

Saint Paul / Ed glared at him in disgust. "I loathe you! Lie down," he commanded. "I knew you were too nosy for my likin'." The man narrowed his eyes, as if he was thinking about what he should do next, and his nostrils flared with anger. Brendan feared for his life.

"It had to have been you who stole my disks. Give them back now!" Saint Paul demanded. His voice echoed as he held the gun closer to Brendan's head.

"Where are they?" Saint Paul roared. Brendan shook with fear.

"I'm sorry, Mr.—"

"You're what? How sorry can you be?" He yanked Brendan to his feet by his collar and shoved him into the corner. Then he opened a drawer, pulled out a silver cord, and proceeded to tie him up with it. Reaching for a piece of cloth, Saint Paul then stuffed it into Brendan's mouth.

"When I'm done with you, you're gonna give me more than my disks back and you'll wish you were never born!" promised Saint Paul.

Just then, his beeper went off. He swore as he picked up the phone with his free hand. His conversation was brief. Brendan couldn't follow it because it was as if Saint Paul spoke in codes. Slamming down the phone, he swore again.

By now, Brendan's heart was in his throat and he had to do some serious thinking about how he was going to get out of his present predicament. Saint Paul loosened the rope from his feet and brought him to the basement, the gun never leaving Brendan's head.

With his hands and feet tied painfully together, Brendan lay helplessly on the basement floor. He heard the front door slam shut and, moments later, a car pulling away.

He had time to think. *Weren't they all supposed to be out of town? As a matter of fact, they had left last night. How could I not have heard Saint Paul come in, though? I was being so careful, so methodical. Did he sneak in because he'd suspected I'd be there? No. There was no way he could have known my plans, because I hadn't revealed anything to anyone.*

How could Saint Paul have known I was here? Certainly, I would have heard some kind of movement if he had come in normally. He must have known that I was here and sneaked in.

Brendan continued to think, *My car didn't give me away, because it is two blocks down the road. So much for that. I have to figure out how I'm going to get out of here.*

As he lay helplessly in the dark on the cold basement floor, Brendan dreaded the moment when he'd hear the door open when Saint Paul, or Ed Coons, returned.

The natural instinct of man is to survive. It is mankind's makeup: the desire to survive and live. If all men were created equal, then who or what gave some the power to "make" rules, and others stripped down to bare nothingness, forced to keep those rules even regarding the question of survival? What are rules, whose are they, and why must they be kept? Certainly, everyone has the right to his own opinion and everyone is different in his or her own way. The right of a man to defend his property as well as the right of a thief to a fair trial are just a couple of mankind's rules of survival.

Given the underlying cause of his circumstance and the hypothetical stance in the judgment hall for his conscious role in the matter, Brendan Clark wondered on which side of the rule book he would fall when that time of judgment arrived. He had a good reason to do what he did, so he thought, as he embraced himself as a citizen in good standing, doing only as duty called. Yet in the back of his mind, there lay the knowing guilt of the fact that he had done something wrong.

How would he hold up before the rule maker of the universe? As much as he would like to admit that he'd done something "good," he knew that he had broken the rule on a huge scale: trespassing, stealing, with nothing to verify his claim of righteous doing.

He fiddled with the cord that held him fast, but only further frustrated himself.

It is indeed sometimes the very consequences of our actions that cause us to think. "Look before you leap," his mother always said. "Weigh the consequences of your actions and know whether or not it's worth your time."

Brendan looked up through the transparency of the basement window and thought real hard of the consequences of his actions surrounding Saint Paul and resolved, *Comes what may, I must survive.*

*****

"I wish, I wish upon a star that love will find me near or far." Kim Futon cast her wish into the night sky and pulled out a strand of her hair and cast it into the air.

Jeannine looked at her oddly and asked, "What was that all about?"

"Sorry, Jeannine, you missed it. You were supposed to cast your wish as soon as you saw the falling star."

"I did cast my wish in my *mind*, mind you. Yours won't come true because you've made it known," informed Jeannine.

"I don't believe that. It doesn't matter if you wish it out loud or not. It's your faith that counts. And by golly, I do believe that one day soon I'll meet my knight in shining armor. He'll sweep me off my feet and carry me to the moon," Kim said most adamantly.

Jeannine just shook her head. Kim asked, "So what *did* you wish for?"

"I'm not going to tell you that. Well, I guess I could because it already came true," Jeannie declared.

"The wish you just made came true already?" asked Kim. "Wow, maybe mine will come true in a few minutes. Let's not go inside just yet. By the way, nothing happened differently since you made the wish. Unless you wish that you keep your sanity." She laughed heartily as Jeannine continued to ignore her.

Then Jeannine said, "I wished that the falling star wouldn't hit the Earth."

Kim returned the odd look Jeannine had given her earlier and said, "What a waste, Jeannine. Seriously, couldn't you have wished for something more important? Stars don't fall from the skies on a daily basis, you know. And even if they did, you wouldn't be lucky enough to see them every time. You might never see one again in your lifetime. Well, too bad, Jeannine. Like I said, what a waste."

"Do you know what could happen if a falling star hits the Earth? It could blow up and we'd all be gone."

"Then there wouldn't be anything to worry about, right?" Kim added. "We'd be gone in a flash, and it would be over before we knew it."

"Your wish came true before you even wished for it, Kim. Brendan cares a lot about you."

"Brendan is just a friend. He's like a brother to me. Let's go inside. It's getting cold out here." They walked through the backyard to the front of the house.

"I can't believe you guys are still playing that game, Mr. Shrouder," said Kim surprisingly. "Aren't you cold? You've been out here for hours!"

"You're cold?" Ben seemed surprised. She nodded. "You're anemic," he replied with a chuckle.

When Ben and his friends got together, they talked about the moon and the stars, heaven and earth, hell and heaven, and everything in between.

These were men with strong opinions, and they held them with high esteem. They were men that had the same cultural experience. They were born and raised to adulthood in Jamaica, yet as their faces differed, so did values and opinion.

"I always wondered if trees and rocks live forever. Those rocks and trees up in the mountains seem to be there forever," declared Hubert.

"Don't be a horse's head, mon. Trees and rocks don't live forever," rebutted Rolston. His face was set, his eyes narrowed, his voice firm.

"That's not impossible. I believe they do," defended Hubert.

"I don't know what you talkin' 'bout, but rocks don' produce rocks. Where you come from, mon?" Rolston retaliated.

As it was with these men, Ben Shrouder wasn't afraid to voice his opinion. "Those same rocks you see now have been around before Adam and Eve," he said, finally joining the conversation.

"You guys talk too much. Let's play some dominoes," said Bob impatiently. "Whether trees and rocks live forever is no concern of mine, but what I know for sure is that I am the don, mon, for dominoes." He slammed his domino hard on the table and said, "Handle that if you can!" He laughed.

"I've traveled back and forth in this country, doing farmwork, before I decided to settle down here, and through those years of travel, I acquired a great deal of knowledge. Traveling brings experience, and experience makes you wise." He laughed at his companions, who'd traveled less. But they just ignored him.

"Pass," said Hubert after diligently searching his hand for a domino to match the one on the table.

These men had left the island physically, but culturally the island was rooted in their hearts.

The little bell jingled in the wind as it dangled from the porch of Ben's house. Ida stood before them with a tray holding four glasses of lemonade.

"Thank you, Ida," said Ben as he grasped a glass of lemonade.

*****

Mrs. Clark wondered why she hadn't heard from Brendan all day. *He's so unpredictable sometimes,* she thought. *He could at least call to let me know he has other plans.*

For some reason, though, she wondered if he was all right. Sometimes she thought she worried a bit too much unnecessarily. She was sure he was fine. She'd had a gut feeling before, as if something was wrong, but nothing had happened that she knew of. He was okay. It must have been one of those days when her motherly instinct had overreacted.

She had a strange feeling when she got up early that morning, and then she felt it again late that afternoon. It was a bit stronger. "I wish he would live with me. I don't know why young people are in such a hurry to leave home—good homes at that," she said, conversing with herself.

She tried to keep her mind occupied with other things because she knew that she would see him soon.

Meanwhile, Ed tapped his fingers impatiently on the desk. His eyes roamed the computer screen. He clicked on the Access icon to open up the database. He scrolled through the files but couldn't find the one he'd created earlier. He could have sworn he'd saved it on the C drive, but it wasn't there.

Maybe he'd saved it onto a disk, but which one? He looked in bewilderment at the numerous disks on his desk. Normally, he'd make a list and note what he had on each disk, but he didn't remember doing that.

He gave a sigh of relief as he clicked onto the Report tab and found the familiar name that he'd called his new file. He reached for a new disk and slipped it into the A drive. He copied the file onto the disk to create a backup, then shut down the computer.

He leaned back in his chair and thought about the missing disks. *Not only am I going to get my disks back from Brendan Clark, but I'm also going to extinguish his life! Nuisances like that shouldn't get a second chance,* he silently told himself. *If they do get a second chance, they sometimes can outsmart you and bring you down.* Ed knew he was now on top of things.

As Ed descended the stairs to the basement, the first thing he noticed was a faint stream of light coming from the small basement window. He stared incredulously at the rope that lay in the spot where he had left Brendan earlier, and exclaimed, "This can't be! How could he have escaped?"

He clenched his fist and pounded the wall, wrenching in agony. He swore to kill Brendan, disks or no disks.

*****

For twenty-four hours, the flaky white stuff fell freely from the sky, piling up drifts as much as twenty inches. It was the highest average of snowfall for Milolta since the blizzard of 1947. They weren't prepared for the handiwork of Mother Nature, and it wasn't because of insufficient warning by meteorologists. Weather such as what they'd predicted wasn't likely for their town.

The city was literally closed. It snowed fifteen inches in one day on top of what was already there.

"When will it end?" complained Jealissa as she stared out the kitchen window. Some power lines and phone lines were down. Fallen trees lay like defeated giants on the ground.

"No marshmallows in my hot chocolate, please!" hollered Jeannine from the living room. Charles helped carry the hot mugs.

"One for me, one for thee, and one for thou," said Charles as he passed them out.

"Jeannine…" Jealissa paused as she gulped her hot chocolate. "Can you please bring me to Jamaica next time you're going?" she concluded.

"It would be great to have you guys come with us the next time that we go," she replied in her Jamaican accent.

"I wonder what the weather is like on the island now," Charles said.

"In the eighties or nineties, I'm sure," Jeannine responded without hesitation.

"Can you imagine if summer skips a year? We'd be in trouble."

Jealissa looked at her brother, cross-eyed at his silly statement. "Good thing you planned on spending the weekend, Jeannine. You wouldn't have been able to go home, anyways."

"You chose the right weekend to be with us, Jeannine," added her brother.

"Why is that?" Jeannine asked curiously.

"Because we could have you cook our meals while our parents are stuck at the hospital." Charles chuckled as he observed the look on her face. She ignored him and reached for a pack of number 2 synthetic hair. She contemplated about braiding Jealissa's hair tomorrow instead. It was late, and she was tired.

"Would you mind if I braided your hair tomorrow instead?" she asked through a yawn.

"I prefer that you braid it tonight, please," Jealissa almost begged. "I've got something that'll perk you up," she added as she rose to her feet and headed for the kitchen. Moments later, she returned with two cans of cola. "I'm sleepy too," she explained like a child who had to give an account.

"Well, this will help," said Jeannine as she reached for the can of soda, knowing full well that after she consumed her soda, she would be awake for hours.

She got started by parting Jealissa's hair, starting from the back, and making small shoulder-length box braids.

"Not too tight," Jealissa reminded her as Jeannine started on the first one.

It was three fifteen in the morning when Jeannine finished the last braid. Jeannine dipped the ends in hot water and curled them into a mushroom, leaving the left side slightly shorter than the right side. She decorated the bangs with silver hair jewelry.

"I like it a lot," said Jealissa as she inspected it in the mirror.

Charles sat upright in the couch and spoke an unknown language. He pointed in the corner and slurred, "Over there."

"Don't mind him," said his sister. "He's a fool when he sleeps."

Charles slumped back onto the couch and resumed his sleeping mode.

*****

Marshall held his daughter's hands in a clasp and kissed them gently. He tried to console her as she complained about his business trip. Kim hated the idea of a weekend business trip. Lately, he'd been having too many "away" meetings, she thought.

"I hate when you leave me here by myself, Dad." She pulled her hands out of his. "Must you leave again this weekend? Can't you miss this one?" she pleaded.

"I really have to be there, sweetheart. I'm sorry."

"I'll be here three days by myself again. It was only two weekends ago that you went on a business trip."

"I know, but something came up," he defended.

Marshall placed his fingers on his daughter's chin and tilted her head back so she could look in his eyes.

"I hate doing this to you. I'll make it up to you. I promise."

A mischievous smile banished the frown that masked her beautiful face. "Oh, boy! I think I've just webbed myself into a fine mess."

She threw her arms around him and pouted childishly. "I know just how you could make up for the agony you've been causing me, Daddy." She twirled like a graceful ballerina and stood on her tiptoes. "I'll let you know what it'll be." She smiled.

"Don't worry, Meeghan will take good care of you," he assured.

"Meeghan? Oh, I thought this was the weekend she was going to visit her family."

"No, it's next weekend."

"So I won't be alone, after all. Well, I'm still going to miss you," she concluded.

"I promise I'll call you as often as I can."

The vivid picture of her mother's face flashed in her memory. What exactly triggered it wasn't known. She remembered her face so well. Charlene Futon was the best mother there was. Although she was only ten years old when her mother died, she would never forget her face. She had a warm smile, big bright eyes, and deep dimples.

Her warm and gentle touch kept Kim in her mother's arms. She couldn't remember a moment when her mother ever raised her voice at her. She was always kind, gentle, and loving.

Kim remembered the many times she would help her mother bring lemonade and cookies to the neighborhood basketball court.

She even cooked meals and brought to some elderly people. Mrs. Duncan was especially grateful for Charlene's home-cooked meals.

"Mom," she sighed. Mother's day was always hard on her.

The day of her mother's death was the gloomiest day of her life. She remembered the day as if it were yesterday. When her father had picked her up from school, she knew that something was awfully wrong even though he'd tried to hide his emotions. His eyes were red, as if he'd been crying.

"What's wrong, Daddy," she asked. Marshall held back the tears as he tried to keep his composure.

"Mommy's in heaven." She stared into his eyes.

"Mommy…died…"

"Died?" she echoed. "Mommy can't die—she just can't!"

Even today, Kim just couldn't understand why her beloved mother had been taken away from her.

Marshall seemed to be doing all right, but Kim could hardly cope with the reality that she would never see her mother again. At her tender age, she was at an emotional strain.

Father Mrozwinski counseled her, but there weren't any word that he or anyone could have said to erase the pain or even to get her to understand.

The cause of Charlene's death was unknown. An autopsy was not conducted. Marshall refused to give them permission to *mutilate* his wife's body, though obviously it would've shed some light on the cause of her death.

It was three years after her mother had passed away that Meeghan had rung their doorbell. She was responding to an ad that Marshall had placed in the paper for a housekeeper. He had interviewed many prospective ones but wasn't pleased with any of them. Kim liked her the moment she saw her.

I wish Mom were still around, she thought. *I miss her.* She sighed again. Marshall noted the look on her face and knew that she was thinking of her mother.

"Sweetheart, can you have Meeghan pick up my clothes from the cleaners tomorrow, please?" He handed his daughter the dry cleaning slip.

"Sure thing, Daddy," she replied.

He kissed his daughter goodbye and rushed to his car. Kim went to her room and threw herself on her bed and switched on the television set. The news was depressing. One of the negative things that stood out was that a death row convict had escaped maximum prison and was supposedly spotted five miles from Milolta. Her father was gone, and she was home alone.

The front door opened, and she jumped to her feet. She peered out her bedroom window and saw Meeghan's car parked in the driveway.

"Oh," she sighed in relief and hurried down the stairs.

"I'm so glad you're here, Meeghan.

For six years, Meeghan had been the housekeeper for the Futons and was like a mother to her.

"What's the matter? You don't look too happy. Did someone take your toy?" she teased.

"Daddy just left for the weekend. He wanted you to pick up his clothes from the cleaners." She handed her the slip of paper.

"Well, there's no time to droop. Let's treat ourselves to something special this weekend."

Kim looked at her. Meegan had a twinkle in her eye.

"What did you have in mind?" she asked curiously.

The forty-five-year-old housekeeper didn't look a day over thirty. She was healthy and strong and hardworking. Kim loved her from the beginning and had grown to love her even more. Over the years, she'd developed a special bond with her. Meeghan was her second mother.

"Let's have a party," she announced.

"A party?" Kim repeated.

"You heard right. Let's have a party."

"Oh, I have an idea," Kim declared with a twinkle in her eyes. Meeghan looked at her in a girlish way and grinned.

"Great minds do think alike," she announced matter-of-factly.

Chapter 8

The Warehouse

Ed picked up the order forms from his desk. It was only 10:30 a.m., and already there were ten orders with a total of 150 computers. It was an average morning, though. He had been working for Dimension Computer Galaxy Corporation for over ten years. Five years ago, he had been promoted to chief executive officer. Ed now oversaw the entire plant. It was an honor that the mother company had granted him with pleasure.

He was excellent at what he did, of course. With 310 employees to oversee, he was right on top of things, which came naturally.

Dimension Computer Galaxy Corporation was known to produce the highest-quality computers for personal and business use. Their excellence in quality, customer service, and customer satisfaction had placed them in the public eye quite often.

Under Ed's new management, sales had increased and the company's ability to assemble more computers and to ship them out at a faster rate had increased tremendously.

New Computer World headed the pile of orders with fifteen xps100 and twelve Dimensions. It was only a week and a half ago that they'd placed a substantial order.

They must be doing really well, he thought. He rose from his desk and closed his office door. He picked up his golden pen, tapped it a couple of times on his desk, then flashed his signature across the signature line of all the orders except for Space World. His eyes scanned each line, reading each detail with a careful scrutiny. Space World was a new listing.

His right hand blindly grasped the mouse on top of his desk. He clicked on the Access icon on the desktop to open it. It immediately prompted him for a password.

He punched in a few letters, numbers, and certain characters, then jabbed the Enter key. Tabs for tables, queries, forms, reports, and modules appeared on the screen. He clicked on the Tables tab and ran his fingers through the alphabetized table. His index finger slowed down when he got to the *S* column. There it was, Space World.

By the time an order form reached Ed, it had already gone through three departments.

First, the telephone operator who took the call-in order entered the information into a system called the Initial Order Form (IOF). She saved the completed order in the IOF file, printed it onto a five-page duplicated order form, kept and filed page 5, then sent the rest to the data entry department (DED).

The DED employees entered the information in Access on the Form field, filed page 4, then forwarded the rest to the editing department. The entire information was reentered on the editing form. The computer beeped if the editing clerk entered any information different from the DED's. Whatever field beeped, it had to be reentered twice by the editing clerk in order for him to bypass the beeping field. The editing department filed page 3, then passed on pages 1 and 2 to Ed.

Ed was required to give his signature of approval, enter his approval code, file page 1, then pass the second and final page down to the assembly department.

Ed right-clicked on Space World, then clicked the Delete button. "Are you sure you want to delete Space World?" flashed the question. Ed clicked on the Yes button, then opened up the trash can on the desktop and emptied it.

He folded both pages in half and placed them in his briefcase and locked it.

As chief executive officer, Ed could access every department file. He immediately closed out the Access file and opened up the IOF file with his password. He located Space World, deleted it, then emptied the trash can again. Next, he deleted the data entry file, then the editing file.

He knew that he couldn't risk forgetting to empty the trash can, because if someone went into the trash can and hit Restore, every order that he'd deleted would be restored and his acts would be detected, careful as careful was.

Now he had to get those duplicated order forms from the IOF operator file, the data entry department, and the editing department.

With him as the CEO, it wasn't unusual for anyone to see him go through the filing cabinets in the departments. Ed went to each department and retrieved all the duplicates of the Space World order.

There was now no record at his company of an order from Space World. He smiled. Mission accomplished, and he breathed easier.

The day was ending. One final job to do before he headed out the door. He opened up the inventory file and checked to see what parts he needed to order or what parts he had enough of. Ed was always on top of things. Never had he ran out of computer parts that put the company on a hold in filling orders.

He flipped through his roller desk and then dialed the number to Golden Gate Experience. After a few seconds, he punched the four-digit extension number of the department he wanted. On the third ring, a masculine voice answered.

"Hey, Luigi, it's Ed. Got a big order for you," he said. "We're going to need a thousand printed circuit boards and 310 mother boards, four hundred CPU chips, two thousand chips number z4376-A; 219 #y1025-s, and three hundred #yy3648-p. Give me 150 8K RAM chips, 150 64ks, and 75 128ks, and three hundred CRTs and only two hundred keyboards. We'll take three hundred pairs of speakers and five hundred mouses. I'm gonna hold off on ordering any printer parts today. And, Luigi," he whispered before hanging up, "I need ten of everything I ordered with duplicate serial numbers."

Three days later, Jiffy Parcel Service arrived with the orders. Trenton and six other men in receiving checked off the packages. Trenton located the conspicuously marked boxes that contained the duplicates and conveniently hid them among the other boxes in the huge storage room.

*****

He had to do something, and fast. Saint Paul was on to him. Brendan paced the floor. He wasn't sure what he must do, but it had to be something, and quick. If only he could break the password lock. He picked up the disk that had the red circular tab. He puckered his lips and slipped it into the disk drive. "Enter password." His veins stood up on his temple. He locked his fingers together and clenched his teeth. "There has got to be a way to open these files," he grunted unhappily.

He slipped out the disks and placed it with the other five disks. He opened up a map that was sitting on the desk. He made a few marks on it and glanced at his watch. He rose hastily from his chair.

He wanted to talk to Jeannine, but he had no idea where to find her. He'd decided to try her house first. He picked up the phone and dialed the number, but Ida was on the other line with her sister Eunice from Jamaica.

"It's nice that you called, but did you have to call now?" Teased Eunice. "It would be nobody but you calling at dis time." She laughed. "Nobody in Jamaica would call anybody at dis time."

"What do you mean?"

"*Dulcimina* on, mon!" she responded. "Everything stops when *Dulcimina* is on. You know that."

"*Dulcimina*?" said Ida incredulously.

"Yes, it is a repeat. After all these years, they decided to put it back on the air."

"Is that why you took so long to answer the phone?" Ida asked sternly.

"Yes. Them playing di good part. Me don't want to miss it at all. Anyways, me wi ask Joycie how it end."

"How is everybody?"

"Well, mi dear, everybody is coping. What can I say but dat we have to learn to cope with situation?" She sighed. "How are my nieces and nephew?"

"Everyone is well, Eunice." Ida heard the front door shut and turned around to see a weary Jeannine making her way to the sofa.

"Oh, Mama, I'm so tired. I went here, there, and everywhere." She plopped down on the sofa and sprawled out.

"Oh, Jeannine just walked in, Eunice." Ida handed the phone to Jeannine.

"How is my favorite auntie?" Jeannine and her aunt shared a special bond. Aunt Eunice would visit Ida and would always have something special for Jeannine. Her excuse was that Jeannine was the baby and she wouldn't understand if she didn't bring her anything.

"I love you, Auntie."

"Me love you, too, darlin'," Eunice replied. "It was so good to see you again, Tibbits."

Tibbits. She hadn't heard that name in a long time. She cleared her throat, as if to warn her aunt.

"You told me you wouldn't call me that name anymore. I've outgrown it, Auntie. It doesn't fit anymore."

The name brought back bad memories. She didn't want to remember the awful day that she'd acquired the name. It was a day that she wished didn't exist.

She was seven years old and was in the country, visiting Aunt Eunice. It was very dark. There were no light posts where Aunt Eunice lived. They used torches.

Jeannine had needed to use the toilet. There was one big problem, as she put it: the toilet decided to live a little distance from the house. *Stupid toilet,* she silently told herself. She'd asked everybody, one at a time, to go with her, but no one budged.

"Just take the torch and walk carefully," her mother told her, but she continued to beg for company.

Not even Aunt Eunice would go with her. They had just arrived that afternoon, and they had a lot to catch up on. They were at an intense peak of a story that Aunt Eunice was sharing: Duppies that could be seen and heard.

Jeannine was afraid, but as she understood, her mother was always right. She told her that there was nothing to be afraid of because there was nothing in the dark that was not in the light. She'd never seen anything scary in the light, except for Mrs. Dillings's bulldog, but he was miles away.

If the theory was right that whatever was in the dark was the same things that were in the light, no more, no less, then she could make it to the toilet and back all by herself.

She made up her mind to go all by herself because she had no choice. She opened the door and looked out. It was nothingness. Absolutely nothing was visible.

Jeannine picked up the torch and stepped out by faith. It wasn't too bad. The torch lit a small area just in front of her. The toilet seemed miles away, though. Now she was in the middle of darkness. Behind her was dark, and ahead of her was dark.

She opened the door to the toilet. It squeaked. She was scared but remembered, *Mama said there was nothing to be afraid of.*

She did what she had to do. She got out, closed the door, and the torch slipped out of her hand.

Okay, where did everything go? The walkway was gone, the toilet was gone, and the house was gone. There were no trees, no rocks. Nothing. Total darkness.

"TIBBITS! TIBBITS!" she screamed at the top of her lungs. Jeannine just stood there and screamed, "TIBBITS! TIBBITS!"

Everyone came running out to the bathroom to see what was wrong. Ben scooped her up in his big strong arms. "What's the matter, J?" She clung to her father like a drowning man.

After they got back inside the house, Aunt Eunice asked, "Who's Tibbits?"

Still shaken, Jeannine replied, "Nobody."

"Then why were you calling Tibbits?" she asked.

"I was scaring all the ghosts away so they wouldn't come and get me, because ghosts are afraid of the word *Tibbits*. It means that they're in danger."

Everyone screamed with laughter, except for Jeannine, of course. Ida tried to regain her composure so Jeannine wouldn't feel too bad, but she couldn't control her laughing fit.

"Who told you that, honey?" she asked between giggles.

"Washburn."

Everyone turned and looked at him.

"I didn't know that she believed me. I was just telling her a story, that's all," he defended.

From that day on, Jeannine was known as Tibbits.

Ida and Eunice talked for about an hour about the good old days.

"Even though we're far apart, there is nothing to stop us from reaching out to each other."

"I know. Just don't take so long," said Eunice. "The human race has come a long way. It's so easy to get from one part of the world to another. Within seconds you could be talking to someone at the other end of the world. How far we've come."

"How far will we go?" added Ida.

"Only time will tell," replied Eunice.

Benjamin Shrouder walked out of his office and into the family room just as Ida said goodbye and placed the receiver on the phone. He was tired and wanted to take a few minutes' break from the computer. He hadn't finished the program file he had started to create. The deadline was tomorrow, and he wasn't anywhere near close to completing it. He envisioned himself at the computer for the entire night.

"Honey, you've been sitting at the computer far too long. You need to call it a night and give your eyes some good rest."

He decided to take her advice and get a couple of hours' sleep and finish it later. He went back into his study and saved the program, suddenly deciding to change the password to make sure the past wouldn't repeat itself. He'd completed an extensive program after working on it for several days. Someone had used his computer and had accidentally deleted the entire program, and that was one sour day for him.

*****

Brendan combed through the books on the shelf, a huge well-braced affair tightly stacked with encyclopedias and all kinds of other books. He wasn't sure of what he was looking for, but he firmly believed that there was something in one of the books that could be of significance.

"What're you looking for so diligently?" Jeannine startled him. He gripped his chest.

"You almost gave me a heart attack. Don't go sneaking up on people like that," he scolded.

"Jeez, I didn't mean to scare you, mister," she said bluntly.

"He's suddenly become very studious," added Kim.

"I'm doing research, and I know these encyclopedias could really help." He gave them a plastic smile. He flipped through the pages of the one he had in his hand as if he were really looking for some educational information.

"Not in here," he said out loud as he replaced the book. Jeannine and Kim looked at each other and shrugged their shoulders.

"Let's leave him alone before he blows a fuse in his head," teased Jeannine. "I have something to tell you, anyways—girl talk, you know." They disappeared around the corner, and Brendan was happy to be alone once again.

As soon as they left the room, he desperately, but casually, resumed looking for the *thing*.

The hunch was strong that Saint Paul was hiding something right there among the pages of one of the books. From Brendan's hiding place, he had seen him walk over to the library of books. He'd glanced behind him to check if someone was watching him, then he'd causally picked up one of the books, whistled, and then replaced it.

It had been a couple of weeks since Saint Paul had caught and tied him in the basement. He'd planned on checking inside the books after he'd searched the study, but he didn't get to do it. He sure was taking a huge risk being in his house after he'd caught him and tied him up.

Brendan had no idea which one of the many books or where on the shelf he'd put something, but because he was 99 percent sure that he'd hidden something in one of them, he diligently hunted for his object. If only he could find it before the girls got back, or Ed, for that matter.

A key suddenly fell out at his feet from the book he was holding in his hand. Luckily, the floor was carpeted, so it made almost no sound. He picked it up. No time to scrutinize it, because the girls were already on their way. He shoved it into in his pocket and replaced the book just anywhere.

"Did you find what you were looking for?" Kim asked.

"Aahm, I think I'll change the title of my research topic," he replied. "Are you girls ready to go?"

"You're acting awfully strange, Brendan. What're you up to now?"

"Men, you can't figure them out," said Kim, and she pulled Jeannine by the arm to get them on their way. "One minute they're normal, and the next minute they're not." Kim laughed as she tossed him a wink.

Later that afternoon, when he was finally alone, Brendan took out the key and looked it over.

It must be a spare key, he thought. Why wouldn't he keep it on his key ring? He had no idea what it was for, but he believed that it was an important key.

Now that he'd gotten a key, he needed to find out where the lock was.

Maybe it was for the front door or the china cabinet. He doubted it. He looked too suspicious when he put it there. *It's a forbidden key, I bet,* he thought. Ed, as he came to find out, was an unpredictable guy.

Now he'd gotten two mysteries about Ed. Maybe, he thought, the key would help with the mystery of the disks. *But how?* he wondered.

*****

It had been almost a week, and Brendan still hadn't figured out what lock the key opened. He'd been watching Ed's house ever since he'd gotten it. As he sat in the car and stared anxiously at the house, Ed pulled up into his driveway and quickly entered the house without looking behind him. Brendan slithered under the wheel of the car and tilted his hat to cover his face a bit. Within a couple of minutes, Ed came marching out of his house and wasted no time getting into his dark-blue sedan. He pulled out of the driveway and drove on down the street.

Brendan started his engine and followed at a safe distance.

Tonight might just be another futile attempt to find out where Ed was doing his scam, he thought, but the pleasure of catching him red-handed evacuated every ounce of impatience. He wasn't the least bit weary of watching and waiting and following. One day, he knew, it would bring him to something big.

Brendan stayed back three car lengths, sometimes four. He kept him in view always. There was no way he was going to lose him.

From one street to another, Ed drove aimlessly, but Brendan kept a hard focus.

He followed him to the outskirts of Delmar. Ed pulled up to a blue-and-white house and alighted from his car. He didn't show any suspicion of being followed. So far, so good, thought Brendan as he maintained his distance.

Ed rang the doorbell, and almost instantly, a man dressed in jogging suit appeared at the door. The two men looked around in every direction before Ed entered the house.

Brendan waited. Twenty minutes later, Ed came out wearing a black baseball hat, black sweat suit, and a pair of black-and-white sneakers.

Brendan's heart skipped a beat. Something was going to happen, and he knew it. Why would he change his clothes and was so conscious of his surrounding?

Ed pulled away. Brendan followed. He must not lose him. Wherever he was going, Brendan had to find out.

After about fifteen minutes of driving, Ed pulled onto a lonely dirt road. Brendan kept his distance. There was virtually no traffic. Every now and then, a vehicle would drive past Brendan, and he was glad for that. If he were the only one on the road with Ed, he would have suspected that he was being followed. Brendan was sure he was watching every vehicle in his rearview mirror, but it was too dark to tell if he was being followed.

Ed turned off onto a narrow road. Brendan stopped in the distance and waited. He wasn't sure if the street led to a dead end. He didn't want to take the chance of running into him. Not that Ed would recognize the car he was driving. He was smart enough to borrow the car from a friend who had no idea about the reason behind Brendan asking to use his car.

Ed's car disappeared around a corner, and Brendan thought it safe to continue tailing him. He drove slowly down the lonely road that suddenly came to an end. A brick building loomed into view, and he reversed the car back to the main road and parked about twenty feet away behind a forest-green pickup truck, as there weren't many vehicles around.

He walked between the shrubs until he came to the brick building. It stood by itself, isolated. The closest building was a quarter of a mile away. Brendan thought about the pickup truck and the two other cars that were parked not too far from each other. He thought it odd that there was no other building close by, yet there were parked vehicles. Maybe they were some of Ed's acquaintances and were waiting for him in the brick building.

Ed pulled up next to two other cars parked at the entrance. His keys jingled noisily as he unlocked the door and entered. He closed it quietly and went inside.

Moments later, the door opened. Brendan ducked for cover. He peered through the shrubs and noticed a man scanning the area.

"We've got a big order for next week," Ed whispered excitedly to his companion.

Big order? Brendan thought to himself. *He's into drugs?* The other man motioned for silence. They headed to one of the cars, but a woman opened the front door and motioned them back inside.

They reentered the building, and Brendan waited. Everything was quiet. He prowled around the building like a lion stalking its prey. A whole hour and forty-five minutes later, six people walked out of the building, Ed included. Brendan thought everyone had now left, because all the vehicles were gone, but he waited another half hour, just to be sure.

Stepping out of the bushes, he made his way to the front door, pulled on the handle, and wasn't the least bit surprised it was locked. He tried the key he'd taken from Ed's house. He turned the key, and to his amazement, the door unlocked. *A spare key? Why?* he wondered.

Slowly he opened the door a crack and peered in. It was dark. There was no sound of life. He took two steps in, closed the door, and waited breathlessly as he looked about. He stuck his head out the door to make sure no one was coming. If only he had someone with him to be on the lookout. He was in a dangerous situation and hoped he didn't get caught, because he was sure Ed would kill him on the spot—Brendan wasn't stupid. He locked himself in and pulled his flashlight from under his coat.

He waited a few moments before he switched it on, allowing his eyes to adjust to the reduced light. There was still no sign of life, and that was to his advantage.

A warehouse. The inside seemed twice as large as it looked from the outside, and it was clear from his first impression that he had hit upon something big. *Now, what is it that he'd been sneaking around and doing?*

He was tempted to switch the lights on for a better look, but he knew better. His heavy-duty flashlight beamed bright enough for him to scope out the building one area at a time without tripping over anything. *Patience, that's all,* he consoled.

The sudden sound of a motor vehicle coming nearer startled him. He immediately switched off his flashlight and stumbled behind some empty boxes.

In a few moments, the door opened and the building was flooded with lights.

His hands shook as he gripped the flashlight to keep it from slipping out of his hand. *Stay calm,* he thought nervously. Rambling voices came closer to where he sat, but he was able to keep his cool.

As the men spoke, a thought came to him. One of the men had a very distinctive voice. Brendan knew that voice but couldn't think to whom it belonged. It sounded strenuous and husky, almost as if something was caught in his windpipe.

He clamped his hand over his mouth and waited breathlessly. He couldn't figure out what they were saying, but at that point, he didn't care. He just wanted to get out alive and go home and never do anything stupid again.

The more they talked, the more he was convinced he knew the man with the scratchy voice. Then it came to him—the helicopter night! It was one of the voices he'd heard from the men that alighted from the helicopter. So not surprisingly, they were definitely connected to Ed. *Oh, yeah, for sure.*

What was it that they had in that chest, and would they use that spot again? He was sure to find out, if he lived through tonight.

He turned his head to the right to move away from the voices, and his eyes fell on a man that sat at a table. His right arm was laid on the table, and his head rested on his arm.

Brendan's breath stopped, his body felt numb, and his brain screamed for oxygen.

The man didn't move a muscle. Brendan slid back and crouched behind one of the aisle separators. *Was this man dead, or was he just sleeping on the job?* Brendan thought. *Death might be a possibility, because he didn't budge a bit when his knee slightly bumped the table. He was probably dead, and Ed and his colleagues hid his body here until they could dispose of it. But why hadn't they taken him with them, because it was dark when they had left the building? And why would they leave a dead man sitting at a table? Doesn't make any sense.* Brendan concluded the man must just be sleeping.

The noise of a forklift sent him flying to his feet. He heard the sound of boxes being moved not far from where the supposedly dead man sat.

I've got to get out of here, Brendan frantically told himself, silently. Though his knees bobbed, he wriggled his way closer to the direction of the front door. He'd only gone about halfway when a box fell in front of him and the distinctive voice swore. Brendan tiptoed in the opposite direction, away from the door, because he knew someone would come to check on the noise and retrieve the box. The loud noise of the forklift covered the sound of his footsteps.

Brendan walked against the wall of the warehouse until he got to the emergency exit door.

He pulled the lever to open it so he could make his escape, sure the alarm would sound once he opened it, but by the time they could get to the door, he would be running like a crazed animal away from the building and into the brush.

To his utter bewilderment, the door just wouldn't open and the alarm let off a screeching buzz, a horrifying, loud noise.

The engine of the forklift stopped and he heard the hustling of footsteps. He yanked on the door again, hoping that it would let him out to freedom. It didn't budge. The alarm continued.

"Lock all doors!" yelled one man. Brendan ran back against the wall and met the man who was lying around the table just a few seconds ago face-to-face. He reached out to grab Brendan, but he swung the flashlight as hard as he could and smacked him dead in the face. He fell flat on his back and lay still, like a corpse.

Brendan ran through the aisles, trying to dodge the men, two of them, not counting the one he'd just knocked out.

While he was going in and out of the aisles, one of them spotted him and fired a shot, but he dived face forward onto the hard tile. He didn't feel anything. Later, when his adrenaline would have been back to normal, he'd probably feel the real impact of the dive. But right now he had to get out even if he had to tear the walls down with his bare hands.

He climbed onto the top of a stack of boxes that weren't too high, making sure his coat wasn't hanging over. The two men searched the building frantically.

"We've got you cornered, scumbag," one of the men said. "Come out, and we won't shoot," one man promised, not to be believed.

"Get in the office and turn on the scanner!" the distinctive voice hollered.

One of the men still stood below while the other went to turn on the security scanner. Brendan aimed and plunged onto the man below him and knocked him to the floor. He knocked the wind out of him, and Brendan raced to the door as if he were on fire.

"He's going towards the door! Get him!"

He unlocked the door and took off down the road like a lightning bolt.

Somehow he was far enough ahead and got to his car without incident, unlocked the door, got in, and quickly switched on the ignition. He peeled out and made for the highway, making a U-turn and heading for his house, hoping he wasn't being followed. He took a couple of detours and purposely backtracked a couple of miles, just to be sure.

At his apartment door, he sighed in relief at his narrow escape.

"That was too close!" he scolded himself. "I need to stop doing this, because I'm not the FBI."

Once inside, he hauled his living room furniture against the door and threw himself on the couch.

He knew the security camera had picked up his image, but wondered if they'd seen his face clearly enough to make an ID. "Maybe it had only picked up my back," he thought out loud.

*****

Kim, Meeghan, and Jeannine put the final touch on Casey's surprise birthday party at Kim's house. Casey was truly surprised when she walked in to pick up her sister and everyone hollered, "Surprise!"

It was a great party except, for one missing link—Brendan Clark. Kim and Jeannine were disappointed. They tried to call him several times and kept watching for his appearance, but there was no sign of him. As a matter of fact, neither girl had heard from him since yesterday morning.

"Brendan really has been acting strange lately, don't you think? Have you noticed that, Kim?"

Kim shook her head in a negative way. "Just a little, nothing major," she hinted.

"Where could he be? I can't believe he missed the party." Jeannine just shrugged her shoulders. She was mad at him for not being at the party and, when she got the chance, was really going to rub it in.

The party was over, and Brendan never showed up.

Chapter 9

A Black-Tie Affair

Jeannine stepped out of her car gracefully and walked to the side of the building and looked around. A grungy old man was the only one there today. Usually, there were a few homeless people at the corner. The cold weather must have driven them away, and she wondered why he was standing there in such harsh conditions. A shelter would be willing to take him in, but instead, he chose the streets.

He looked lonely. Hurt. She took out a twenty-dollar bill and handed it to him.

His eyes bulged, a grateful thanks wide and clear. He raised his hand, but only to wipe the stringy gray hair from his eyes, as if to clear his vision. He looked into her face. His eyes trailed from the top of her shiny black hair to her blue suede shoes.

She was young, very young, and also very pretty. He stared into her radiant brown eyes. The eyes, they say, are the windows to the soul, and in that case, her soul looked pretty good.

Why, he thought, *would someone of such obvious class stop to look at me, let alone give me money? She was kind, thoughtful, sensitive, an unselfish love.*

"Here, for you," she said softly. Her feminine voice was reassuring, full of life, compared to his frail, weak voice, the victim of aging and weak from hunger.

He looked into her eyes again. She smiled at him patiently, a warm smile, not mischievous—truly genuine.

"Here," she said gently, still patiently.

He reached out his hand and took the bill, always keeping his eyes on her face. His hand shook. "Thank you," he said in a deep but weak voice, "thank you very much. Thank you."

"Get yourself something to eat."

He watched her walk away. *She is an angel in disguise, I'm sure of that. People like that just don't exist,* he told himself.

She didn't seem to have experienced any hardship in life to say she'd been there and understood. No. She was just…an angel.

Jeannine was happy. She had done a good deed. She'd help someone today, and it made her feel good inside.

Then, a surge of sadness swept over her, and she thought, *No one should suffer like that. So many people have their money sitting in banks while people go homeless and hungry. No. It shouldn't be.*

It wasn't the first time Jeannine had helped a homeless person, or someone who was in need. She genuinely loved people, and her volunteer work at the nursing home was very fulfilling for her.

She anticipated taking the social worker exam given by the county social services, and hoped beyond hope she'd get hired as well. Going back to the car, she returned with a coat in her hand, and when she placed it over his shoulders, he began to sob, saying, "God bless you."

"It's warmer than the one you're wearing."

Jeannine made a quick stop home before heading to the nursing home. She informed her mother, "I'll be back in a couple of hours. I'm going to the county nursing home."

"Okay, honey. I probably won't be here when you get back, but I won't be gone for too long. If you get back before I do, can you fix dinner? I took out a pack of chicken from the freezer and put it in the refrigerator to thaw. Make some brown stew and rice and peas. Thank you."

"Bye, Mama."

*****

Away at college, Washburn, too, was experiencing a similar sense of fulfillment as had his sister. He faced a schoolmate in dilemma.

Jerry had walked into the room and dropped his books on the floor in frustration, shoulders slouched and head hanging in despair. "I'm sick and tired of school. I'm doing so badly. My GPA is only 1.75. A stupid mouse can get a 1.75! I'm about ready to quit—it's just too hard for me, and I can't handle messing up."

Washburn picked up his books and motioned Jerry outside. Jerry reluctantly followed him to the side of the building and blurted out, "Wash, I'm past helping. I don't have a clue as to what's going on in my accounting class. I just got a 35 on my pop quiz, and that's horrible!"

"I know it gets hard sometimes, but you have to keep at it," encouraged Washburn.

Jerry's face was flushed with embarrassment.

There was something very common among the Shrouder children. Determination was a quality engraved in them throughout life. Quitting was never an option. No matter what it was, they had to endure to the end.

There was a well-known story about Washburn among his friends. It seemed that when Washburn was about eleven years old, his parents had signed him up for clarinet lessons. From the first day to the last, he hated every moment of it, but he had to stick it out until term's end.

His mother had said to him, "How do we know you weren't created to be a clarinet player? If you quit, then you'll never find out."

"You have the power to endure, and you've got to prove that to yourself," his father counseled. "Never quit something good, even if you think it's not for you."

Like her brother, Jeannine also had a firm determination that didn't let up. She wouldn't stop at anything until she had proven she had control over every situation. That was what made the Shrouders stand out.

Jerry strutted to his next class with new hope. The few words that Washburn had spoken to him were like fuel added to fire. Someone who cared had offered to help. He was now willing to face the challenges associated with college life with a renewed dignity, knowing he had the power within himself to win or lose.

A few weeks later, Jerry smiled wide and happily because he had made it through his season of depression, and Washburn was glad he had been able to encourage him and be his friend.

*****

While Washburn had two years left in college, Jeannine was only in her first year, which had gone fairly smooth to this point at Milolta Community College. It was finals week, and she could hardly wait for the semester to end. She had no intention of going to summer school, none whatsoever. Her grades were great, and besides, she thought summer school defeated the whole purpose of a glorious summer.

"I want to do something exciting and memorable this summer," she announced to her friends one day.

"Like what?" Jealissa mused out loud. "I know," she replied to her own question. "Let's do something…something…daring!"

Jeannine waved her hands violently and declared, "I'm not the daring type. The only daring thing I ever did was to climb trees in Jamaica!"

"You're no fun! That's what makes things memorable." Jealissa pouted. "Oh, I have a brilliant idea!"

Jeannine rolled her eyes at the sound of those traumatic words that came from Jealissa's lips, and commented, "The last time you had a brilliant idea, we ended up screaming for help!"

"Don't dig up bad memories," said Charles. "Let's sleep on it, shall we? We have plenty of time to decide. Summer is still a few weeks away."

"I might be busy this summer, anyways," said Jeannine. "I'm excited about the social services exam I took a couple of weeks ago."

"What's so exciting about working at social services?"

"For one thing, it's challenging. I love challenges, and not the dangerous ones," she added quickly, watching Jealissa's face. "For another thing, it's different from the other temporary jobs I've had. I just know I'll enjoy it because it gives me the opportunity to meet a lot of people and to help them…well, at least try to help."

"Yeah, a lot of crazy people…" Charles twirled his index finger in a circular motion to his head as he walked out of the room.

"Whatever," she declared.

*****

"You are nothing but dead meat if you don't return those disks!"

The phone went dead.

Brendan hung up slowly and slumped down onto the couch and thought to himself, *I've got to know what's on the disks!* He stopped suddenly in the middle of the floor. He slid his hands in his trousers pockets and shut his eyes so tight that little, tiny dots swam back and forth behind his eyelids. *How could I possibly get access to the disks?* His head throbbed. He knew that he didn't have much time before Ed would finally catch up with him. Then it was over.

On second thought, from what I sense from the phone call, they seem to be of more importance than I can understand, he told himself. *I don't think he'd kill me before he got them back, and there is no way he could ever know where they are. It doesn't seem that he has any copies of them…or else, he probably would have burned down my apartment while I slept. Obviously, he has no copies and feels like a fish out of water without them. Obviously, he is desperate to get them back, so he won't kill me before he gets them back—which will be never!*

It wasn't long before Brendan received yet another threat. He pulled the small sheet of paper from under his car windshield wiper and read it out loud. "You are wearing out my patience!" He looked around quickly and then hopped into his car. This time, Brendan was beginning to get worried. Ed knew his home phone number and address. *He might just kill me and keep looking for the disks,* he told himself. *Not a very secure position to find myself in at the moment.*

Brendan was very careful about how he went in and out of his apartment. He wanted to tell Kim and Jeannine what had been happening, but his instinct told him not to do so. "Maybe I should just go to the police and have them figure out everything else," he thought out loud, taking in the surroundings in the rearview mirror.

He looked at his watch and realized he didn't have much time to get ready for the black-tie-affair banquet. Calling Kim, he asked her to take a cab over to his apartment and they'd go to the banquet from there. His excuse was that he had quite a few errands to run and they wouldn't make it on time if he had to go across town to get her. Actually, his real reason was, he wanted to keep a low profile and avoid getting caught by his pursuer.

Kim didn't mind and understood. He thought, *She is understanding, and we would make a good team, and her a good mother. A good mother for sure, but children drive any sane person bonkers.* He'd seen some kids in his day. Little brats, he called them. He'd seen a three-year-old speak so harshly to her mother that if it had been him he would have smacked her so hard she would have been speechless for weeks.

"Give me my bottle now!" the little girl had demanded with both hands on her hips. Her mother had spoken in too soft a tone for Brendan's liking. "Now, honey, that's not the way to ask for something."

Smack her, will you? Brendan had said to himself. *Smack her hard!*

On another occasion, when he'd seen a little boy slap his mother dead in the face, he had prayed, *God, don't give me children, please! I don't want to be a murderer!*

Brendan reassured himself.

*****

Kim arrived in the cab, and he was all ready to go. He strolled down the long hallway and into the ballroom with her on his arm.

"Hi, Kim," said Jeannine excitedly.

"You're looking mighty fine, young man," Remington greeted Brendan with a smile.

"Not too bad yourself, cowboy," he said with a grin.

Brendan's white shirt and soft mint-green bow tie enhanced his black tuxedo. Kim's floor-length evening gown gently clasped her upper body as it loosened at her hips and flowed freely to her ankles, further complementing Brendan's look. Her spiral curls flowed down her shoulders and bounced gently as she moved.

"I can't stay in this room with that lowlife," muttered Zaire Campbell as he stared in disgust at Brendan.

"Are you having a good time?" Remington asked Brendan.

Just then, someone tapped Kim on the shoulder. When Brendan turned around, he found himself staring Zaire in the face.

"May I have this dance?" Zaire asked Kim.

"Get lost!" snapped Brendan between clenched teeth.

"I was talking to the beautiful lady."

"I said get lost."

Kim intervened and said, "It's okay, Brendan. It's only a dance. Really, it's okay."

"No, it's not. Stay away from her, you lowlife!" Brendan's eyes burned with anger as he threatened Zaire.

Throughout the whole time, Zaire complained about how Brendan had stolen his girlfriend and he hated him and wished him dead. He gave one last look at Kim, and then a disgusted look at Brendan, as he finally walked out the door.

*****

Ed read the message, typed on an eight-and-a-half-by-eleven fluorescent-blue sheet of paper:

> *There are two customers with the same serial number, Harry Jones from 1425 Ruthland Avenue in Fionasville and Erica Boneau from 16 Sarah Ann Drive in Conners. Both are from different states with different computer problems. Harry called last week with a simple issue: couldn't connect to the internet.*

> *That was taken care of immediately. His information was in the system, but today when we got a call from Ms. Boneau and asked for her serial number, it brought up Harry's information. The computer showed Harry's last technical phone call was placed last week.*
>
> *According to Ms. Boneau, she purchased her computer in September, and when asked if she knew Harry, she stated that she had no clue who he was and that she didn't know a soul in Fionasville.*
>
> *Our system showed that Harry purchased his computer in May, which tells me that he is the legitimate purchaser. But grab this! Ms. Boneau was convinced she'd purchased her computer from us, so to prove it, she faxed us a copy of her receipt, and sure enough, she told the truth!*
>
> *Ms. Boneau was quite annoyed and insisted on speaking to the top manager today. Harry has no idea about all this, though. He doesn't need to know, I suppose.*
>
> *Susan R.*

"Okay, Susan, thanks for writing a book," he said to himself with a smile. "As Jamaicans would say, 'No problem, mon.' Good thing I'm the CEO."

Ed opened up the database that he'd created for such a problem. Since he was the only one with access to the database, he had named it Solitaire. But actually, it was a database with flag numbers. He'd randomly created numbers for people who'd called in with the same serial number as others. It wasn't often that a problem arose.

After thinking about it awhile, he picked up the phone and called Erica Boneau.

"Good afternoon, this is the CEO of Dimension Computer Galaxy Corporation. May I speak with a Ms. Erica Boneau, please?"

"This is she."

"First, I would like to apologize for any inconvenience that we may have caused you because of the misunderstanding of the serial number on your computer."

"Oh, yes, your company had me scared for a moment there. I hope we can resolve this issue today. I do hate problems."

"The problem is already solved. From now on, if you ever need to call us with an issue concerning your system, disregard the serial number on the back of your tower and use the flag number that I am about to give to you. Are you ready to take down the number?"

She was amused by his mannerism and professionalism. "Oh, yes, I've got a pen," she said.

"Here we go: B5281CSR. Now, in a few days, you will be getting this number in the form of a sticker. I would like for you to peel the sticker off and place it over the serial number. In addition to that, I will send you a disk for free internet service for one year. Pop it into the A drive and it'll prompt you through the simple steps of setting up your free internet service for the year. That's our way of saying forgive us and we hope we won't lose you as a valued customer."

"Oh, my! I wish all problems could be solved this simply! I promise, with your professionalism and prompt attention to my request, I will always be a customer of Dimension Computer Galaxy and I will be more than happy to give my recommendation to those I know."

"We appreciate your business. You have a great afternoon."

"Thanks!"

Ed entered Erica Boneau's information into the field next to the flag number he'd given her, saved the file, and then closed it. Then he opened up the technical support database he'd created and entered her information. This way, if she called back with an issue and gave her flag number, her information would appear on the screen and the technical support operator would be able to resolve her computer problem.

Ed leaned back in his chair and sighed contentedly. He had, once again, met a customer's need and probably gained tenfold because of it.

Chapter 10

Wedding Bells

Ed had put two and two together and figured out that Brendan was the one that had been in the warehouse. He replayed the surveillance camera that picked him up seconds before he disappeared out the door. No doubt. He'd recognize that back anywhere. He'd seen him enough on the tape to recognize him, even a silhouette.

He pounded the desk. "I can't believe that one stupid, mangy boy is giving me such a hard time." Ed swore he'd kill him at all costs, day or night.

*****

After the banquet, Brendan hadn't been able to see much of anyone. He knew that Ed was furious and his life was in danger. He had gotten enough warnings. He wanted to go to the police but figured he didn't have much of anything to lodge an accusation. He didn't know what to accuse Ed of doing, and the police couldn't take Ed's disks and force him to give them the password when they had nothing on him. On the other hand, if Ed found out that he'd gone to the police, he would be in an even greater danger, because Ed would surely kill him, if the police didn't lock him up for stealing someone else's property. A true catch-22 situation.

He didn't have anyone he could talk to—at least no one he thought would be able to help. He didn't know what his next move would be, but he knew for sure that he had to stay away from Ed. So much for proposing to Kim. With a wedding, invitations, a date and time, what easy prey he would be for Ed, so that would be a wrong move. Right in front of the minister, he imagined, he would have fallen over on his face, splattered with red stuff all over a white tuxedo. So much for hiding out and being cautious. Well, no time to play chicken. It wasn't getting him anywhere.

He had to get back to the basic problem. He had to get to the house and find the passwords, somehow, even by a miracle. They had to be in the study or somewhere in the house. The only other place they could possibly be in would be at his job or the warehouse. Most likely, they would be at home, in the study somewhere, more private and very personal. He and only he entered that little room (in his mind), except for Brendan, of course.

He had to find out when his next business trip was going to be. Getting into the house when he was out of town was safer. A week-end business trip or a day-out-of-town trip would do. How would he find out if he was out of town? Easy, all he had to do was ask his daughter. She wouldn't suspect anything. So far, she had no clue what Brendan had found out. She trusted him so much that she wouldn't even dream of Brendan snooping around the house, trying to nail something on her wonderful father. Brendan picked up his notebook and sat down to make some new, rather-drastic plans.

*****

Ida sat on her porch, enjoying the lazy afternoon. Lost in thought to the newspaper that sat on her lap, she didn't hear the footsteps that came through the gate.

"Any good news in the paper today?"

She looked up to find her handsome son reaching out a dozen red roses to her.

"Surprise!" he said.

"Washburn! I wasn't the least bit expecting you! Didn't I just talk to you twenty minutes ago?"

"Modern technology, Mama. That was from my cell phone." He turned and beckoned to a young lady who was sitting in the car. She walked shyly to the porch and joined them.

"Mama, I'd like for you to meet Jenna. Jenna, this is my mother, Ida."

Jenna was nervous. She didn't know what to expect of Washburn's family even though he'd assured her of their many positive influences in his life.

She soon came to find out that Washburn was more than just right. Ida was a pleasant lady with such a bright countenance and a true pleasure to be around.

After that, Jenna ended up spending more time with Jeannine and her friends than she did with Washburn. It was an instant bond. Both girls had a lot in common, and when Jenna was with Jeannine, it was as if they were identical twins. Washburn was happy. *Step 1 accomplished. Step 2 just ahead,* he told himself.

*****

Finals week was coming to a close, and Jeannine and Osaris sat together in the cafeteria and talked about Tom Hankias.

"He's right over there," said Osaris. Jeannine wanted to turn and look at him, but she dared not.

"He's so cute!" The girls giggled.

"He won't take his eyes off you for a moment," said Osaris, who had all the privilege of looking at him because she was wearing her shades. Tom hadn't the faintest idea that he was being watched.

"He hasn't blinked for a moment," Jeannine said.

There were three days left until the end of the semester, and Jeannine sort of hated that because it meant she wouldn't be able to behold Tom for a while.

"Does Tom have a girlfriend?" Jeannine asked, hoping Osaris would say no.

"No, he doesn't," she replied bluntly.

"How do you know?"

"I just know. Guys that good-looking usually don't have girlfriends. Girls think that they've already been taken because they are too cute to be single, so they just admire them from afar, like you, Jeannine."

Jeannine gave her a plastic smile.

Jeannine couldn't keep her mind off Tom's handsome face. As she made lemonade for her father and his friends, her mind kept wandering back to him.

"Don't spill that on me, Jeannine," her father warned. "You look like you're in a daze. I was just going to ask you for a favor, Jeannine, but how much help can one be with a dazed mind?" He chuckled.

Washburn couldn't wait to marry Jenna. They'd only known each other for eight months, but Washburn knew she was the love of his dreams.

"Jenna and I are going to get married next month," he said to Casey.

"You're what?" Washburn's older sibling asked. "Washburn, you've only known her for a few months, and besides, you still have a little while to go in college. I don't think it's a good idea," she said firmly.

Ben and Ida didn't quiet agree with their son's sudden burst of wedding fever. They wanted him to wait until he'd graduated and have established himself somewhat, but he was determined. He was in love and was sure Jenna Campbell was the girl for him.

"You need to wait a little and get to know each other better. Marriage is a serious thing," his mother counseled.

"We have seriously thought about it, Mama, and we think it's the right thing to do."

Ida exchanged glances with her husband. They knew there wasn't anything they could do to make him change his mind, so why try?

"All right, son, if you feel this is right for you, then we are behind you all the way," his father said with a sigh. "You're of age, and that's your decision to make."

Jeannine and Casey wanted to help Jenna pick the right wedding gown. They targeted two bridal shops and knew for sure that they wouldn't need to shop any further because Marion's Bridal Shop and Sarah's Wedding Bliss had exquisite bridal gowns.

Marion's Bridal Shop was the first target. "They're all so gorgeous. It's hard to choose," said Jenna after trying on the third gown.

The fourth one was a hit with Casey. "Ooh, I like this one a lot," said Casey. "It looks great on you," she said with glee. Jenna scrutinized it in the mirror and agreed.

"This is perfect!" she exclaimed. "I am happy with this one."

"It's beautiful," Jeannine agreed.

The Shrouders and Campbells combined together and prepared for Washburn and Jenna's big day. When it finally arrived, Jenna had butterflies in her stomach. The twenty-one-year-old Afro-American stood before the mirror and stared at her image. Her palms were sweaty.

"Are you sure that this is what you really want?" she asked the image.

She imagined herself walking down the aisle and became nauseated. Of course she loved Washburn, but many other couples started out loving each other but still ended up in the divorce court.

She wondered if she was doing the right thing. *If I get married, it's for better or for worse, till death do us part,* she told herself. *That's a long haul, indeed.*

She'd gotten advice from friends that she ought to wait. "You have your whole life ahead of you."

She mused on the advice she'd gotten. Some thoughts were encouraging, and some were not.

"I love to see young people doing the right thing," one neighbor said. "People these days just go from one person to another, but people ought to choose their mates carefully and then make a commitment."

"My prayers are with you, dear," another neighbor had said. Was it that bad that she needed prayers?

She had mixed feelings, really nervous emotions. *Washburn cares for me a whole lot, which is quite clear. He loves me, and I know that without a doubt. Isn't that why people get married in the first place? But...then...why do they have problems later?*

Washburn stood at the altar, sweating profusely, as Jenna lingered in the dressing room. He'd been standing there, waiting, for what seemed an eternity and thought, *I have no doubt about marrying her. Wonder what's taking her so long. Hope she hasn't changed her mind. I'll just pray to die right here! Imagine having to tell all these people to go home because the bride didn't want to marry me. Bad scene…*

Come on, Jenna, where are you?

Finally, the music began to play. Washburn turned and looked to see Jenna standing at the door, and his heart melted. She stood there a moment and waited for the organ's cadence to pick up. She then nodded to her father that she was ready to make the long walk down the aisle. As the music played, she steadily made her way toward an exuberant Washburn.

She smiled stiffly as she met the gaze of the audience. Her face shuttered. The aisle seemed long, but Washburn was at the end, staring at her with pride.

Her elegant white gown was lined with white pearls from the shoulders to the bust. The sleeves were puffed at the shoulder, then enveloped her arms to her wrists. Her shoulder-length white veil was attached to a white crown that dazzled with faux diamonds.

You are so beautiful, he said to himself without much effort.

Finally, Jenna made it to the altar and the minister began his words. "Who gives this young woman away?"

"I do," replied her father. Then a soloist began to sing "Forever Love."

Ida cried.

"Nobody died, Ida. He's still our son."

The sermon was short. Mr. and Mrs. Washburn Shrouder walked down the aisle together. Their faces glowed.

After the three-hour reception, the limousine took them to the airport, where they caught a flight to Florida for a two-week honeymoon.

*****

He was in. He knew every inch of the house. Brendan knelt down next to the safe and slipped the coin into the slot and pulled the lever. *Click.* He heard the sound that let him know it was open, but then it also reminded him of the click of Ed's revolver. His pulse raced. He was caught once, and if he got caught again, he knew he could just say goodbye to life, because luck would not be his friend twice. He felt goose bumps all over his body.

If only Ed's daughter knew what he was up to, but it would never have crossed her mind that Brendan would be trespassing and searching the house as if he were an official investigator. Though she knew and trusted him, his current actions would have bothered her.

He opened the safe slowly. It didn't have much in it. A few sheets of lose papers lay at the bottom. He quickly scanned through each one.

He unfolded an eight-and-a-half-by-eleven sheet of paper and stared in awe at the bolded, underlined words at the top of the paper: *Floppy Disks Passwords.* His eyes popped wide-open. A stroke of luck. He couldn't believe that he had actually found them after all the effort. It was too easy to be true. The paper listed the disks by their color tabs and the password for each color.

This thing could have been over a long time ago, he thought. *If only I hadn't gotten caught the first time.*

Someone spoke from the living room, and it startled him. For a moment he'd forgotten he was snooping around. He folded the sheet of paper and tucked it in his pocket, hurriedly closed the safe, and pulled the lever. The clicking sound told him it was locked. He closed the study behind him and walked away, sighing in relief as he made it safely out without being seen. He'd made headway and must determine what Ed Coons was so eager to get back. He cut his visit short again because he couldn't wait any longer to see what he now had in his possession.

He cherished the sheet of paper as if it were a ticket to heaven. He noticed the time as he drove past Milolta Savings Bank.

"Oh," he uttered. He had told Kim that he would meet her at his grandmother's house. If only he hadn't made that plan. He made a U-turn and headed south to his grandmother's house. He was already ten minutes late, but his grandmother was a sweet old lady and Kim would be well taken care of until he got there.

Kim was already at the house on time. She hated that Brendan had suddenly developed a bad habit of being late.

She peered through Ms. Abbey's cracked window. Ms. Abbey seemed to be in a deep sleep, and Kim decided not to wake her by knocking. The old woman sat motionless as if she were a mannequin. An open book sat in her lap. The receiver hung freely at the side of the chair. She must have fallen asleep while talking on the telephone, Kim thought.

Kim made a decision to knock lightly on the front door, but Ms. Abbey didn't respond. She stared at the building as if she'd seen it for the first time. She suddenly became aware of its rough texture, as if the carpenters had haphazardly tossed slabs of mortar at it. Wild trees covered most of the house, a structure that looked as old and frail as Ms. Abbey herself.

"Ms. Abbey, it's me, Kim, Kim Futon." She tried the lock, and the door opened. She took a step inside, and the wooden floor creaked so loudly it scared her.

She had only met Ms. Abbey once. One day, Brendan had introduced her when they were driving by the house and had stopped for just a short while.

This was her first time inside the house. It was dim inside, the room being lit by the light that came through the windows.

"Ms. Abbey?" she whispered, trying not to wake her if she was sleeping, yet loud enough for her to hear her—if she had her hearing aid on. She wouldn't want to startle an old lady and give her a heart attack if she found that someone suddenly appeared in the middle of her living room.

Kim slowly walked to where Ms. Abbey sat comfortably in her rocking chair. She didn't mind waiting for Brendan to show up.

The floor seemed to cry out in pain at every step she took. She reached out and touched Ms. Abbey gently, but there was no response and Kim knew that she was fast asleep. A noise from upstairs startled her. Who could be in Ms. Abbey's house besides Brendan and Mrs. Clark?

She heard footsteps descending the stairs and instinctively knew the person present didn't hear her come in. There was no way that she would let whoever that person was know that she was there. She hurried past the dining room, into the kitchen. There were two doors, and she quickly opened the one on her right and slipped in and closed it behind her.

She hadn't the faintest idea that the door she had chosen would lead her to the basement. Before she could retreat her steps, she heard a thud in the living room. She glided down the stairs and stood panting at the bottom.

It was dark, and she was frightened at the thought of being trapped in the basement with an intruder lurking upstairs. She waited a couple of minutes, listening to the sounds upstairs, and hoped that the feet would just leave the house.

A dragging noise trailed from the living room to the kitchen. Beads of sweat dampened her forehead. Her hands shook as she bit on her nails anxiously. To her utter dismay, the basement door opened a crack. She hurried into the farthest corner and crouched behind a rug that was leaning against the wall.

The door creaked louder as the intruder opened it wider. She stayed still. A series of bumps followed on the stairs and came to a halt at the bottom. She held her breath.

The footsteps ascended the stairs. There was a pause, and then the basement door creaked open and then slammed shut.

Her heart pounded wildly in her chest. *Don't lock the basement door,* she thought as her body shook uncontrollably.

She heard the front door open, and seconds later, an engine started and a vehicle pulled away.

She waited for what seemed like half an hour before she decided to retrace her steps. She stood, and tiny needlelike sensations ran through the bottom of her feet and up her legs. She flinched as she rubbed them to allow the circulation to flow again freely.

She cast her eyes at the bottom of the stairs. A gray bag lay almost under it. She walked over and pulled on it, and Ms. Abbey's head popped out from the opening.

She screamed a long, blood-wrenching scream and ran up the stairs like a lightning bolt, through the kitchen and living room, and directly outside—straight into Brendan's arms. He was opening the front gate.

"Hey, calm down, where are you going so fast?"

"Your grandmother's dead! She's in the basement in a bag!" she said bluntly.

"What?" Brendan asked incredulously and ran into the house. The horrified look on her face verified that she wasn't playing games. He knew that something was terribly wrong. He ran into the house to see about his only grandmother. She had no vital signs, and giving her mouth-to-mouth resuscitation didn't help.

Brendan called the police and his mother. Mrs. Clark stumbled, then fainted, when she got to the house and learned her mother was dead. Brendan didn't tell her all he knew, that she'd died when he'd called. As it was, he'd only told her she was unconscious.

"She's been murdered!" she declared hysterically after the smelling salt brought her back to consciousness.

There was a piece of paper in her hand that had one word scribbled on it: *disks*. Brendan was sure that Ed was the cause of her death. He didn't say anything to anyone about the meaning of the note. It didn't even occur to the police the note had any kind of meaning.

I'll get you for this, he vowed as he held back the tears. He was distraught and angry, and he was going to do something about it.

Later that day, he made a phone call from a pay phone to Ed. "You murderer!" he hollered into the receiver. "You want those disks so bad, you're going to have to get them from the police." He slammed the receiver down and walked away.

A chill ran up his spine. He knew he had just doubled the trouble he was already in but had sense enough to avoid his apartment. He was certain that someone would be watching to track his comings and goings. He wanted to get the disks and bring them to the police, but for now he had to stay hidden. The disks were safe, in a little combination box in a hole in his unfinished basement and covered with an Oriental rug.

"I'll fix you good," he promised. "I'll make sure your empire comes crashing down, scumbag!" he yelled.

Mrs. Clark lived at the other end of town. Brendan was glad for that. Ed didn't know where she lived, he hoped.

He remembered the day he had a hunch that someone was following him when he was on his way to his grandmother's house. He had shrugged it off, but now he thought that maybe his hunch then had been right. He'd thought that maybe he was overreacting because he had gotten a couple of threats. Apparently, he wasn't. How he regretted not following his feelings.

He made sure this time that he had not been followed, and he went to the basement cautiously and retried the disks. With cloudy eyes, he opened each disk and viewed the contents. The sweetness of obtaining the passwords diminished as he mourned the loss of his grandmother. He really didn't feel up to going through them, but he'd waited long enough, and just in case something further might happen, he wanted to know what Ed was up to.

The first couple of disks didn't make much sense to him. There were long lists of numbers with names, addresses, and phone numbers. He didn't know what to make of them, as no one else would either. But slowly he began to make sense of the disks when he found files that were more explicit. His mouth hung in sheer shock as he scrolled through the files on each disks. Ed's entire operation was on the six disks in explicit detail. The police would have everything they needed to convict and put him and his men behind bars for life. Brendan hoped he'd be able to get to the police before one of Ed's henchmen got to him first.

Brendan and his mother officially laid his grandmother to rest, and he could now focus on how he would recompense the murderer for killing his precious grandmother.

*****

"Six whole hours it took me to create those files. I am finally done!" Ben said out loud to himself, jubilant about his success. "Now I know I can really go to the meeting tomorrow." He rubbed his burning eyes and kept them closed for a few seconds. He hadn't had much sleep that past week, and he was exhausted. "It was worth it, though," he told himself. He was finally done and was pleased.

"Ben?" Ida said. She opened the door to his study and handed him the cordless phone. He hadn't heard the phone ring. He watched her petite figure disappear around the corner.

"Hello?" he said in a raspy voice. A strange look came over his face as he listened to the caller.

"We must get rid of him," he finally said. "He's nothing but a hindrance."

His expression lightened. "So you do agree that we should get rid of him?" He smiled as he said, "This is long overdue."

The conversation was brief, but he was pleased.

"Ben?"

"Yes, Ida."

"Won't you come to bed? It's late."

He shoved the chair back to give himself room to get up. "I'm coming."

Bed, covers, sleep—too inviting to give up. Tonight, he thought, *I can really get the rest my body craves.*

CHAPTER 11

Whereabouts Unknown

Brendan's whereabouts were unknown. He hadn't contacted anyone to let them know he was all right. There was no telling where he was or if he was dead or alive. There were no leads to his disappearance.

Kim was becoming a nuisance to her father because of the constant mention and worry over Brendan. Marshall flicked out a disk and snapped in another one. He barely heard a word she said.

He punched the keypad professionally as his daughter rambled on.

"Have you heard a word I've said to you?"

Marshall stopped and turned toward her. He looked at her impatiently and apologized half-heartedly. He felt bothered.

Kim walked to her room and sat on her bed. She stared at the phone until her eyes crossed. She hoped it would ring and Brendan would be at the other end of the line, but another day was done and Brendan hadn't called. She retired to bed with him on her mind and woke up the next morning with a splitting headache from the nightmares she'd had about him.

She wasn't the only one who was worried sick about Brendan. Mrs. Clark was hysterical. She hadn't seen her son in almost three weeks. She knew that that wasn't like him. Plus, to think of it, she'd noticed how strange he was acting the last time she'd seen him.

"I talk to him every day. He's always coming over. He's not picking up his phone, and when I went to his apartment, his mail was flowing over in the mailbox," she told the police, who listened with interest.

"He hasn't been to class either," added Jeannine.

"How old is he?" the officer asked.

"Twenty-two."

"He's an adult, then. Do you think he just might have wanted to get away for a while?"

"No, no, that is not like my son. He's my child. I know him."

The police took her report and filed it with the missing persons' list. They made a search of his apartment and came up with only a note that said, "Return my disks."

Even though it was hard to tell if the note was a threat, Mrs. Clark was bothered by it. "I have a horrible feeling that something terrible has happened to my son. He's probably dead somewhere."

Ms. Abbey had been murdered, and now Brendan was missing. That didn't add up to a happy day. Ms. Abbey was a good woman. She had gotten along well with everyone, a quiet old lady. There was just no apparent reason that anyone would have wanted to harm her. Yet she was murdered. The autopsy revealed she had been injected with a lethal dose of something that Mrs. Clark couldn't even pronounce.

Now that Brendan was missing, she didn't know what to think of the situation. She wondered if the person who killed her mother had done the same thing to Brendan. Who in the world would target her family in such horrible crimes? Was Brendan really missing or too grief-stricken to stay around? Maybe he wanted to get away and sort things out, rebuild his life. But that wasn't like him. Those thoughts just wouldn't leave her alone. She was worried sick and didn't know what to do next or, worse yet, or whom to turn to.

Jeannine tried to comfort her. She stayed with her all day, just listening to her and being in her company. Mrs. Clark sat by the phone, hoping and praying that Brendan would call and say he was all right, but each day ended in hopeless despair.

Kim still hadn't had a clue about what was going on with him. He didn't tell her anything, and she knew he wouldn't skip town without telling her. If it were to the point he had to leave, he would let her know one way or another, but she hadn't heard from him at all.

"Something awful has happened," she sobbed.

Marshall tried in vain to comfort his daughter.

"You don't even seem to care that he might be dead somewhere, Daddy," she said.

"I do care. I hope he is all right, but I have enough things to worry about than to worry about someone who might have just taken off because he was sick of everybody."

*****

Today was just another fretful day for Mrs. Clark. She paced the floor back and forth. The thought lingered for the longest in her mind that her son might be *dead*. She tried to stay calm down but couldn't. What if he's been murdered? It was a frightening thought. She wouldn't be able to live if she knew that her son was dead. She couldn't think of anything that would lead them to where Brendan might have gone. She summed up everything and came to the conclusion that something had happened to him. She shivered.

She waited impatiently for the Missing Persons Investigating Department to get back to her. "I don't know what's taking them so long," she complained as she picked up the phone and dialed the number.

"Oh, Mrs. Clark," Officer Spunk said gently into the phone, "I was just about to give you a call."

"Any leads?" she interrupted abruptly.

"No."

She let the phone slide from her hand onto the receiver. No other words from his lips mattered.

It wasn't long after she'd spoken with the officer that Jeannine rang the doorbell. Jeannine made it her duty to visit her almost every day. She was glad for the company. Jeannine leaned over in her chair and placed a hand on Mrs. Clark's arm.

"It's gonna be all right," she consoled.

She smiled in response. Her teary eyes had a glimmer of hope, as words spoken by angels.

"Maybe he's alive."

She managed another smile; this time, she didn't strain too much to offer it. Her attention shifted to the picture she held so tightly in her hands.

"I can't lose him, Jeannine," she muttered.

"I believe in miracles," Jeannine replied.

Mrs. Clark passed a finger over the picture and wiped away a teardrop that had fallen on his face.

It was his high school graduation picture, and he was dressed in his cap and gown. Brendan smiled broadly. The background of books accented his personality. He was a very studious young man.

Jeannine wished there were something she could do. If only she had a strong sense of intuition to seek him out and find out where he was. She hoped he wasn't lying in a ditch somewhere, hurt, badly hurt. She pondered about the homeless man she'd helped a couple of months back. He surely must have moved on to some other spot more conducive to surviving. She sure hoped so. She shrugged her shoulders.

She didn't mind helping people at almost any cost. She wished she could help Mrs. Clark by taking away the pain as they waited each day for Brendan to return unharmed.

The inevitable nature of pain comes in all forms and affects every life force. "Oh, Mrs. Clark, I'm praying for him," she burst out. "I believe he's all right. We don't understand, but I believe that there is an angel watching over him wherever he is."

*****

Ed looked at the caller ID on the telephone, and it read, "No caller ID." He picked up the phone and answered in a calm tone.

"Ed?" asked the voice at the other end of the line.

"Luigi?" replied Ed.

"Yeah, we need to talk. For the risk I'm taking, you're not paying me half enough. If they find out what I'm doing for you, I'm done. It's a serious crime, man, and it would cost me a lot if I get caught. Probably my whole life behind bars, if not the electric chair, man. Why should I risk all that for the pennies you're paying me? If you don't up my reward 100 percent, I'm out."

"Listen, Luigi, don't say things like that on the phone. Don't you have any sense? Let's meet and talk privately." Ed paused. "Can you meet me tonight by the riverfront?"

"By the riverfront for a private conversation? Are you kidding?"

"The weather is a bit cool, and not many people will be at the riverfront late tonight. There might not even be anyone there. Is elven thirty good for you, Luigi?"

"Yeah, man, and you'd better bring some money with you too. I got bills to pay and a family to support."

"See you at eleven thirty, Luigi."

*****

Luigi was at the riverfront area by eleven o'clock. He couldn't wait. After all, Ed ought to know that what he was asking was, at the very least, pretty reasonable. *A man putting his neck on the line for another is worth a million bucks, and you know it, Ed,* he thought. He knew he had the upper hand over Ed, because who else would do this for him? He further mused, *If he brought this to anybody else, they'd probably turn him in.*

He was the only one at the riverfront, and he knew no one else would be there, because who would find it thrilling to hang out by the river on a chilly night, wind chill to the bone? *Good,* he told himself, *my butt's covered.*

A black Mitsubishi rolled up behind him. The person inside opened the car door and stepped out. The glare of the headlights prevented Luigi from seeing a clear view of the person, so he cupped his hand over his eyes.

Luigi fixed as best as he could on the man approaching him. "Oh, I thought you were someone else," Luigi said apologetically.

"Luigi?" the first man asked.

"Do I know you?" he asked tensely.

"Oh, no. Ed sent us. He wanted us to give you a message. A .32-caliber message." One of the men pulled out a small gun from his waist and said, "We know where you live, twerp. We know your wife and children."

"Do your job with joy or…or else…you fill in the blanks, dude," the other man said.

Luigi's knees wobbled. One of them kicked him in the stomach, and he bent over with a groan. The other hit him hard on the back of the head with the gun. A few punches and a couple of flings to the ground left Luigi helpless and hardly able to move. Blood oozed from his mouth.

"That's how serious we are. If you don't do your job, we can easily kill you and everyone connected to you, and we'll just find someone else to take your place. You choose."

They left. Not too soon for Luigi, who lay on the ground, helpless. He crawled into his car and waited for whatever strength he had left to return.

*****

It had been more than two months since Brendan was last seen, and still no one knew his whereabouts. Mrs. Clark was becoming weary with a police department seemingly unable to find an ocean liner at a port. Brendan had not been in any of the hospitals in the tri-city area. Mrs. Clark's patience was worn. She sat on her porch with a crochet needle and some thread. She brushed away a tear that had escaped from her eye. "Son," she groaned, as if to scold him and, at the same time, hasten his return.

She picked up her glasses and gently placed them on her face, pulled out the thread, and began to make a stitch. She still hadn't really decided what she wanted to make, but whatever it turned out to be would be just fine with her. What was important was that she made something.

"Mrs. Clark?" Officer Pringle stood tall and confident in front of her, his wide shoulders and firm chest making him look invincible.

He removed his shades and took a few steps closer, his gentle manner a vast contrast to the ruggedness of his appearance.

"Yes? I'm Mrs. Clark." She looked searchingly into his eyes and hoped he had good news. His expression gave no clue.

"There is a young man at a hospital thirty miles south of here that fits your son's description," he continued. "He was in a car accident, and he had no form of identification on him."

New hope. Could it be her son?

"He is in an unconscious state, but once in a while, he'll mutter something the attendants can't make out. We thought maybe you'd like to take a look at him to see if—"

She rose immediately, and halfway into the house, she muttered, "Yes, of course."

She rode nervously in the officer's car to the hospital, wondering all the while if she should hope to hope. What if it was Brendan? What kind of physical state was he in? What if it wasn't Brendan? She didn't think she could handle disappointment well at all. Not that she wanted her son to be hurt, but a hurt son was better than no son at all.

Down the long hallway she walked at the officer's side as she tried to keep up with his long strides. The smell of hospital nauseated her.

"D-16," the nurse at the nurses' station told the officer. As they got to D-16, she stood hesitantly at the door and just stared at the limp figure that occupied the tiny bed.

"It's all right," said Officer Pringle as he tugged at her arm to get a little closer. She walked slowly to the side of the bed but momentarily hung her head in disappointment as she looked at the stranger in the bed. "No, that's not my son," she said in a whisper and began to cry.

*****

"Someone just called and hung up on me," complained Marshall. "The first time was acceptable, as I figured someone had the wrong number. I'm beginning to get curious because it happened three times within the past two hours."

An hour later, the phone rang and Kim answered it. She was in her room, and Marshall was downstairs.

"Kim!"

"Who is this?"

"It's me, Brendan."

"Brendan! Where—"

"I can't talk for long. I'm on a pay phone."

"You have all of us worried sick about you, especially your mother. Where are you?"

"I have to keep a low profile. Don't worry. I'll be fine. Tell Mom I'm just fine."

"You haven't called your mother?"

"I can't explain anything over the phone. I have to see you. Don't leave the house today. I don't know what time I'll be there, but I will."

"What is going on, Brendan?" Her worried voice seemed to echo through the phone line.

She heard a click and then a dial tone. She called Mrs. Clark right away. Mrs. Clark squealed in delight at the good news that her Brendan was all right after all. Her spirit revived. Kim watched two hours slip by, then four, and still Brendan didn't show. Mrs. Clark prepared a delicious meal and watched the door for his return, but Brendan never showed up there either.

*****

Petrified and furious at the same time, Ed Coons still couldn't believe the disks had fallen into the wrong hands. He knew it could cost him his life or, worse, he could spend the rest of his life in prison. He wondered if threatening Brendan was the wise way to go about getting them back and thought of making him an offer. *Will fifty thousand dollars weaken the kid's resolve?* Everything had always been easy to take care of, and if there was anything that challenged him, it wasn't much of a challenge. But Brendan was different. He couldn't get a grip on him in the ordinary way. How could he have been so careless to allow the disks to be stolen in the first place? The more he thought about how young Brendan was and how valuable the disks were, the angrier he got. "No deal!" he muttered to himself. "The kid's gonna die! And those worthless men! They're good for nothing. They couldn't catch one mangy boy in a stinkin' warehouse!"

So far, it didn't seem as if the police knew anything about the operation. Nothing suspicious had taken place. Maybe Brendan hadn't been able to access the files, and besides, he was afraid of getting killed and might not even understand what he was looking at even if he was to access the disks.

Besides, Ed knew the disks were going to be in his hands again, and soon. Everything would be back to normal, and it would be business as usual with a little hiccup.

"Ed," Margo said for the first time since they'd entered the room. Ed looked up suddenly, as if Margo's voice reminded him that he had company. With a distant look in his eyes, he tried to stay focused on Margo's face, only to be lost again in deep thought while Margo's lips flapped on.

"And that's what I think we should do, yeah."

Those were the only words Ed heard Margo speak.

"Uh, what?"

"All this time I was just talking to myself? Thanks a lot, man."

Whatever the strategy or basic plan, the bottom line was that the disks had to be recovered at any cost.

*****

Brendan took every precaution as he headed to Kim's house, doubling back, even taking wrong turns on purpose just to see if he was being tailed. Eventually, he made his way there.

"Brendan," she said, sobbing, "where have you been? We've all been worried sick about you!"

"For a very special girl," he said, handing her an arrangement of roses. "I can't talk about it right now. I'm fine. Don't worry. I can't stay. I came because I just had to see you." Five minutes was all he needed to behold his Kim. As he turned to leave, Zaire pulled up in the driveway, got out of his car, and closed the door. He leaned against the door with his arms folded, as if he were surveying an island all his own.

"What're you doing here?" snorted Brendan. Just then, something came over him, and within seconds he jumped on Zaire and started throwing wild punches.

Meeghan heard the uproar and came running out the door. She didn't know what to do and so screamed at them to stop, but they were going at each other without hesitation.

Kim screamed at the top of her lungs, but they ignored her completely. Brendan and Zaire rolled on the ground in a deadlock. Mr. and Mrs. Jenkins, who lived next door, heard the commotion and came out to see what was happening. Mr. Jenkins was bold enough to get between the two and pulled them apart.

"You'd better stay away from Kim, or I'll kill you!" Zaire shouted angrily. He got in his car and sped away.

Brendan wiped the blood from his face with his shirt.

"You'd better go to the hospital," said Meeghan shakily.

Kim was hysterical. Brendan staggered to his car and left Kim crying in the driveway. He couldn't believe that Zaire had the nerve to go to her house, and wondered how many times he'd seen her since he had been in hiding.

*****

He was barely at the apartment door when two men approached silently and grabbed him from behind. One man covered his mouth as the other held his hands behind his back.

"Where are the disks, Brendan Clark?" whispered one of the men through clenched teeth as he painfully wrenched him. He tried to free himself to see who had him pinned from behind, but to no avail.

"I'm not Brendan," he replied in a shaky tone as he felt something hard at his side.

"Keep your voice down!" Someone opened a door down the hallway. They quickly let go of him, but he could still feel the point of a gun in his side.

"Hi, Brendan," a middle-aged woman called out as they walked past her on their way to the parking lot. He glanced at her, nodding, and walked cooperatively to the exit.

"Don't make a sound or I'll blow your brains out!" whispered one of the men. They led him to a tinted dark-blue car, shoved him in the back seat, and drove away, one of the men keeping a watchful eye.

In a few minutes, they pulled into a dark alley and stopped.

"I'm not who you think I am—"

He had begun to say more but was slapped in the face.

"Unless you're going to tell us where the disks are, you have no right to speak," one of the men snarled. "You can make this as easy as possible on yourself, or…it's your move."

"Give us the disks!" the other man barked.

"Yeah, and we'll let you go." The other laughed sarcastically under his breath.

His knees began to shake. The horror of death confronted him in no uncertain terms. "I don't know what you're talking about." One of the men smacked him hard in the face with the handle of his gun. He could feel the warm blood trickling down the side of his face.

"We'll get you to talk." The other man kicked him in the stomach with the leading edge of his hard boot.

The young man moaned and slumped over, but they yanked him upright by his collar and beat him heartlessly.

His only hope was that someone passing by somehow would come to his aid and rescue him.

*****

Jeannine was glad that her workday was over, and felt relieved when seeing the number 33 bus just half a block away. She was on her way to Jealissa's house and wished she'd chosen another day to visit because today she was exhausted.

"I hate not having my car," she murmured. She glanced at her watch, almost 7:00 p.m.

"Oh, I'm sorry," said a deep, husky voice that jolted her back to the present. He had accidentally stepped on her foot, but she was too much in a trance to realize it.

"It's okay," she replied with a smile. She gingerly climbed onto the bus and settled down comfortably at a window seat, closed her eyes, and tried to block out all the events that had happened that day.

It wasn't long before she began to doze.

A jolt of the bus awoke her. She couldn't tell where they were, but in a moment her mind cleared and she was relieved to know she hadn't passed her stop. She now fought hard to stay awake.

The bus stopped at Tinball Avenue, and she wearily poked her way through the thick column of passengers and exited the bus, then walked casually down the semidark street in the direction of Cranshaw and Myrtle Avenues. Just ahead, a muffled sound caught her attention. It was coming from the alley on the right. She walked closer with caution.

As she got closer, she stopped and hid behind a tree and listened. She could see the silhouettes of three people. Two men spoke in whispering tones, while the third stood limp with his arms behind him. The men sounded very angry.

"Oh my god!" she exclaimed, staring down the poorly lit alley in disbelief. She couldn't understand what her eyes told her was going on.

"That's Brendan!" she exclaimed. Even though the ally was poorly lit, there was enough light to recognize someone she'd known for years.

What is he doing with those men? Out of the blue, after disappearing for months, Brendan appears in a dark alley with two angry men, she thought. It just didn't make sense.

The men closed in on him, talking in a low, whispering tone. One of them shook a small handgun in his face as he talked.

She couldn't get a good look at either one of the men because Brendan was the only one facing her direction. She strained to hear the nature of the conversation. She moved closer, cautiously.

"Give…will do…disks!" one of them snorted a little louder than he'd probably intended, and she was able to pick up just a few words.

"Oh god, please don't hurt him!" she prayed frantically. "What can I do?" she said, pleading with herself. "How can I help?" She knew that she was no match for the men, so she had to find a way to save him.

She heard a thud and a moan. He was knocked to the ground. He wrestled with the men but was pinned on his face to the ground.

On impulse, she screamed with all her might and yelled, "Over here, Officer, over here!"

The men swung around, and one of them hollered, "Grab her, Cooper. But if it's the cops, we have to get out of here!" Without hesitation, she ran as fast as she could down the dark street toward the intersection.

A shot was fired. She had no idea of the bullet's origin or target. "Oh, God, please help me!" she prayed frantically. Her heart pounded as she ran headlong toward the intersection and yelled, "Officer! Officer! Over here!"

She glanced over her shoulder, and to her relief, she saw no one behind.

She made it to the intersection and hurried into the grocery store. It was a busy night, and she knew that they wouldn't dare follow her there. She was okay. She checked herself and was relieved to learn that she hadn't been shot, just shaken up.

Brendan! Her heart sank. He must have been the one they'd fired at. She wanted to scream. She wanted to run back and see if he was all right, but she was aware that it was too risky to chance it.

Jealissa was just around the corner from the intersection, but she dared not walk any farther. She was two blocks within Brendan's apartment.

She walked to a pay phone and dialed 911 and told them what had happened.

She called home. It took her a few moments to remember her own phone number. There was no one at her house, or at her sister's house, so she called for a cab.

"Good timing," said the man at the other end of the phone. "There's one in your area."

Brendan might be dead, she thought. She felt a sense of failure. *My friend needed me, and I wasn't there for him. Coward, that's what I am.* She began to sob.

She knew that the men had seen her, and she wondered if they'd seen her well enough to recognize her. A tough guess.

She called his mother, but there was no answer. She locked herself in the bathroom and waited for her parents to get home.

The police and paramedics arrived at the alley within minutes. They found the victim, and he was pronounced dead at the scene. The head officer picked up anything he thought might be of help. They laid the corpse in a body bag and zipped it shut.

At the morgue, they laid the bag on the cold, hard table. *A young man with his whole life ahead of him was suddenly cut down like a tree,* thought the detective as he shook his head, never really getting over death of any kind.

*****

At the sound of her mother's voice, Jeannine unlocked the bathroom door and went downstairs. She cried uncontrollably as she related everything that she'd seen.

"Where's Daddy?" she asked between sobs.

"I don't know. He's probably working late at the office." Ida couldn't believe what she'd heard. *Poor Mrs. Clark,* she thought. She sighed and sat back in the couch. Every muscle in her body felt numb.

"I have to go and see Mrs. Clark. Would you like to go with me?"

Jeannine shook her head. "You go ahead. I'll be fine."

She locked the doors after her mother and made sure that every window was shut and locked.

*****

Mrs. Clark opened the door with anticipation. She couldn't help but notice the look on Ida's face and knew she didn't have any good news.

"I think you'd better sit down." Ida told her what Jeannine had said. Mrs. Clark let out a scream that pierced Ida's ears.

"I thought I'd tell you before the police did, so I could be here to support you."

Mrs. Clark would have missed the police at the door, but the shrilling sound from inside the house let him know that she might have been informed. Officer Pringle waited and then rang the bell again.

Ida rose to open the door. She stared the officer in the eye and then motioned him inside. Mrs. Clark's teary eyes stared pitifully at the officer, as if to beg him to say that it was all a mistake.

"I'm sorry, Mrs. Clark," he said in a monotone voice. "Someone called us about your son. They also gave us your address and phone number. When we got there, he was dead, shot in the head. We do need for you to come and identify the body." It was just as hard for him to stand there and tell her that her son was dead as it was for her to hear it.

It was as if she'd heard the news for the first time. Her eyes rolled over in her head, and she fell backward. Her lapse of consciousness lasted only momentarily. She sat upright and stared around. She followed the officer to his car like an obedient child.

Ida went home to see about Jeannine because Mrs. Clark insisted she was all right and didn't need Ida to bother herself.

The ride to the morgue was traumatic. She didn't speak a word, and neither did the officer. She stared down at her dead son and swallowed hard. He had a disappointed expression on his face, as if to say, "Why?"

She nodded in confirmation. It was Brendan. Just what she'd feared had happened. She lost him and knew as well she'd lost all strength to go on.

She didn't remember much of her trip back home. She awoke with a throbbing headache after sleeping a bit. She tried to raise her head from the pillow but gave up. She pulled the covers over her head and let go of every ounce of strength she possessed, crying for hours until her eyes were swollen shut.

*****

Jeannine stared blankly at the television screen as the newscaster reported the incident that she'd stumbled upon. She trembled. Brendan was in danger, and she didn't help him. She was his friend, and she'd failed him. She remembered the last time he sang to her. The song rang back in her ears. *"Count on me, I'll always be there…"*

But you couldn't count on me, could you? She sighed in resignation.

She choked on the thought that she, too, could have been killed. A flood of confusion swept over her. She couldn't understand why he was murdered. She had no clue whatsoever under the sun why he was brought to that fate. The Brendan she knew was a good, law-abiding citizen. Maybe they had him mixed up with someone else.

She wanted to help the police in whatever way that she could. It was the least she could do to make up for failing to help him.

*****

Kim stared at Jeannine incredulously. What she heard just wasn't possible. She noted the seriousness in her face and knew it was true.

"No! No!" she screamed vehemently. Jeannine joined in, and the two girls cried until they lost their strength.

How could Brendan be dead? Kim wanted to know. He didn't deserve to die. Everything seemed foggy. How could life be so cruel? Was everyone she cared about going to die and leave her all alone? What was next? She had lost her mother, and now she'd lost a very special friend. She knew that she would have someday married him.

Maybe she should have told him yes when he'd proposed to her. Maybe that would have changed things and he would not have been killed. She blamed herself for the loss of his life. If only she weren't so selfish in thinking about herself.

Kim Futon was never the same. She had withdrawn. She barely ate or slept. Life to her was nothing but misery and grief.

The police were doing all that they could to find Brendan's murderers. They searched his possessions to see if there was anything that would lead to the men. Upon the information that Jeannine gave them about the disks, they took his disks to the station and found nothing but school projects on them. Nothing of any significance to the case could be found on the disks.

Jeannine tried to resume her normal, everyday life. As long as she stayed occupied, she was okay. Kim and Mrs. Clark were always in her thoughts. She breathed a prayer for them that they would make it through the tragedy that had disrupted their lives, a prayer she repeated many times during the day.

*****

"We've got our man," the man said in an affirmative voice.

Ed's eyes widened a bit. "Are you sure?" His jaw was set. "You're sure about that?" He wanted to make sure. "Is he really dead?" He had a distant look in his eyes, as if he were looking at some faraway country.

"Yes. As dead as one gets, that is."

"And the disks?"

The two men that stood in front of him took a breath and held it. "We have a lead," one of them said as he released his breath.

"Give us some time, we'll have them. That's a promise," added the other man quickly. He tried not to say anything, but he thought that he had to say something of comfort so that their boss wouldn't send them to a bottomless pit for being a failure.

As if a sign that he was satisfied with what he'd heard, the tightness in Ed's face lessened. He spun his chair around and turned his back to the men. It was a hint that the meeting was over. They walked out the door with an earnest determination to retrieve the disks, wherever Brendan had them hidden. It was just as dangerous if they fell into the wrong hands as it was for Brendan to have them.

*****

As their meeting had ended with Ed, Detective Schennenburger stood on the other side of Jeannine's door, waiting to meet with her again.

"Hello, I'm Detective Schennenburger, and I'm here to see Jeannine Shrouder," he said to Ida, who opened the door.

"Certainly, Detective, come on in," she replied. "I'm Ida, Jeannine's mother."

Jeannine was nervous, and rightly so, and she wondered why he was there.

"Yes, Detective, how can I help you?" Jeannine said.

"I just wanted to do a follow up with you on the incident that you reported to us. We just want to know if there have been any new developments." He pulled out his tape recorder.

"Do you mind if I record our conversation?" he said, not really caring about the response. "Has anyone approached you, or have you been followed? Any suspicions about anything?"

A mixed feeling of relief and disappointment swept over her. She would have loved to hear that the men had been caught, but she would have hated to have to identify them.

She painfully recalled the incident again to the detective, who recorded the conversation.

"I remember clearly that one of them used the name Cooper." Something she'd never thought about suddenly struck her, and she said, "If they knew Brendan, then it's a possibility they might know me. Is that right, Detective?" He nodded, and she shuddered.

The meeting took about an hour. She was glad when it was over. "What a nightmare," she mumbled as the detective ambled out the door.

"Thank you, Ms. Shrouder. We'll keep in touch."

*****

The church felt cold and somber. Faces masked with black veils hanging from black hats and bodies dressed in full black complemented the general mood.

It was a dark day for Mrs. Clark, a day imprinted on her heart as one of the saddest days of her life. She wanted to be dead; that much was clear. Dead people didn't feel. Dead people didn't cry. She didn't want to feel the pain of an everlasting curse.

Her only child was ripped away from her. This recent trauma was one, she knew, that would never go away. For the rest of her life, she would grieve.

The air seemed to whistle a sad tune. Life seemed hopeless and gloomy. A sense of eeriness dominated the church.

Brendan, the center of attention, lay in his coffin at the front of the church. How could life be so unfair? He was so young. Why? He was robbed of life, a good kid that didn't deserve to die.

The minister rose and walked to the podium, his long robe trailing behind. His voice echoed in the huge church as he spoke in confidence, as if a surety from God. "Life, a gift from God," he began, "is one of the most treasured gifts one ever has…"

Mrs. Clark was present in body, but her mind was gone, understandably back in the past, when Brendan bloomed from a child to a young man.

All of a sudden, her voice pierced through the somber service.

"No! No! No!" She kept screaming it over and over.

The minister paused. He smiled with compassion. With great patience he stood, waiting for her to calm down.

She finally regained her composure. The minister resumed his duty and carried on with the service. The procession was short. Mrs. Clark caught a few words of encouragement from the minister as she slipped in and out of attention. The grief-stricken mother barely held on.

She didn't feel anything while they drove to the cemetery. She stood still between two women who supported her physically and emotionally. As they lowered the coffin into the ground, it struck home once again that her Brendan was really gone. He would never be seen again in this life.

She gave a holler that didn't sound human, and then she fell to the ground, and again they tended to another traumatic attack. They thought this time her heart had given out. She had no pulse. The paramedics came within minutes. She wasn't dead, but close to it.

Jeannine was grief-stricken as well over the death of her friend. She'd never had the experience of losing anyone close to her before, and it was hard dealing with it.

After the graveside ceremony, she went over to Kim's house to comfort her and to be comforted. She had no idea what to say, but just being there helped.

Death was the ultimate bad hand. What could anyone say to the bereaved that would make the pain go away? Not one word could come close to soothing the wound of losing someone as precious and dear to her as Brendan was.

The phone rang, and it was Detective Jake Schennenburger, asking Kim if he could speak with her again. He promised her to be brief. She agreed. Schennenburger figured that he needed to get Ben Shrouder into his office before he spoke with Kim. Ben wasn't too thrilled about the idea of being questioned, but he knew that he had to cooperate.

He sat across from Detective Schennenburger at the oblong table and said impatiently, "I do have an appointment. Please make this brief." Schennenburger shuffled a few sheets of paper without looking up. Ben knew that he heard him but held his peace.

"Where were you the night Brendan Clark was murdered?"

"I beg your pardon?" he replied with hostility.

"Don't tell me you need an interpreter, or are you playing deaf? Where were you the night Brendan Clark was murdered?" he snapped, his voice rising impatiently.

Ben's face softened a bit. He had an obligation to himself and his family to clear himself of all suspicion.

"I think I was at work or something. I don't remember what day he was murdered. Come on. Why are you questioning me, anyway?"

"We have reason to believe you might have something to do with his death."

Ben sat upright in his chair. "That's not possible. I have nothing to do with his death. He and my daughter were close."

"Tell you what? I'll give you a hint. Your debit card was used just a few blocks away from the crime scene that night within the same hour that Brendan was murdered. I could go on."

Ben knitted his brow. "Listen, don't even try to set me up. I just happened to be in that area. I have nothing to do with that boy's death. This is absolutely ridiculous!"

Detective Schennenburger rose from his chair. "Well, you think about it. The next time I speak with you, you'd better come up with a good alibi, or I'm going to have to book you until I do get one."

"What—"

"Have a good day," the detective said and walked out of the office.

Ben rubbed his face with the palm of his hand and sat for a moment before he proceeded to leave the station.

Schennenburger wasted no time getting to Kim's house. Jeannine had already left because she knew he wanted to speak with Kim alone. As the detective had promised, his visit with Kim was brief.

*****

Ed accessed his job's computer system from the warehouse because he'd set it up via a LAN system. He made it virtually impossible for anyone else besides him to access the warehouse database from his job computers.

He heard a beep, and the computer alerted him that there was a networking connection.

"What?" he blurted. "Who is connecting to my system?" he asked himself nervously. He tapped frantically on the keyboard to lock out the intruder but was unsuccessful, because Harry Genre had already made it through the firewall safety net.

Dimension Computer Galaxy Corporation had four computer programmers. Harry was one of them. He was at his desk, getting ready to write a new software program for the company's new line of computers, the XPS-500. His assignment was to create a computer software program that would bring computing to a new level. The

XPS Series Galaxtra was a new and highly intriguing software bundle that Harry was going to create to enhance modern computing to untold levels.

"Uh?" said Harry in amazement as he stared at the bold red letters that announced the approval of a networking access.

"What network?" *Entering Myra's Thrift Shop,* it informed. "How in the world did I do that?" He grabbed a sheet of paper and scribbled down what he thought were the steps and codes that he'd used to access Myra's Thrift Shop. He hoped he'd be able to access it again.

"Very interesting. How did we get Myra's Thrift Shop on our system? A thrift shop and our computer company have nothing in common," he stated with curiosity. Harry tried to access files, but everything needed a password for access.

"Dogonnit!" He haphazardly landed into the file that Ed had opened, and Ed tried hopelessly to close it but couldn't. He was frantic.

Harry's face froze as he threw his head to the side and looked at the screen in shock.

"Who in the world is responsible for this? Thrift shop, uh? Yeah, right. Some thrift shop! Something's going on. Okay, Harry, calm down," he whispered to himself. He knew that he'd be able to access this again, even if he had to play around with it. But he had the basic idea.

Ed sat frozen in his seat. Because Harry had accessed his files, the computer main drive was frozen while being used by Harry. Ed did the Ctrl+Alt+Del routine and shut down his connection to the server, but it didn't affect Harry, who was still logged on to the server's hard drive.

Realizing his dilemma, Ed bolted from the chair and rushed out the door. He had to get to the office before whoever it was had intruded sufficiently into his file and found out too much.

He sat rigidly around the wheel, gripping tightly. His adrenaline raced, as he had to get there on time.

He cut through cars and ran amber lights, hoping that luck would keep him from getting stopped by the police.

He pulled into the parking lot with a screech and walked as casually as he could to the building. With such a big building, it could take him the whole day to figure out the identity of the intruder.

Zone 1 had six offices. The first four belonged to the four computer programmers, set next to one another as you entered the front door. Sid and Memphis were at a conference, and Bilda was out sick, only leaving Harry. He glanced quickly into Harry's office and saw his eyes locked in a gaze on the computer screen. He knocked on the door, and Harry looked up quickly, beckoning him in.

So you're the one, he thought as he opened the door. Before Ed could say anything to make his showing up appear casual, Harry blurted out, "You won't believe what I've stumbled upon, boss. Finding things out like this could get you high honors." He had a twinkle in his eye.

Ed took it as a sign that he hadn't found out he was connected to the files. He looked in fear at his files, which Harry was drooling over.

"Very fascinating," he said to Harry, trying to sound thrilled. "I'll be back in a second."

"Don't take too long. You don't want to miss anything."

Ed slipped out of the office and went into Bilda's office across the hall, closed the door, and made a thirty-second phone call on his cell, then hurried back to Harry's office.

"We need to call headquarters on this," said Ed. As soon as the last word fell out of his mouth, Harry's phone buzzed.

"Yes?" he shouted into the speaker.

"Hey, Harry, I just passed your car in the parking lot and tried to open the door to turn off your lights, but the alarm went off when I pulled on the door. It's making a horrible sound out there."

"Oh, shoot! I'll be right back."

"Hey, take a scroll, will you? See for yourself," he invited as he rose hastily from his desk. He ran out the door, keys in hand.

Ed closed the file and immediately changed the codes, software, and keyboard sequence to get into the networking.

"The lights aren't on," he said out loud. Harry extended his hand and pressed the deactivating button to turn off the noise. As he turned to leave, shots rang out.

Harry lay dead in the parking lot of Dimension Computer Galaxy Corporation.

It happened so fast no one even knew where the shots originated.

Someone ran into the building, screaming, "Call 911!"

The police were there in minutes and questioned Ed, as well as everyone else.

"I have no clue what happened," Ed confessed. "We were in his office and someone buzzed him and told him that his lights and alarm were on, so he went out to take care of them. Next thing I knew, someone came in screaming that he'd been shot."

The police asked everyone as to who buzzed Harry. In the end, there were no initial breakthroughs, either in trying to get key witnesses to change their stories or to force Ed to reveal perhaps more than he was willing to tell. At the end of the police questioning, Ed left. He picked up his cell and dialed a number.

"Good job. Take the cloth off your plates."

"We did that four blocks away. Don't worry about a thing."

No one but Ed knew what Harry had inadvertently discovered. "That was close," he sighed in relief. "Yeah, real close."

Chapter 12

The Unidentified

No matter how still he tried to be, the pain was excruciating. He tried to raise himself up so he could get out of wherever he was, but the pain engulfed his body like flames of fire. He moaned deeply from the core of his soul.

His mind a total blur, he wanted to be out of his misery, one way or another. He wished the pain to either leave his body *now* or that he died on the spot. Well, on second thought, who wanted to die, anyway? He didn't know what lay ahead in the *other* world or even if there was such a world. So he decided that living was his desire.

"Mom!" he called in a whisper. He pictured her face and the tender look she'd give him if she were to see him in this condition.

"Help!" Was he dying? He really didn't want to die. He hoped the wish he'd made earlier wouldn't come true. He pleaded again for his mother, and still no answer. He prayed, "Oh, God, help me, please! I want to live. Let me live. Take away the pain. Let someone find me. Please help me." He moaned over and over and then went silent.

*****

"My legs! My legs! I've lost my legs!" he hollered. Someone shook him by the shoulders.

"It's all right. It's all right." It was a voice that wasn't familiar, a feminine voice well intentioned. She kept shaking him gently, trying to wake him from a nightmare, but he only faded back into a deep sleep.

Back at the cabin, heavy wind and rain beat against the structure of the building, making her shudder. She sat at his bedside and waited, watching the clock and noting how long it took him to wake up—two hours and fifteen minutes. He fluttered his eyes open and looked around the room. There she was, sitting on a wooden chair at his bedside, peering into his face.

"Hello?" she said.

He didn't answer, just stared back at her with glossy eyes. She wondered what type of state he was in this time. At least he was calmer. He woke up without making a sound.

"Ah!" The pain was coming back. He clutched his legs and tried to raise himself up.

"It's all right, really. I'll get you some pain reliever. It's about time for another dose, anyway."

Another dose? he wondered. When did she give him a dose? How many times had she given him doses? *By the way, what year is it, and who is this woman?*

He tried to remember things, anything. He couldn't think of anything. His brain hurt from trying. He gave up and relaxed his body. She rose gingerly and walked over to a shelf across the room. There were tiny bottles, which he figured were medication. Within minutes she was back with a plastic cup half-filled with water.

"Here, this will ease the pain." He looked at her questioningly. She read his thoughts. "It's all right, I won't hurt you." She gently placed her palm on a huge lump on the right side of his head and frowned.

"Must have been a hard blow you took," she said compassionately. "I'm Cecelia. I'm going to help you get better. What is your name?"

His face looked blank.

"It's all right. We'll get into that later," she said reassuringly.

She looked trustworthy. He raised his head. She popped a capsule into his mouth. He puckered his lips and received the water graciously. He gulped until there was none left. He dropped his head onto the pillow and took a deep breath. He closed his eyes as if he wanted to work magic and make the bad disappear and the good appear.

He suddenly became aware of his surroundings. "Where am I, exactly?" he managed to ask.

She didn't answer. He turned his head and saw the chair was empty.

He was on a bed that took up most of the space in the room. The wooden floors looked somewhat decent. It was old and weather beaten, but it looked good from whatever she scrubbed it with to make it look shiny. The wallpaper was peeling off the walls, exposing the dry, rotten wood beneath it. The only lamp in the room sat on a…on a…

What is that? his mind asked curiously. *On something…who cares what? It's doing its job, and that's all that matters.*

Something was brewing. *Homemade soup? Mmmm. Smells good.* The aroma of chicken and spices dominated the room. He was hungry. He couldn't wait to eat. Things were jingling in what seemed to be a kitchen. He could see a portion of it from the doorless room that he occupied. A wooden stove with blazing fire under a midsize pot sent a twirling of steam from the semicovered pot.

Her hip brushed the table as she walked past it, and it almost toppled over. It shook violently. He could only see two of the legs. They wobbled for a few seconds and then resumed to their stillness.

He must have fallen asleep. He didn't know for how long, but there she was again, sitting in her little wooden chair next to him. This time, she had a little bowl in her hand with a spoon sticking out of it.

Was I right? So he was. *Just as I thought. Soup, medicine for the soul.* He couldn't wait to dig in. He was too weak to sit up, and the pain hadn't completely left his body yet. She offered to feed him. He had no objection to that kind act.

She fed him. Not fast enough, he thought. He was ready for another spoonful, but she just sat there and waited. *For what? Till the first spoonful is digested, perhaps?*

C'mon, feed me…

He dared not say it out loud. He nodded to let her know that he was ready. *Like, right now,* he thought.

The soup was…he didn't know. *Was it good?* He couldn't remember what it tasted like. Whether good or bad, he had to eat.

It was loaded with stuff. Some things he recognized, others he didn't. He kept his eyes closed most of the time so that he wouldn't see anything that he thought he might not want to eat.

He rested. The pain had subsided greatly. Whatever that stuff was that she gave him for the pain, he hoped she had a lot more. It was good. He felt somewhat new. He was pain-free. The soup did help him too. He felt a bit stronger.

What now? She sure seems quiet. She hasn't asked me a question since I woke up in this little…whatever the place. A cabin, maybe?

He had no idea what time it was, if it was night or day, or even what month it was. He must have fallen asleep again. This time, he woke up to the sound of voices. Tiny voices. It sounded like hundreds of them. His eyes popped open.

"What's going on here?" he called out. *Forget the humility. I need answers. After all, it's my life. I ought to know.*

The woman walked in and smiled at him. It was the same woman who had been there all along. He didn't remember eating anything after the soup. He couldn't tell how many days had passed since or if it was the same day. *That's messed up,* he thought.

"You look so much better now."

He fumbled for words. *Where do I start?* "Thank you," he replied. That didn't sound like his voice at all. He turned his head to see if someone next to him had spoken. No one else was there. Just the two of them.

"Where am I?" he asked. *That's a start,* he thought. *A great conversation opener.*

She sat down in her chair. "Well, we found you in the wilderness under a shrub. You were unconscious."

We? he thought. For all the time that he was there, he'd only seen just her. Anyways, he had no idea how long he'd been there. It could have only been for a half an hour, for all he knew, or even months, for that matter. It was dreadful not knowing.

She interrupted his thoughts. "My husband and I were hunting, and we found you. This is our hunting cabin."

Husband? Okay, he knows about me, so it's not likely for him to burst in here and finish me off.

"I was awakened by children's voices and thought I heard them again."

"No, there are no children here."

He took a deep breath and stayed quiet until he fell off to sleep.

Chapter 13

Tragedy Struck

Ben was preoccupied and had a lot of things going on in his mind. Jamaica was one of them. The beautiful scenery of Averill Park triggered memories of Jamaica.

The chirping of birds, the rushing streams, surrounding trees and wildlife, and the landscape sceneries all brought back memories of his life in Jamaica.

Jamaica, however, wasn't the only thing on his mind. His son was now a married man. He was no longer his little boy. He remembered so well the day that he was born.

He'd always wanted his firstborn to be a son, but instead Casey came along. When Washburn was born and the doctor told him it was a boy, he was ecstatic.

Four weeks later, Washburn became deathly ill. Ben was sure he was going to lose him.

Washburn had lost a significant amount of weight in a short period. When Ben and Ida brought him to the hospital, the nurse had told them that another hour at home and he would have died. He was admitted and fed intravenously.

Ben returned to the hospital to visit his boy. "Ward number 8," said the nurse.

Moments later, he returned to tell the nurse his son wasn't there. The nurse took him to ward number 8, and surprisingly, the meager baby was Washburn. Ben groaned as the suffering of his son hit him hard.

Barbara stood over Ben with her hands on her hips. "I've called your name three times, and all you did was stare into space."

Ben apologized. "I was daydreaming about Jamaica."

"Again? I think we ought to just ship you off to Jamaica for good."

"We're short one person. Ben, won't you join us?" called Marlo. Ben vibrantly accepted the offer and joined the men on the basketball court. It had been too long since he'd done any form of exercise. Since Washburn went off to college, he hadn't spent any time on the court. He could hardly keep up.

"Nothing beats trying," he said, laughing. Every year, Ben's job planned an outing. For the second year in a row, they'd gone to Averill Park.

Ben had a good time. Especially when he taught them how to play dominoes. It felt good passing on a Jamaican game.

"If you can't hear the dominoes connecting with the table, then you're not playing dominoes." He laughed.

He taught them another game: the egg-and-spoon race. With one hand only, each person carried a hard-boiled egg on a spoon to the finish line. The object of the game was to be the first person to reach the finish line with the egg still on the spoon. If the egg fell, they would have to go back to the starting line.

Ida was busy conversing with the women about husbands, home, and kids. She never had a problem fitting in. She got along with everyone.

It was a well-spent day at Averill Park. The employees of Memphis Technology packed up their belongings and headed home.

Catherine led the way. Twenty minutes into the journey, something went horribly wrong.

Without warning, the driver of a silver two-door car suddenly cut in front of Catherine. Out of the blue he'd decided to change lanes. He was inches away from her, and Catherine swerved to the right to avoid hitting him. In the process, she lost control of her car and ran off the road. Her car flipped over twice before landing upside down. She was thrown some eight feet from her car.

Ben, Ida, Catherine, and her husband were involved in a horrible car accident that took a life.

Someone had dialed 911 from their car phone, and within fifteen minutes the paramedics were on the scene. Three of the victims were rushed to the nearest hospital, where emergency surgery was immediately performed.

The fourth person was bagged and taken to the morgue. The paramedic said he died on impact. The others that followed closely behind Catherine narrowly escape the accident.

Ben lay in a coma from a massive head injury. His brain was swollen and was continuing to swell. The doctors worked extensively to drain fluid from his brain, and they couldn't say whether or not he was going to make it. It seemed unlikely he would. A life-support system sustained his life.

Ida suffered a broken back, and both legs were broken. She was in a state of shock that worsened her condition. She kept asking for her Ben, but they wouldn't bring her to him. They assured her that he was fine, but she didn't believe them. She didn't trust them. She wanted to see for herself, and she wanted to see him now. As she lay motionless in the trauma unit and stared blankly at the ceiling, tears streamed quietly down the side of her face at the thought that Ben might be dead.

Catherine also suffered from broken bones all over her body. A severe spinal injury left her motionless from the waist down.

"She might never walk again" were the harsh words of the doctor.

Jeannine was the first to receive the message about her parents. She was hysterical. She called Casey, and then her grandparents in Jamaica.

Carlton was dumbfounded when she gave him the news. His knees knocked together, and he grabbed the couch and plopped down into it. He placed his head in his hands and cried. He hadn't cried since he was a boy. It took a lot to get a man to cry where he came from. It took something of this nature. His son was at the point of death, and it cut through his heart.

Mildred had left for the market when he got the news. He regained his composure and refrained from telling her. He was afraid of how she would take the news. He hoped for a drastic change in his condition. He would tell her about the accident when Ben wasn't so bad.

If their son didn't recover, then that would kill her, he was sure. "Dear God, help our son," he groaned.

With the death of her best friend and now her father dying in the hospital, Jeannine knew that she just couldn't go on. Her days seemed meaningless and empty. She couldn't understand why those things had to happen. She didn't want to blame God, because she knew that it wasn't his fault. Deep in the back of her mind, though, she wanted to ask Him why he'd allowed such horrible things to happen to her.

She didn't want to anger Him. Maybe He'd allow an even worst thing to happen, like her parents not recovering from their accident.

She prayed for peace but just couldn't seem to get any from God. She was depressed every day and a nervous wreck.

The sound of the telephone set off a nerve. She feared that the hospital might be calling to give them bad news. She couldn't imagine life without them.

Her circumstance pressed her to heavy gloom. She fretted constantly about their condition and grieved every moment over Brendan. The three Shrouder children couldn't really give support to one another because they needed a shoulder to lean on.

Eventually, Ida was changed from critical to stable condition, and Jeannine was happy for that. Life without both parents would be unbearable.

*****

Just before game time, the guys got popcorn, sodas, and chips. It was crowded in the lounge of the Vaughenden College of Business in Remseyville, and the girls present in the lounge stood no chance of watching anything else on television while the basketball game was on.

Vaughenden was a private college with a student body of eight hundred, the perfect size for Washburn. He hated to be in a school situation where he was only a designated number. At Vaughenden, the average number of students in a classroom was thirteen, a perfect class size.

"C'mon, you guys, we want to watch something else," pleaded one of the girls.

"In your dreams," said Tony Zelata. He chuckled as he slapped a fellow student a high five.

A few rooms down the hall, Mike pounded on the door to wake up Washburn. "The game's almost on, man. You sleep like a woman. Get up and let's have some fun."

Washburn Shrouder swung the door open and responded with a grin, "Excuse me, but I have a game to watch." He closed the door behind him and whistled his way down the hall to the lounge to join the more than thirty maniacal basketball fans. Mike shook his head and trailed behind him.

"Sometimes I wonder about you, kid," he said when he'd caught up with him.

At the other end of the campus, Ted tried to get his roommate off the phone.

"Bonehead is on the phone again," he said to Hardy, who was busy admiring himself in the mirror.

"Whom are you preaching to this time?" asked Ted. "I think the world has had enough of your Jesus stuff. Give it a rest, will you?"

"Ted," said a voice from behind him. He turned around to find a six-nine giant standing before him.

"Ooh, don't hurt me, please." He shuddered jokingly.

"Are you guys ready?" Dough asked. "The game's on."

"I am," replied Ted wearily. "Just thought I'd remind the preacher about the game."

"Bye, Mama."

"Ooh, he's a mama's boy!" All this time he was talking to his mother. "Didn't you see her last week, boy?"

"Okay, let's go. I think I look smashing!" interrupted Hardy.

"You know, Hardy, I know that there is no woman on this planet or any other planet that would want you. Stop wasting your time, kid. You can't look good no matter what you do."

"I'm about to rearrange your face. Somebody please hold me back," teased Hardy.

"You know, guys, each one of us has been created in God's image."

"All right, it's really time to go. We're about to be sermonized," said Hardy.

The boys raced down the hall, out the back door, across the campus, toward the main lounge, which was located on the first floor of Piason.

Breathlessly they slumped down on the floor in front of the twenty-seven-inch color television set.

As Washburn headed back to his room after the game, he found a note taped to his door. It was from Jeannine. The message was marked Urgent. He hated messages like that. He couldn't help but think the worst, but he made himself believe that everything was all right at home. He took a deep breath and dialed home.

Jeannine answered the phone on the first ring.

"You've got to come home, now," she pleaded, her voice quivering.

"Why?" he asked nervously as he noted the tone of her voice.

"Just come home now." She wouldn't tell him why, but he knew something awful had happened.

"Who is dead, Jeannine?" he hollered.

"No one, just come home."

He felt like all his strength was gone.

She broke down and began to cry. "Mama and Daddy are in the hospital," she finally gave in. "There's been a terrible accident. I can only hope they'll be all right," she reassured him in faith.

Washburn caught the next flight to Milolta to see his parents. His uncle Jesse hopped into his car at the news and drove three days to Milolta.

Everyone who knew them was distraught. It was hard for coworkers, families, and friends to cope with the tragedy.

Jeannine didn't know what to do. She spent endless hours going back and forth from her mother to her father.

She stood over her father and watched his mannequin-like body. He seemed lifeless. His head was swollen. It hardly looked like him. She felt faint.

She couldn't remember a day when her father was ever sick, not even with the flu. He was a strong man. Always on the go. Always working hard, taking care of his family, just as his father did when he and his sibling were growing up.

She bent over and whispered in his ear. "Daddy?" she sobbed, hardly able to stand looking at him in his condition. "I need you." She rubbed his face gently.

She visited her mother. Ida was awake and alert.

"What's your father's prognosis?" she demanded. "Jeannine, please tell me," she said on a softer note.

How could she lie? She knew that it wouldn't be good for her to know the truth, but she was persistent.

"Oh, Mama. Just concentrate on getting better. Daddy will be fine. He's going to need you, so get well soon, Mama. We all need you."

"Is he really alive?" she asked with a horrified look on her face.

"Yes, Mama, he's really alive. I wouldn't lie to you."

Ida sighed in relief. She believed her.

Jesse picked up two speeding tickets as he headed to Milolta. It didn't stop him from driving even harder to see his brother, though. He couldn't believe his eyes at the sight of Ben. He stared at him with a somber look on his face. He shook his head in grief. A gloomy mass seemed to press their spirits to the lowest level.

Jeannine's eyes were dim with tears. Her petite body leaned heavily against the windowsill as she stared blankly out the fifth-floor window.

Washburn sat with his arms folded and his head directed toward the floor. He didn't know what to say. He wasn't sure of what he believed. If faith could bring his father back to as good as new, then he knew that he didn't have that faith to make it happen. He felt a sense of hopeless fear. What if he never woke up? Then what would he do? *God almighty,* he silently groaned in deep distress.

"Washburn," whispered Casey through sniffles, "want to go downstairs for a little bit?"

He rose from his chair and walked out the room without saying a word. Casey followed behind him.

"Remember the time when we were little boys and Pop had taken us with him to Rain Field?" Jesse began. Maybe, just maybe, if he could remind Ben of the good old days, then that might stir up the fighting power he already had in himself. "He'd wanted to check on the new growth of his crop, and we begged him to bring us along with him. We were about eight and nine years old then." He stopped and watched Ben's face, hoping to see some kind of sign of acknowledgment.

"He had left us by the huge rock and had told us to stay right there until he returned," he continued with a little difficulty. "Our perception of time was way off. We got so scared that Pop wasn't coming back for us that we'd decided to walk home. It had seemed like he'd been gone for hours. We later learned that it had only been about twenty minutes to a half hour."

"Anyway," he said as he let out a gush of air, "from the woods we started running home. We ran the five miles it took to get home. I don't remember if we ever even stopped to rest. Everyone we saw, we'd ask, 'You see Papa?' They all said, 'No.' We cried so much our eyes clouded with tears."

"I don't know how we found our way home, but I do believe that the big man upstairs directed our feet in the right direction. I believe He is still watching over us, Ben."

He paused again and brushed a tear from his cheek. "We need you. You have to make it, Ben." He sighed deeply. "I'm so glad that you were with me that day. I probably wouldn't have made it home." He rubbed the back of Ben's hand with the palm of his hand. "We've come a long way together, and I don't want to lose you now."

He felt another tear trickling down his right cheek, but he ignored it this time. He didn't care about the stereotypical idea that men didn't cry. He hoped Ben could hear every word and that they would make a difference.

As the days went on, Ben made basically no progress. Ida and Catherine were coming along gradually. They were still not well enough to leave the hospital, but their health had progressed satisfactorily.

*****

Carlton couldn't hold back the bad news any longer from his wife. It had been four days, and their son was still in a coma. He was hoping that his condition would improve and that he'd be able to give her better news, but he hadn't changed and he needed her support. He couldn't carry the weight of the tragedy alone anymore. He'd finally gotten the courage to break the news to her, and when he did, she fainted. Just as he'd thought, that she wouldn't handle the news too well.

The smelling salt revived her. "I have a terrible headache," she mumbled and held her head. She didn't show any sign of remembering the news that her husband had related to her.

"What happened? Why am I in bed in the middle of the day?"

Mildred never took naps. She was always doing something. There were just too many things to do for her to be in bed in the middle of the day.

"Mildred?" he asked. "You remember what I told you 'bout Ben?"

"Ben?"

She held her chest and gasped. "Yes! My god! It can't be! It just can't be true!" She sat up in the bed and looked searchingly in her husband's eyes. "Are you sure?" Without waiting for her husband's answer, she turned her head upward and began to pray.

"Please, God, save my son's life. Touch him and heal him. Please, O God. He needs us," she said, sobbing, "and we've got to be there for him. Oh, Ben!"

Mildred was a born-again Christian and believed in the power of God through faith. That night, in prayer meeting at her church, she told them about the accident and requested prayer for all three victims.

They booked a round-trip ticket for the next possible flight, which was a week away. They called Jesse, but he had already heard the news and was at Ben's side.

The day had arrived when Carlton and Mildred would fly to the US. She was apprehensive. She'd never flown before.

Carlton had flown many times in his younger days, when he'd traveled to the US as a farmworker. Flying never bothered him.

"Calm down, Millie, you'll be just fine. God will bring us there safely."

She was a little embarrassed. She was the one that always talked about God and what God could do, and here her husband, who was not a Christian, was assuring her of what God could do.

Mildred was relieved when the plane touched down its wheels on the runway of the Milolta International Airport. Jeannine and Washburn were waiting for them.

Ben had a good family. They never skipped a day in visiting him. Their strong family ties kept them together.

Despite his mother's advice to finish the semester, Washburn refused to go back to school, knowing that his parents needed him. "You both need me, and I'll be here for you," he had told his mother.

Jenna agreed with him that they take some time off from school until the ordeal was over. He was relieved to know that his wife was with him in the decision.

Casey really wasn't doing too well, but together as a family, they mustered up their strength and hoped for the best.

As time went on, Ben's prognosis changed somewhat. The doctor had said that his condition still wasn't good, but at least there was some positive change. There was a very small sign of brain activity. Mildred stayed close to his side and offered up prayers constantly.

Jeannine remembered how her grandmother had taught them about God and the Bible all through their childhood years.

Even though her parents didn't go to church much, they were sent to church every Sunday. She remembered the pastor always saying how much Jesus loved and cared for all people.

"Cast your cares upon Jesus. He will carry you through." She sure needed someone to help her bear her burden.

Since they'd moved to the United States, they hadn't gone to church too often. A lot of things that she'd learn during her childhood seemed to be coming back to her. She knelt down to pray but felt guilty that she hadn't prayed in so long and now that she needed help, she was turning to God in prayer. She knew that the God of the universe was a forgiving God, but that didn't stop her from feeling guilty.

Washburn pushed his mother in her wheelchair to the elevator. He punched the number 5, and the elevator door closed slowly. She was nervous. Her clammy hands were proof. She was on her way to see Ben for the first time since the accident. It had been a miserable three-and-a-half-week ordeal. She braced herself and pulled back the curtain. What she saw wasn't her Ben. It couldn't have been her Ben. He had the face of another man.

Ida screamed. Washburn held her and offered comfort. "Mama, he's doing better now. He looks bad, but his body is healing gradually. He's coming along, Mama."

She began to hyperventilate, and Casey was sure she was having a heart attack.

Time slipped by slowly. Ben's family anxiously waited for his complete recovery. It was amazing how tragedy could halt one's routine. They had their plans and schedules and were busy doing things they chose to do, but when tragedy struck, everything seemed to come to either a complete halt or had slowed down dramatically.

The Shrouders were struck full blast with something that halted their normal, everyday activities. Their lives were placed on hold as they sat and waited for Ben to come out of his coma.

Jeannine felt weak. *It's not real,* she thought. She was in a dream, and she just needed to wake up and everything would be all right. She'd tell her parents how she had had a bad dream and how her father was in a coma and Brendan was murdered.

It was all a bad dream, and she knew it. Things like this only happened to other people, not them.

She took a walk to the park and sat on the grass and meditated. A deep breath expanded her lungs. She held it. She didn't feel like breathing. Maybe if she held it long enough, she would wake up coughing, but the pressure of her breath forced its way out of her lungs. Her shoulders dropped. She looked up to the heavens. "God, I believe you're aware of my father. Please help him. Make him better, as good as new."

There were children using the swings, people walking their dogs or just lying out on the grass. Life was moving on regardless of what state of mind anyone was in. She couldn't picture life without her father, so at the present moment, life was on the halt for her. From the day she was born up until that very moment, she hand never gone away for long from her father except for when she went to Florida for two weeks. Life without him would be no life at all.

In hope, Jeannine and the rest of the family waited impatiently for Ben to make a turn for the better.

Ben was eventually moved to another hospital that specialized in what he was going through. It was his parents' turn to be at his side. Ida was there three hours ago and was home to shower and rest. Washburn sprawled on the couch and placed his head in her lap. She tried to watch a movie but was only staring into space.

She couldn't sleep, so she just sat there on the couch, thinking. She knew that she was a walking miracle. She hadn't recovered completely from the accident, but the inner strength that she had put her on the road to recovery.

What could she have done to prevent this tragedy? *Driven my car is one possibility,* she thought. *Why, why, why,* she wept silently. *I'm sorry, Ben. Please forgive me.* Tears silently rolled from her eyes.

Washburn looked up at her. "Mama, he's going to be all right. You've got to be strong for him, and for you and for all of us. We all need you."

She took several deep breaths to calm her aching soul. "It's just so hard, son. I wish I could go back in time and change our plans."

There was not a Shrouder who hadn't prayed for Ben. Prayers were offered from Florida, Milolta, and Jamaica, Canada, and

England. *God's got to hear somebody,* thought Casey. *If he's not in Milolta to hear those prayers, He's got to be in Jamaica or even Florida.*

Ben lay like a lifeless corpse on the hospital bed. "Ben Shrouder is well. Ben shall live and not die. All is well with Ben Shrouder. Jesus took all of Ben's sicknesses. He is healed by Jesus's stripes." Mildred read scripture after scripture in her son's ears.

"CDPC is waiting for someone like you!" shouted the man on the other side of the curtain. He was tired of listening to Mildred read to a man that couldn't respond.

"Jesus loves you." Mildred had no idea what CDPC meant, but she knew he was angry.

"Sure he loves me, that's why I'm suffering!" he snorted.

"Millie, don't say a word. Just keep your voice down. You are disturbing the man."

Later that day, Mildred asked a nurse out of curiosity what CDPC meant. "Capital District Psychiatric Center."

"Psychiatric! He's the crazy one!"

"Calm down, Millie!"

Ben began to show a little bit more progress. He was responding by squeezing fingers that were placed in his hand. Ida was elated.

Catherine finally left the hospital. She was beginning to have a little tingling in her legs. With the help of a psychiatrist, she was able to cope with the loss of her husband.

*****

"Your husband's condition has relapsed. He's taken a turn for the worst. His brain is not responding. His chance of survival has gone from slim to no hope."

The words came as a sharp sword. They cut her to the core of her heart, and Ida felt like her heartstrings had been severed. Not her Ben. They must have been mistaken. Her Ben couldn't die. She'd never thought of him dying. Not for a moment. She knew that he was human and fallible, but it just never occurred to her that he could *really* die.

"Ben is strong and vibrant and full of life. Besides, it's not fair. What has he ever done to deserve this? What has the family ever done to deserve this kind of heart-wrenching experience? Murderers and wicked people live long and healthy lives, but why do good people have to suffer and die?"

Distressed and heartbroken, Ida cried bitterly day and night. Mildred never gave up hope despite the hopelessness of his condition. She was distressed but hopeful.

"It is no secret what God can do," Mildred would often say. "He can do the impossible."

"I am believing God for my son," added Carlton Shrouder as he stared down at him.

"He will live! He will live!" his mother said over and over. A tear fell on his forehead. With such strong faith in her God, Mildred stayed by her son's side endlessly, expecting a miraculous turnaround.

Chapter 14

Farewell

Ben was rushed to the operating room for the second time in one day as fluid gathered around his brain, again. The doctors worked six hours draining the fluid and massaging his brain.

It was only a few months ago that Jeannine and her father enjoyed the summer weather in Jamaica, basking in the tropical sun. Now she sat in a room whose atmosphere was dark and heavy. Ida stared down at the seemingly lifeless body of her husband. It was amazing how she was even conscious.

Dr. Gregowski lowered the bar at the side of the bed so she could reach him more comfortably. He looked as though he was ready for burial.

She gently placed her hand on his cheek as tears fell from her eyes onto his face.

"You must come back, Ben, you must!" This was it. Ben was as good as dead. The doctors gave him over to death. He told Ida to be prepared because he didn't have much time left.

Kim felt really bad for Jeannine, as she was still grieving over Brendan. Everything seemed to be happening so fast she didn't know what to do. Jeannine needed her, but she didn't have any condolences to offer. She was grief-stricken and needed comfort herself and didn't know what to do. Also, she felt guilty about not being there for Jeannine and worried she might be the reason Brendan was dead. She didn't know exactly what was going on with him. Why he had become so secretive was beyond her understanding, but to take a wild guess, she'd wager it to have something to do with Zaire. But how and why?

Zaire called and made known his wish to see her, but she refused to see anybody, not even Jeannine. He begged, but she stood firm.

"I'm really sorry for what happened to Brendan, but I want you to know that even though I was angry at him, I would never kill him."

"I just want to be alone," she replied and placed the receiver on the hook. He understood, though. He was willing to wait patiently until she needed someone to stand by her side.

Ben had made a remarkable turn for the best, and they wished this time he wouldn't give them such a scare. "We're as surprised as you are about his turnaround. What can I say but that it's a miracle?" Dr. Gregowski had told Ida.

Ben was pulling through; believe it or not, Ben was pulling through. Slowly, he began to make steady progress, finally showing signs of recovery. He had increased activity in his brain, and his vital signs constantly got better.

As the weeks turned into months, Ben's brain began to heal itself. He became fully aware of his plight. He knew that something was horribly wrong. He tried to shake himself awake but couldn't. He didn't know, however, how bad his chance of surviving was, but he knew that he wanted to live, and that seemed to be making the difference.

His mother's voice, his father's, and all the other voices of his loved ones were like medicine to his soul. The combination was a tremendous help. It was effective. Dr. Gregowski had told them that Ben needed that, and he got just what the doctor had ordered.

"Your husband has a very strong will to live, Mrs. Shrouder. I think he's going to pull through." Ida felt a weight lifted. The burden didn't seem so heavy anymore.

Ben fought for life. The doctors had become hopeful, and a more cheery mood was everywhere present.

"A person can determine if they live or die?" she asked the doctor.

"Yes, in some instances. If they don't want to live, the mind will give up on life, and because the mind does, the body will also."

A glimmer of hope—she felt encouraged, and so she fought with her husband.

Ida spent hours at the hospital. She slept on a chair next to his bed and refused to go home. She wouldn't mind if she had to sleep on a rock. She just wanted to be there for her darling Ben.

*****

Ben opened his eyes slowly and looked around. The surrounding wasn't familiar.

Ida sat on a chair next to his bed. She had her hands clasped by the edge of the bed, with her head resting on her hands. She heard a sound and raised her head to see Ben's eyes wide-open and his head turning from side to side, almost in normal fashion.

"Where am I?" he stuttered.

"Ben! Oh, Ben!" she squealed. "Nurse! Nurse!" she called, continuing to press the call button. She was ecstatic. With no apparent warning, he had snapped out of his coma, muttering to himself. The nurse came running in.

"He's awake! He's awake! Oh, Ben! How are you feeling?" She trembled with excitement and cried tears of joy.

She wanted to hug him tight, but she knew that he was still in a delicate condition. She talked rapidly to her husband, asking questions and making statements without even giving him a moment to respond.

It was a miracle, a flat-out miracle.

One minute Ben was lying lifeless in a coma, and it seemed the next minute he was raising himself up in bed.

The doctors came in to examine him, and Ida had to leave the room. Twenty minutes later, they came out and called her. Mrs. Shrouder?"

Ida didn't like the look on the doctor's face. She felt something was wrong and wondered if he had slipped back into a coma.

"Yes?" she answered anxiously.

"He doesn't remember anything, not even his name."

She looked at the doctor, expecting him to say more. He waited for her response.

"That's it?"

"For now," he responded.

"I thought it was worse than that. That's not too good, but that can be worked out."

"You see," the doctor continued, "he might never remember his life before the accident. He might have to start life all over again."

Ben couldn't remember his name, let alone anyone else's, and didn't want to see or talk to anyone. He looked at his family and frowned. "Who are you?" he asked Jeannine with slurred speech. Ben grabbed ahold of the Help button and pressed it hard. The nurse came running in. He wanted the stranger out.

"Please leave," he ordered faintly but firmly. The nurse escorted Jeannine from the room and explained his prognosis to her.

"Right now his brain is like a city that is lit in some areas and dark in others. We don't know how much he will eventually remember, but he needs to take it very slowly."

How would they handle it if he never recovered his memory? The thought of that happening made her sick.

Casey's husband, Barry, was glad he was in town for good, because his wife needed him more than ever. He was stationed at the base in Milolta just minutes from his house. Ben thought his life looked bleak. The accident was bad, but not remembering your family or yourself was probably even worse.

The day finally came for Ben to be released from the hospital, but he didn't want to go home.

"I hate to intrude," he said to his wife. Jeannine cried until her eyes were puffy. It was an awful feeling to know that her father didn't know who she was.

The doctor told them that Ben needed his family more than he'd ever needed them before. He would need the help of his family to overcome the milestone of regaining his memory.

*****

The long process of healing at the home of the Shrouders had begun. It took great patience and endurance to cope with the tragedy of living with someone whom they'd shared so much with and who had lost every bit of his memory before his accident.

Ida gathered together all the family albums in hopes of jogging his memory. He looked at pictures that were decades old to the most recent.

"That was when you were twelve and playing in the school band at Saint Benedict's Catholic School in Saint Andrews. That's instructor Maestro."

Ben stared at the pictures blankly. He tried hard to remember. "These are great pictures, but I'm afraid I don't remember anyone, or any event." Forty-seven years of his life seemed to have been erased as one would erase writing on a chalkboard.

With a sense of victory, Mildred and Carlton boarded the plane back to Jamaica. They knew everything was going to be all right. If God could bring him out of a coma and defy the doctor's prognosis, then God could finish the work He'd started and bring about a complete recovery, memory and all.

*****

Tears clouded Jeannine's eyes as she drove to the cemetery. She knew that she had to let go of him in order to function, but it was too hard to let go. She missed him terribly. She tried to refrain from crying but just couldn't help it.

She was angry. She clenched her teeth and gripped the steering wheel. Whoever killed her friend should be thrown in jail forever or, better yet, die by the electric chair.

She sobbed loudly and uncontrollably. She glanced at her puffy face in the rearview mirror.

"Brendan, oh, Brendan! I miss you!" She blew her nose in a tissue and, for a moment, forgot that she was driving. An angry motorist swerved away from her and held up a fist as he sped past. Shaken, she pulled over to the side of the road. She lay across the seat and allowed all the tears that had bottled up inside her since he'd die to flow freely.

After a few minutes, she resumed her driving and made her way to the cemetery. She studied every tomb that she walked by on her way to Brendan's. People of all ages were laid to rest on the beautiful burying ground of Memory Lane.

She knelt down before Brendan's tomb and stared at it in unbelief. She felt numb all over. It was hard to believe that he was really gone. She felt a tightening in her chest. She gently laid the flowers she'd brought on his tomb.

"Brendan, I miss you. I've got to let you go so I can move on with my life. Farewell, my brother, farewell." She sobbed. She could almost smell his cologne, as if he were standing right next to her. "You'll always hold a special place in my heart," she whispered.

A rush of wind sent a few fallen leaves twirling in the air. Her voice faded into the night as the wind carried her voice to the distant sky. "Farewell, Brendan, farewell," she repeated solemnly.

A voice from behind her spoke her name. It startled her. It was Remington. She rose to her feet and wiped her eyes with the back of her hand.

"How'd you know that I was here?" she sniffled.

"I had a feeling. I know how hard this is for you. No one knew where you were, so I thought I'd check here. Are you okay?"

Jeannine nodded and walked with Remington away from the memory and to the parking lot and the car.

Chapter 15

The Great Outdoors

Someone was following Jeannine, and she couldn't lose the silver sports car that duplicated her every turn. *Now I'm sure they're after me, but why?* She was gripped with fear while keeping her eyes glued to the road and her rearview mirror.

Traffic lights and roadwork played a large part in hindering her from losing her stalker, and she didn't know what to do. She tried to get a good look at the person behind the wheel, but whoever it was stayed smart and kept a distance of at least two car lengths.

She tried to think who could be doing this to her while, at the same time, doing her best to evade the persistent car. *I have no enemies that I know of, except for the men who murdered Brendan. I'm quite sure they didn't get a good-enough fix to recognize me. That's it! Maybe I'm being mistaken for someone else.*

Then Jeannine got angry and said out loud to the unknown pursuer, "You want to follow me? Let's go!"

Precinct 2 was only a mile away. Even though it was in the opposite direction of her house, she felt it was the best place to head to. "Let's see how bold you are!" she said, giving another verbal challenge. The mysterious car followed her until she was within a block of the police station, then the car made a sudden left turn and dropped out of sight.

She parked by the entrance of the precinct and just waited. As she'd thought, they weren't bold enough to follow her there. Her hands shook as she reached into her purse for her mace and placed it into her shirt pocket, just in case she might need it.

Then she pounded her fist into her palm as she thought, *I have enough going on in my life. I don't need anything more to add to my distress! On second thought, I wonder if I was really being followed or if it was just my imagination playing tricks.* Now she wasn't sure. Ever since Brendan's death and her parents' ordeal, she hadn't been herself. She bit her lip, trying to hold back the tears. "What a nightmare!" she sobbed.

Just then, someone tapped on her window, startling her. Seeing it was a policeman, she rolled down her window. "Are you all right?" he asked kindly as he keenly observed her face.

"Yes, I am, thank you," she replied. With a watery smile, Jeannine put the car in gear and drove away.

*****

"I really think it would be a great idea for you to get away and clear your mind from everything that's happened lately," said Jealissa to her nervous friend.

Jeannine wasn't about to leave her father, though. He hadn't fully recovered yet, and she wanted to be there just in case he might need her. "I can't do that," she replied as she slumped onto the sofa, locked her fingers together, and placed her hands on her head.

"Don't do that," said Jealissa superstitiously.

"Don't do what?"

"The way you have your hands on your head means mourning. You might be calling grief into your life, like someone dying or something," warned Jealissa.

"I don't believe in superstition."

"I'm telling you, Jeannine, it's happened."

Jeannine sighed. "What else could go wrong in my life? Everything is already wrong."

"You need to get away so you won't go crazy."

"I have to be with my father in case he needs me," Jeannine insisted.

"Your mother and the others are taking good care of him. You just need to relieve your mind before you lose it or have a nervous breakdown," counseled her good friend.

Suddenly, Jeannine sat up straight; her eyes twinkled, and her face glimmered with a smile. "You know," she said abruptly, "I think I'll go somewhere! That way, if those criminals who killed Brendan ever figure out I was the one who saw them, they won't know where I am!"

Serenity. She wanted to live in tranquility, in a wonderland, where everything was beautiful and calm. The more she thought about going away, the more enticing the idea became. She also wished she could be in heaven with Brendan, but that could wait. Brendan had been a good kid, and she knew he was in heaven, because people like Brendan didn't deserve to go to hell.

In her opinion, Brendan was an angel in disguise. God had sent him to touch people's lives in a special way, and indeed, he had touched the lives of all with whom he'd come in contact. That is, except for those evil men that didn't appreciate anything good. He had obviously touched their lives, but evil people hated good, plain and simple. Jeannine couldn't help wondering what it was that Brendan could have done to them that had caused them to take his life. She knew he hadn't been selling drugs; neither was he involved in anything that was against the law.

Between Brendan's death and her parents' tragedy, Jeannine had been left emotionally and physically drained. She accepted the fact that she did indeed need to get away in order to refresh her spirit, mind, and soul.

Jeannine wished she knew more about Brendan's murderers so they could be brought to justice. It was unthinkable that people could be so cruel and yet be let to live in peace.

Her mind drifted back in time, and she remembered the good fortune she had had in Jamaica when she had uncovered a murderer's secret. Maybe God would help her uncover this dreadful secret.

*****

For the next few days, Jeannine and her friends made preparations to spend some time at her friend's cabin that was away from the hustle and bustle of everyday life.

"I'm so glad our parents are letting us use the cabin," said Jealissa.

"I hope they have a wonderful time in Paris," added Jeannine.

"Oh, by the way, I spoke with Remington a few hours ago, and he said he'll be able to come after all. He had a change of plans," said Charles.

"That's great!" Jeannine was delighted. At least Charles wouldn't be the only guy on the trip. If the men were truly after her and knew where she lived, it would definitely be safer if she was not around for a while, and so she had no reservation about taking the trip.

When her thoughts turned to her parents, Jeannine let out a sigh that left her body limp when she thought, *They might try to hurt them to get to me. What have I done to deserve all this?* She had been complaining inwardly yet to the world at large. *I can't afford to let anything happen to them. If something did, I would never be able to forgive myself. I just hope that they don't know who I am. O God, what should I do*? Her mind was full and running almost on pure adrenaline.

Taking a deep breath, she tilted her head back and rested it on the sofa. Then she tried to think positive and pleasant thoughts, but everything was floating in her mind all at once and she just couldn't settle on one thing.

Her parents' safety was of vital importance. If she chose not to go, how could she protect them? After all, she had no physical or supernatural powers to handle those dangerous men.

"Do you know what they do to people who get on your nerves in Jamaica?" she asked Charles.

"I don't know. Knock them out?"

"Nope. When they find them, they chop 'em up with a machete."

He gave her a weird look, tapped his knuckles on her head, and said, "Hello? Is Jeannine home?"

"I haven't lost my mind," she said as she brushed his hand away. "They do that for real," she said convincingly.

Once again, her mind wandered back to the murder scene. The men had had no idea she was there all the time they had interacted with Brendan. They had been taken aback when she had let out a shrill scream but had known better than to chase her to the busy intersection.

I don't think they knew who I was or where I live, she tried to reassure herself. *There is no way they could know.*

*****

Dressed in blue jeans and sneakers and a short-sleeved white blouse dabbed with blue flowers, Jeannine hurried from the house, through the door, and into the SUV that was awaiting her.

"Do we have everything?" she asked excitedly, her dark-brown eyes sparkling with excitement. "Who has the list?" she asked as she climbed in next to Jealissa.

"I do," said Charles as he unfolded it. "I went over it more than once, and we seem to have everything that's listed."

William Pratt's cabin was two and a half hours away, and Jeannine and her friends drove happily along the back roads that would lead them to it. Remington's SUV was perfect for the trip.

At 4:35 p.m., they turned onto a narrow dirt road that left a trail of dust behind them. The SUV rocked from side to side as its wheels rolled over the dry, unpaved road.

"This reminds me of the country roads in Jamaica," Jeannine said as she bounced around.

"It sure looks like a real desert. Seems as if it hasn't rained for years," said Remington as he swerved around a rock that was lying in the middle of the road.

About a mile and a half up the hill was as far as the road went. They parked the vehicle in the open space under an oak tree, the sun still burning brightly.

"A breath of fresh air, oh, how sweet it is!" exclaimed Jeannine as she climbed out of the vehicle and stretched as she looked around. "It sure seems like no one's been in this neck of the woods for a long time."

"No footprints, nothing," added Remington.

"The big, wide-open spaces," Jeannine breathed out. "I like it. I like it!"

Just then, a butterfly landed on a limb next to her, and with swift hands she gently cupped it and giggled as she said, "Oh, that tickles!"

"Let that poor butterfly go, will you? Live and let live." Charles frowned.

"I had no intention of killing it," she said in a girlish tone as she let it flutter out of her hands. "I just wanted to hold it and look at it for a minute."

Several trails lay before them. "Which trail do we take?" asked Remington in his deep, husky voice. "Who's got the map?"

Jealissa unfolded the map her father had drawn. After scanning it for a few minutes, she replied, "Oh, yeah, this one," and pointed to the one that led westward.

Filled with a sense of serenity and newly found peace, the campers unpacked their bags from the Jeep and headed up the trail that was almost covered over with grass. It led them around corners, up steep hills, and then down again. About three quarters of a mile later, they were all standing in front of the old log cabin. It was located in a beautiful meadow overlooking the horizon. Jealissa and Charles hadn't had any trouble finding it because they were already somewhat familiar with the area.

"Wow!" exclaimed Jeannine.

The sixteen-year-old cabin stood between two great mountains and surrounded by tall trees that seemed to form a protective shield over and around it. Wild plants ran up and down its structure, making the logs that formed it barely visible.

The surrounding area was nature in its most natural state, uncultivated and unsettled.

The weather-beaten cabin stood alone in the vast wilderness. Its outward appearance denied the fast-growing growth of modern carpentry and architectural beauty. It stood like a three-dimensional picture against an imaginary background.

The mixture of wildflowers and green shrubs accented the atmosphere in which it sat seemingly unwelcomed. Framed by logs from strong acacia and sycamore trees, the little cabin looked vastly inferior, as if captured by an elf and tossed into its surroundings.

Lilies, daffodils, tulips, roses, and other beautiful plants were a part of the scenery that gave it the marvelous sense of freedom.

"Well, here we are. Long time no see, baby," Jealissa said to the cabin as she dropped her bags and gave an all-around look, as if to once again become familiar with the area. "Oh, no, I forgot the keys," she said in bewilderment.

They all looked at one another in dismay.

"You what?" Charles asked incredulously.

"Gotcha!" Jealissa teased with a big grin.

"I see you like to play games, Ms. Thing! Better watch your back," Jeannine warned.

"Oh, I shudder with fear," Jealissa responded with a mock shake.

"All right, let's get moving here. I must get on with my life, you know," teased Remington.

Jeannine walked through the cabin and noted every aspect of it. Unlike with the outside, a homelike atmosphere lingered on the inside and gave them a sense of ease. It was clean, except for some dust that had naturally settled after it had been unoccupied for quite a long time. The cabin contained one room and a loft. Surprisingly, it looked more spacious inside than it did from the outside.

A half-wall partition of wood separated the kitchen and the main room. Cold gray ashes filled the woodstove.

There were stones piled high in the left corner of the kitchen area, creating a fireplace. A half-barrel of wood chips sat neatly next to it.

Two moose heads, with eyes wide-open, hung over the fireplace, giving a sense that one was being watched.

A single oil lamp and a flashlight sat on a wooden table that was tilted with age. It sat almost in the middle of the kitchen. The three wooden boxes that were used as chairs were tucked neatly under the table.

Jeannine stood and admired the two amateur paintings that hung on the wall. In one of the paintings, a little girl of about ten years old stood next to her mother, who was wearing a flowered apron. Jeannine pictured herself as the little girl and the woman as her mother.

The little girl was looking up at her mother with a twinkle in her eye as her mother held out to her a basket filled with steaming cinnamon rolls. There was a smile of gentleness and warmth on her mother's face as if to say, "Especially for you."

In the other painting, a vase of freshly cut flowers sat on a wooden table. A bowl containing apples, pears, oranges, and grapes sat at one end, while inexpensive plates, bowls, and utensils were neatly set in place.

Such a humble life, Jeannine thought as she was drawn into the spirit of the paintings, her eyes roaming from one to the other.

A tiny window on the east side of the cabin allowed a small view of the outside world. There was only the one door that allowed access in and out of the cabin. At the back of the cabin, there was a small porch that was stacked with firewood. In order to get to the firewood, one had to go out the front door and walk halfway around the cabin.

Jeannine opened the door and walked around to the back. The stone stacked chimney Siamesed the left side of the cabin.

Just down the slope from the cabin was a well. A rope was attached to a bucket that was used to retrieve water.

It was mid-July, and the weather was just right. The aroma of flowers was released by the combination of sun and, sometimes, the rain.

The sweet whistling of birds invaded the silence of the deep woods.

"Oh, let's never, ever go back!" exclaimed Jeannine as she stepped back inside.

"What a beauty! No job, no school, absolutely nothing. I wish I were an animal of the woods, like a tiger or something," said Charles.

"A monkey or a baboon would fit you well." Jealissa giggled.

"Oh, yeah, and you would be a bug and I'd step on you."

After a light snack of peanut butter crackers and juice, they headed out the door to explore the area. The sun was beginning to set, causing orange and yellow rays to beam freely over the horizon.

"Which way should we go, east, west, north, or south?" asked Remington excitedly. They created paths as they walked on untrodden ground.

Charles and Jealissa didn't know much of the surrounding area even though they'd been there a number of times. Their parents hadn't been the curious type to go searching the wilderness around them, and they certainly weren't brave enough to go out on their own.

"Hey, you mongrels down there!" called Charles from the top of a tree.

"Mmm. What'd we have here? Why, it's a ripened mango. You know what we do in Jamaica to a mango that is ripe and is still hanging from the tree?"

"No, what do you do?" asked Jealissa

"We throw stones at it until we hit it out of the tree."

"Huh?" Charles's eyes widened as Jeannine picked up a stone and tossed it at him. "C'mon, guys, help me get this stubborn mango, will you?" They all grabbed a stone as big as their fist, but Charles leaped out of the tree before they could get a chance to toss them at him.

It wasn't long before they came upon a stream as clear as crystal. The cool water refreshed their weary bodies as they washed their arms, legs, and faces in the running stream.

Jeannine sat on the ground and dangled her feet in the water. They had Slim Jims, peanut butter crackers, and juice before they moved on.

"Look!" Remington pointed to a cave just ahead. Upon closer inspection, the group found a small pile of wood lying loosely in the center.

"Looks like someone has been camping out," declared Remington. "It's probably from last year or even longer," he added.

"Or could even be recently," said Jeannine.

"Hello!" Jeannine stuck her head in at the entrance and shouted. Her voice echoed back. "We enjoyed doing that back in Jamaica."

The sun had sunken behind the horizon, and it was dusk by the time the hikers returned to the cabin.

"I am exhausted! All that climbing and reaching made my muscles hurt!" complained Jealissa.

Suddenly, Remington stopped in his tracks a little distance from the cabin and just stared at the ground. "I hadn't noticed those footprints before," he said with a frown.

Jeannine's first thought was, *Maybe someone followed us here!* She shuddered. For a short while, she had felt free and happy. Now she found herself regretting taking the trip. After what had happened lately, Brendan's death, the fear for her life returned. There was no one to help them if they got in trouble way out there.

"Those are some big prints. Maybe someone was just passing through," Charles said in comfort as he noted the look on Jeannine's face.

"I agree. People do hunt in this part of the woods," added Jealissa. But Jeannine's mind seemed to block out every reassuring word her friends uttered. Her thought was, *And if you're wrong?*

Jeannine couldn't shake the fear that gripped her and thought of the possibility of Brendan's murderers finding her in the middle of nowhere, where no one could rescue her. She felt a knot in her throat but managed to ask, "How far is the closest cabin to this one?"

"I'm really not sure. I never cared to find out," admitted Charles.

With a sudden burst of renewed hope, Jeannine interrupted with the assurance that there might very well be another cabin in the region that was occupied by hunters, and said, "People do hunt this time of the year."

"They probably had been here before us and had gone hunting and wound up here. I'm sure it's nothing to worry about," Jealissa said, trying to be optimistic. "We've been using this cabin for many years, and nothing's ever happened to us or anyone in this area."

"I really don't think we should spend our time worrying about footprints," said Remington impatiently. "Let's get inside and stop worrying over nothing."

The smell of burning wood reminded Jeannine of the time she had visited her aunt in the country. She often thought that using a woodstove was what made Aunt Eunice's food so exceptional. Her mother made great meals, but Aunt Eunice's meals could not be matched.

"I didn't know that Americans used kerosene oil. I thought everything was strictly electric," she said as she poured more kerosene oil on the wood. She had completely forgotten about the footprints that had been the center of their attention earlier. The flames suddenly shot up in the air, and Jeannine stepped back in surprise. "A bit too much kerosene, I guess," she confessed to the room at large.

As the warmth of the fire began to make its way around the room, Remington laughed as he observed, "I've never seen anyone use a fireplace in the summer."

"Well, when you're deep in the woods even during the height of summer, it can be a bit chilly at night," said Jealissa.

Jeannine sat as close as she could to the fire and stared into its rising flames. She felt safe, until her mind wandered back to the footprints they had seen outside the cabin.

"I think it needs more wood," said Charles.

"Just grab some from the pile over there," said Jealissa, pointing in the corner.

"We'd better cook all the meat we brought, because the ice is melting in the cooler and meat can last longer when it's cooked," said Remington.

So they proceeded to fry all the steak and chicken and cooked the hot dogs they'd brought with them.

For dinner, the girls fixed pepper steak, rice and peas, lettuce and tomatoes with French dressing. It was so good they went back for seconds.

"One usually doesn't think of eating food this good while staying in a cabin in the wilderness. Cheese and crackers are the norm," said Charles between bites.

"Jeannine, how did you learn to cook so well?" asked Remington as he licked his fingers. "You cook like a grandmother."

"As is the Jamaican custom, girls are taught to cook at home, also to clean and take care of a house from the time they are knee-high. I've been cooking since I was nine years old."

"Hooray for the Jamaican people!" Charles chuckled. "I want a Jamaican woman."

The hours slipped by unnoticed as the foursome played every indoor game they'd ever learned. Charles looked at his sister and stifled a grin. Jealissa pretended not to notice how silly he was acting. Remington didn't seem to notice anything. Charles placed his index finger on his lips and motioned to Jealissa, cleared his throat, and coughed just before saying, "Jeannine, can you please get me a drink of water?"

"I'm in the middle of a game, so get it yourself!" she replied.

"Please, pretty please," he begged. She rolled her eyes and ignored his plea as she tossed down a "draw four" Uno card for Remington and grinned in victory.

Remington grimaced as he added four cards to the thick pile he had in his hands. Charles continued to beg. As she rose to her feet to do her nagging friend a favor, she suddenly found herself flat on her face. Charles had secretly tied her laces together. Jealissa couldn't help but join in the uproar of laughter.

"You knew that he was doing this to me and you didn't tell me?" Jeannine asked her friend.

"I couldn't say anything," confessed Jealissa. "He's older than me," she added in a girlish tone. Jeannine banged him over the head with a cushion.

It was way past midnight when they all decided to turn in for the night. It didn't take Jeannine long to drop off to sleep, but then, suddenly, something awoke her and she instantly sat up. She thought she heard a crackling noise and whispering voices, or did she? *Maybe it was my imagination,* she thought. *Jealissa was probably talking in her sleep…I hope.* After what seemed like forever, she finally fell asleep.

At daybreak, Jeannine was the first one to awake. Remembering her unexplained awakening the night before, she chided herself for being so foolish and becoming worried over nothing. She reminded herself that they were in the middle of a wilderness and people were probably all over the place, hunting, climbing, and doing what they enjoyed. But she couldn't help wondering, *But that late at night?*

The others were still asleep, and Jeannine tried her best not to disturb them. It was about 6:00 a.m. when Jeannine walked out the door and took in a deep breath of the fresh morning air that carried a faint hint of damp wildflowers.

The sun was just coming up, and she enjoyed the light and shadows on the scenery around her, thinking of them as an accent to nature's beauty. She thought, *What a scene for a photographer! The morning is alive with the chirping of birds and busy insects and squirrels gliding up and down trees as they pass the day away. Oh, and butterflies all around!* She reached out to touch one, and it fluttered away and circled around nearby. Then she noticed beetles and bugs of all kinds also enjoying the early-morning sun.

"Oh, nature is so beautiful! I wish the rest of the world were as beautiful and kind," she whispered aloud. Looking around, she saw no pain and no hurt in that small part of her world. "If only people would stop hurting one another and cherish the beauty of nature." She was overcome by the beauty of the wilderness and enjoying being alone, where there was no one and nothing to bother her.

She began walking, and in a few minutes, she was at the pond. It was filled with frogs and tadpoles, and when she put her hand in the water and scooped up some tadpoles, she then raised her hand to the surface and let them fall through her fingers.

"I won't take you from your home of security," she verbally promised before continuing to walk along the banks of the river and gaze into the bright morning sky. Thousands of thoughts flooded her mind. She had questions for just about everything she saw. There seemed to be plenty of questions, of which there seemed to be no answers.

Thoughts about death came to the forefront of her mind, and she wondered, *Why do people and things die? And where do we go after we leave here? What is the purpose of life? And is there really life after death?*

It was natural that her thoughts shifted to her father, and she couldn't help wondering how he was doing. She believed that God did exist, but wondered, *What else is there about Him? On second thought, does He really, really exist?*

Next, Jeannine's thoughts drifted back to her childhood days, as if they were only yesterday. *Every Sunday my siblings and I went to church. But why did our parents stay home while they sent us to church? Evidently, they thought that Christianity was a good thing, but they never showed they truly believed it enough to actually take up the lifestyle of the Christian people.*

Suddenly, something jumped in front of her, and she screamed. Looking down was the cutest squirrel she'd ever seen. She continued to walk and think and reason for a while until she'd decided it was time to go back.

They must be up by now and wondering where I am. I'd better go back, she thought.

For a while Jeannine walked but didn't seem to be getting closer to the cabin. *I should almost be there by now,* she thought. She walked on some more, but nothing looked familiar.

Fear gripped her, and the thought of being lost in the middle of nowhere caused her to shudder. Evidently, she had so completely let go of herself and had become caught up in a fantasy world where there were no cares, no pain, and no fear—nothing unpleasant—that while daydreaming she had walked and kept on walking until she had gone too far. Now she searched diligently for the cabin she'd left about an hour and a half ago.

Tall trees surrounded the area, thus making it hard for her to see where she was heading. Then she decided to climb to the top of a tree, and to her dismay, she could not see anything but more trees, hills, and rocks. The cabin was not in sight, and she became numb with fear.

Meanwhile, at the cabin, Charles had prepared breakfast and called, "Hey, girls, breakfast is ready!"

"Is it time to get up already?" Jealissa asked while stretching and yawning. The night seemed like but a moment, and she felt as if she were just getting ready to have a good sleep. Raising her head and looking around, she saw, indeed, it really was morning. The room was lit by the brightness of the morning sun.

"You guys can stay in bed all day if you'd like, but we'd rather spend our day in the great outdoors!" hollered Charles.

"Yeah!" responded Remington, slapping him a high five.

"Where's Jeannine?" asked Jealissa as she climbed down from the loft. Surprised, both boys just looked at her.

"We thought she was still sleeping," replied Charles.

*****

Four hours had passed since they'd been up, and Jeannine hadn't returned from wherever she'd gone. Remington tapped his foot nervously. They were all now beginning to worry.

"Something might be wrong. She might have walked too far and have gotten lost," Jealissa said. "We've got to go and look for her."

They all agreed and walked and called her for two hours, but to no avail.

"Let's go back to the cabin. She might have returned," said Charles anxiously.

Upon returning, they found the door wide-open. "I knew she'd be back," said Remington excitedly as he hurried to the cabin.

But Jealissa just stared at the lock on the floor. "The lock's broken!" she exclaimed. Then they all stared in dismay at the ransacked cabin. "We've been burglarized!" screamed Jealissa. The mattresses were thrown off the beds, and their bags were emptied onto the floor. It was as if a storm had passed through the cabin.

Jealissa began to cry. "I am scared! Is someone trying to hurt us?" she blurted. "I want to go home now! They probably kidnapped Jeannine!"

Upon quickly checking the cabin, they found that nothing seemed to have been taken. "I had some money right here on the little table, and it's still here, untouched," Remington declared.

"If they didn't want our money, then what did they want?" cried Jealissa. "Our purses were emptied out, but everything seems to still be there…our money, our credit cards. This is too spooky."

"It might be a bunch of kids doing this for fun," Charles said, trying to comfort her, but his voice quivered.

"What do we do now?" Charles asked Remington.

"I can't stay here. I am scared," Jealissa stated as she nervously leaned against the wall. "Oh, God, no!" She began to hyperventilate. Between breaths she whispered, "Please, let's go home." Charles tried again to calm her down and went into the kitchen to get her a glass of water.

"What about Jeannine? We can't leave her here," said Remington.

"Oh my god! They're going to kill us!" Jealissa violently cried. "They probably have guns and are probably watching us right now!"

Remington held her. "Jealissa, we've all got to stay calm so we can think clearly."

"Now what do we do?" she asked shakily.

They waited in fear for Jeannine to return. They didn't want to leave her, and they were afraid to start the search for her again, because they were afraid they might run into the intruders. And who knew what kind of weapons they might have?

Together they waited huddled in a corner of the room. Each had something they might use as a weapon if their unwelcomed guests were to return.

Charles finally broke the silence. "They must have been watching the cabin this morning, because they broke in after we left."

"Yeah, they might have been in the bushes, watching when we came back," added Remington.

They were weak with fear, worrying about who "they" were, what their intentions were, and what type of weapons they had. These were just a few of the fearful questions that were running through their thoughts.

By two thirty in the afternoon, there still was no sign of Jeannine, and it had now hit home to the three in the cabin that something must be terribly wrong. Charles said, "We can't wait any longer. We've got to go for help. But that means we will have to break up, though. Onc of us has to stay here at the cabin, just in case Jeannine does find her way back."

"I'm sorry, but it won't be me. I can't stay here alone. I'm scared for my life," announced Jealissa.

It was left for Remington to volunteer to stay. He said, "You two go find help quickly," as he tossed his car keys to Charles.

Remington was worried sick about Jeannine and constantly wondered what might have happened to her. *Oh god!* his mind seemed to yell. *First, Brendan was murdered, her parents had a life-threatening accident, and now she is missing. What else could go wrong in this girl's life?*

Charles and his sister put on their heavy boots and packed a small bag with two bottles of water and some snacks.

"Be careful," Remington cautioned as he watched the two cling to each other as they walked down the narrow trail toward the vehicle.

On that walk back to the car, they jumped at every sound they heard and constantly looked all around them. It was the longest walk they'd ever experienced. Finally arriving at their destination, they quickly tossed their bags in the back and Charles jumped behind the wheel. He couldn't wait to get moving and drive like a maniac out of that remote and, what now had become to them, dangerous wilderness area.

Quickly he slid the key into the ignition and turned it, but there was no sound of a strong SUV motor coming to life. "Ah!" he gulped. He turned the key again. "Come on, come on, come oooonnn," he implored. Jealissa silently watched him with wide eyes. "Come on, you stupid hunk of metal!" Charles begged.

He slid out of his seat and popped the hood. "Oh, no!" he exclaimed in sheer horror. "Every wire has been cut!"

Jealissa now became frantic.

"This is really too much," Charles said in disgust. "What do you want from us, you jerks?" he hollered. "There're some awfully disgusting people in this world," he snarled.

After venting his frustration, Charles took a moment to think about what the best course of action for him and Jealissa to take would be. Then he decided and told her, "We're going to have to walk." With them they took the map, their packs with water, and some snacks.

Meanwhile, Remington had gone inside the cabin to wait for Jeannine. He said a prayer for her, for himself, and for Charles and Jealissa.

Charles and Jealissa had been gone about forty-five minutes when Remington heard a noise outside. He ventured to peek out the window but changed his mind. *I'd better expect the worse,* he thought. Then he crouched behind the little table and waited, cocking his ears and listening as best he could. The noise grew louder, and he could hear his heart pounding in his chest. Beads of sweat dampened his forehead, and his mouth grew dry. But he stayed very still, so still that his body ached.

Then he heard the door slowly creaking open. Chancing a peek from his hiding place, Remington hoped it was Jeannine, but instead his eyes saw a tall slinky, hairy man whose beard reached halfway down his chest. The hair on his head sat like a tangled mass of weeds. His eyes swiftly and wildly roamed the inside of the cabin.

A hermit? Remington wondered. *Was he the one that had trashed the cabin?* He clenched his teeth and angrily thought, *I'll teach you a lesson!*

Watching for the right moment, he waited until the man's back was toward him, and in a flash, he leaped from behind the table and jumped on the man's back, knocking him to the floor. Remington pinned him to the ground with his stronger body and immediately demanded, "Why did you break in and trash our cabin?"

"I didn't do it. It's my first time in here. I just needed something to eat, that's all."

The man wrestled like a wildcat with Remington until he was able to break free. Then he dashed through the door like a whirlwind and left Remington sitting on the floor, breathless.

In a couple of minutes, while still sitting on the floor, trying to make what he could out of his recent encounter, he heard another sound. Listening carefully, this time he was sure he heard voices, male voices. Again, he slid behind the table and waited. The voices came closer to the door of the cabin and lingered, but Remington couldn't make out what they were saying.

Suddenly, a shot was fired pretty close, and involuntarily he let out a holler and fell flat on his face. It didn't matter, though, because they were just as taken aback as he was that they didn't even hear him holler. He could hear them running through the bushes.

Then one more shot was fired, and Remington stayed in hiding for about two hours.

Since that second shot, Remington hadn't heard anything, not even the movement of small animals. He couldn't help wondering, *Had the shots been from hunting rifles and had been fired at an animal?* But then he couldn't make sense of anything that had happened since the day had begun. Especially, *Who was the man I wrestled with, and who were those men that had been talking just outside the cabin? Who fired the shots I heard? And did they fire at the men, or were the men just scared from not knowing who had fired those shots?*

Remington didn't know if he should be grateful or not for those two shots. *Yes, they had gotten rid of the men, but could they have been intruders, or even better yet, could those men have been of great help? Life is wretched,* he thought.

*****

Brendan was moving back home, but only in spirit and not in body.

Mrs. Clark sat on her son's bed and stared at herself in his dresser mirror. Her mind had finally gotten around to accepting the fact that Brendan would no longer come back to his apartment.

Whoever had killed her son, she fervently hoped God would never forgive them. It would give her great pleasure to know that they would burn forever in hell. She believed there was such a place as hell. There had to be. Because the wicked just *had* to be punished. She was quite sure God pitied her and that heaven would be her eternal home. *Of course it would,* she was convinced. *After all, I've been a decent, law-abiding citizen all my life,* she credited herself.

Standing, she picked up one of the empty boxes on the floor and walked over to the dresser, where she began placing the items in the box, one at a time. Next, she pulled the dusty curtains down, gave them a vigorous shake, and then folded them neatly before placing them also in the box.

It took her half the day to pack up his few belongings, but it was finally done. It seemed that almost as soon as she had finished sealing the last box, the moving truck arrived.

Staying out of the way, she watched dispassionately as the strong men moved the heavy furniture from the apartment and into the truck.

She took one last look around at the empty apartment. The men didn't waste any time bringing Brendan's things into her basement.

When she was alone again, Mrs. Clark went back to wondering how long it would take for the police to bring her son's murderers to justice. She couldn't help herself and called Detective Schennenburger. He was very understanding of her grief and offered her words that momentarily consoled her.

After hanging up the phone from speaking with Mrs. Clark, he folded his arms and leaned back in his chair, deep in thought. He pulled his pen from behind his ear, and as he fiddled with it, his cheekbones tightened. The grim look on his face mirrored the tension in his body.

"People who willfully murder someone should spend the rest of their lives in prison," he muttered under his breath. "Better yet," he concluded, "they should be tortured for the rest of their lives."

He'd been on the force for twenty-five years and had personally experienced the cruel hand of crime when he lost his own son five years ago. To say the least that his son was an innocent bystander would be the understatement of the year.

JR had only gone half an hour to visit his friend Marve. As they were standing in front of Marve's apartment, talking, a group of hoodlums fired shots from a car during a joyride. One of the bullets hit him in the head, killing him instantly. His friend Marve, on the other hand, was fortunate to have walked away with only emotional trauma.

The morning before the death of his son, Detective Schennenburger had had an uneasy feeling in his stomach that he couldn't explain and couldn't shake. He didn't understand it but felt as if *something* awful was going to happen, but what do you do? How could he have known? So the detective had shrugged his shoulders and tried to ignore the feeling.

He had been so proud of his father-son relationship with JR. Oh, how he loved his only child. His son was his life. Seventeen years previously, he had lost his wife through a divorce when JR was only six months old. But he had fought for custody, had won, and upon moving to Milolta, had started his life all over.

Who could have foreseen he would only have seventeen birthdays with JR? He played the mental game. *If only I could go back in time, if only I could have known the future, I could have avoided a lot of things. If only I had known my intuition was right, I could have done everything in my power to ward off and avoid the tragedy. That day, we both would probably have stayed home until the day had passed.*

Should I be blamed for not protecting my son? After all, I'd done a good job for seventeen years. Why had I failed him then? I had always been there for my boy, but not the time when JR needed me the most.

He continued to reminisce about the fishing trips, the basketball games, and the many things they'd done together. Then he remembered how he had been cheated and thought, *How dare those hoodlums rob me!* gripping the desk so hard his fingers became white, and as he raised his brow, a ripple of lines ran across his forehead. *They don't deserve to live! I hate them!*

He could taste the revenge he longed for. But what made it worse for him was that the culprits had never been caught, and he was left feeling frustrated, hurt, angry, and worst of all, impotent and powerless to do anything.

But now he had someplace to aim his anger. For now he felt driven to check out every nook and cranny in order to find Brendan Clark's murderers. With a purpose, he sat upright in his chair and shuffled a few pieces of paper. Then he called out, "Hey, Ronnie, can you call Jeannine Shrouder and ask her if she could come down to the precinct?" His voice quivered with anxiousness. "There are a few details I would like for her to try to recall, very important details."

Detective Schennenburger leaned back in his chair and wondered why the killers had mentioned something about disks before they had killed him. He figured they either worked with computers or had been hired by someone who did a great deal of computer work.

Ronnie called for Jeannine, but to no avail. Ida told him she was out of town. When informed, Detective Schennenburger slammed his hand down on the desk in angry disappointment.

Then he wondered if he should call Kim in again, but as suddenly as he'd thought about it, he dropped the idea. Mainly because he knew Kim wouldn't give him the time of day. She was still quite angry and didn't want to talk to anyone about Brendan.

*****

At the time Detective Schennenburger was thinking about her, Kim was home, preparing a special meal for her father, and probably wouldn't have let the police ruin the mood.

"Dinner is almost ready!" she called from the kitchen as she stirred the forest-green pot.

"Darling, I'm sorry, but I will have to save supper until later. I have some errands to run," explained her father.

"Oh, Daddy, this late?"

"Yes, I know, but I won't be long. It'll be quick," Marshall reassured her.

"I've prepared your favorite, chicken bouillon, scalloped potatoes, string beans, and homemade rolls. It'll only be a few minutes more," she wheedled.

"Okay, I'll stay," he agreed with a deep sigh. Marshall didn't want to disappoint his daughter, so he sat down at the table and waited for her to serve him.

"I know this must be hard on you, losing Brendan. How're you doing?" he kindly asked.

She avoided his gaze as she responded, "I'm fine, Daddy, really."

But she hurriedly changed the subject because she dreaded getting emotional. "I haven't been seeing much of you lately. I think you're working too hard at the office. It'll catch up with you after a while. You've got to slow down, Daddy."

"I never dreamed it would be so soon that my little girl would grow into such a fine young lady who would counsel me on life." He smiled as he continued, "You are beautiful within and without. No matter how old you get, though, you'll always be my little princess."

"Even after I turn ninety?" She laughed.

Marshall enjoyed his supper and the company of his daughter so much that he almost forgot he had to go out. "That was excellent," he declared as he rose from the table. "Thank you, honey."

"Be home before midnight," she teased as he walked out the door.

*****

The door to the elevator opened, and as Zaire exited, he made a right and headed for apartment 7B. He had one thing on his mind, and that was to call Kim. Once inside, and as soon as he had closed the door, he sat down next to the telephone. Before he could use the phone, there was a knock on the door. Grunting, he stood and opened the door. He was surprised to see two police officers standing at his door.

"Are you Zaire Campbell?" asked one of them.

"Yes, I am. Why?" he replied with raised brow.

"We have a search warrant for your apartment."

"What for?" he demanded.

Without another word, they pushed past him and made their way into the apartment and began their search.

"Did you have a fight with Brendan Clark the night he was killed?" one of them asked.

"Y-yes," he stuttered. "But if you think that I have anything to do with his murder, you're mistaken."

Zaire trailed behind the two men and watched impotently as they turned his apartment upside down while searching every nook and cranny, wearing latex gloves.

"Looks like you're in hot water, son," said one of the officers, who came striding from Zaire's bedroom. He displayed Brendan's charge cards and checkbook. "How did you come into possession of these items?"

He looked at them incredulously and indignantly responded, "I didn't have those, and you know it! Don't you be planting any evidence in my apartment!"

Ignoring him, the police officer quoted, "Zaire Campbell, you're under arrest for the murder of Brendan Clark."

"What?" Zaire bellowed. "You have no proof that I killed anybody, and besides, you had those with you when you came in!"

"There're other evidences that point to you" was all the officer said as he pulled out his cuffs and handcuffed Zaire's hands behind his back. While he finished reading him his rights, Zaire only vaguely heard the officer due to being in shock.

He was also angry and wanted to resist the arrest but knew it would only be another charge to add to his "crimes."

"You killed that boy so you could have his girlfriend!" one of the police yelled in his face. "You lost your ex-girlfriend to him, and you couldn't get her back, so you murdered him in cold blood!"

Zaire felt numb as he rode in the back of the police car to the station. He didn't know of a good lawyer to call, so he spoke to one of the legal aid lawyers that the county provided for people who couldn't afford a lawyer.

Six hours after he'd been at the police station, they released him for transportation to the county jail. He rose to his feet and walked the steps it took to get to the door of the van, and as he climbed in, he looked around. The atmosphere was unfriendly in addition to being very crowded. It had only two small windows on either side, so he could barely see outside. To Zaire it felt as if it was the port of death. Like, goodbye forever.

Taking notice of everything they passed, he felt as if everything was slipping away from him, even the hope of marrying Kim.

Six other men occupied the van, but Zaire chose to focus on an Afro-American young man who sat to his immediate left. First, he noted that his hair was braided and was shoulder-length. Next, he saw that his pants were way too large, as was his shirt. He could tell he was more like a boy, probably no more than fifteen years old, and was tall and slender even though he held his head low. The eyes were distant. *His mother must be crying herself sick,* Zaire thought.

When the van stopped, the officer swung the doors open wide. With his feet shackled and hands cuffed behind him, Zaire had to slowly and carefully descend the steps. A voice in his head said, *Welcome home.* He quietly groaned to himself because he had never seen the inside of a jail before, and he admitted he was scared. With that admission, he felt a cold chill.

"This is your cell, D6." The guard then proceeded to give him a rundown of the rules. Zaire mutely nodded in response. He had no statement, no questions.

The word *inmate* was printed on the back of his forest-green jail shirt in huge white letters.

His first night in jail was the longest night in his life. He didn't sleep at all. How could he? Basically, they had inferred he would lose his life, and he couldn't pretend as if everything was all right.

He couldn't help but wonder, *What will my life be like? So many people have gone to jail and, after that, have never seen the outside world again.*

Zaire just sat on the hard bed and stared at the walls and bars that enclosed him. They were only inches away from him. Clenching his teeth, he whispered, "Now, Brendan, I hate you even more! You deserved to die!" Then he pounded his fist in his hand and vowed, "I've got to get out of here! I just have to!"

Visiting days came and went, but no one visited Zaire. Hours, days, and weeks slipped by as he sat in the county jail, hoping for just a single piece of mail from Kim. None came. He figured she must still be grieving over Brendan. Zaire spent hours each day just lying on his bed and staring blankly at the ceiling.

"Zaire Campbell?"

But he didn't hear his name the first time because he had given up hope of any mail or anyone coming to visit him.

"Zaire Campbell!"

This time he thought he had heard someone call his name, so he stood and asked his neighbor, "Did someone call me?" But his neighbor just ignored him.

"Last call for Zaire Campbell!" came a louder call.

"Yes," he replied quickly.

"Got a visitor," the guard told him.

All the while he hurried down the hall to the waiting area, he wondered who it could be. A smile lit up his face when he saw Kim Marie Futon sitting at a table in a corner.

"It's so good to see you, Kim. How have you been?" he beamed.

"Okay, and you, Zaire? Really, how are you?" she said sincerely.

"So-so. I've missed you a lot and was worried sick about you. I can't believe they set the date for my trial so far away. In here, they don't care about anybody, even if you're innocent." He stared into her eyes. "You do believe I'm innocent, don't you, Kim?"

She nodded. "Yes, I believe you."

"The police confiscated my computer, but I have refused to give them my password to my disks. I told them I was too stressed and that was probably why I couldn't remember it."

"Kim, I did not kill anybody," he said firmly, hoping to remove any doubt that she might have.

The visit was too short, but Zaire enjoyed every moment of it. It was the first time he'd spoken to Kim since he'd been arrested a few weeks ago. Now he felt relieved to know she thought he was innocent. He began to have hope and to even think that after this chapter of his life was over, he and Kim would live happily ever after.

*****

Schennenburger and Ronnie discussed the Brendan Clark case fervently. "My guess is that he killed him because he wanted his girl," said Ronnie. "But how the disks come into play is a mystery to me. It just seems 'logical' that Campbell killed him. He was killed only a few hours after the argument, and the autopsy showed Zaire's blood on Brendan's body and Zaire's hair under his fingernails. But where does that put Ben Shrouder?"

Jake Schennenburger moistened his lips and took a long, deep breath. "I think he's in this somehow. I can't prove anything right now, but he might have played a part in the murder."

"How do you figure that?" asked Ronnie.

"Well, we know Zaire was already angry with Brendan. So what if someone knew that and made him a good offer to do away with Brendan for reasons not revealed to him? Hey, you never know. All they had to do was supply the weapon, money, and the rest, as they say, is history. Jealousy is a deadly thing, and you only think *after* you act."

"Remember, though, the young lady saw more than one person."

Detective Schennenburger shrugged his shoulders. "He had an accomplice," he replied matter-of-factly. Then he angrily slammed his pen onto the hard desk as he said, "Well, we might never know the truth, since Ben is now a mindless fruitcake."

*****

They interrogated Kim again and again, trying to see if she could shed light, any light, on the case. She was made to feel as though she was the criminal, as they demanded answers to their questions. Kim hated and resented every moment she spent at the police station, being subjected to their probing questions.

Jeannine had also spent a great deal of time at the police station because she was the key eyewitness to the murder. If she hadn't left on her trip, she would probably have been there every day to answer more and more questions.

What Detective Schennenburger wanted to know was if Jeannine would recognize Zaire as one of the men in the alley. But now that would have to wait until she got back from her trip. He knew she had told him she hadn't gotten a good look at either of the men, but the detective thought that maybe after seeing Zaire, it might trigger a recollection, like his build or voice.

Was Zaire a murderer? Was it just a coincidence that after a brawl with Brendan, someone else murdered him and then framed him? But if Zaire didn't kill Brendan, then who did and why? Also, what was on the disks that the men had demanded from him? Was Brendan in a gang? Those were some of the questions the police department had tried to answer, but they were at a dead end.

Detective Schennenburger thought he might be able to get some valuable information by going over to the basketball court and questioning a few guys who knew both Brendan and Zaire. But that idea didn't pan out; no one seemed to know anything.

After the detective had left, Tom asked Jahquad, "What was that all about?"

His friend answered, "He was just asking questions about Zaire and Brendan. By the way, man, have you seen Zaire?"

"I ain't seen that kid in a minute."

"Maybe he's all broken up over Brendan's death," said Tom. "Yo, man, I think he's hibernatin'."

"Broken up?" Jahquad said. "Didn't you know?"

"Know what?"

"Brendan stole his girl and Zaire threatened Brendan several times, man, and promised to snuff him out if he didn't stay away from his girl. They even had a fight the night Brendan was killed. There were witnesses too. The next morning, they found Brendan dead someplace. He hated Brendan."

"Oh, word?" said Tom, surprised.

"Word is bond. I believe the brother killed him, man," Jahquad said.

"Well, we don't know that for sure. It might not have been him who killed him, though."

"Are you guys ready to play, or you're gonna stand there and converse like sissies?" someone yelled.

"Yo, watch your mouth, man!" Jahquad shouted in answer.

"The game is on! Let's play some b-ball!"

Chapter 16

Captured

Charles and Jealissa were getting weary. They'd been walking for hours and still hadn't found another cabin or the main road. The map really only covered the area of the cabin and a little beyond, so they were not sure where they were and suspected they might be walking in circles.

Charles wanted to keep going, but Jealissa was too exhausted to take another step. "Okay, we'll camp for the night, sis. Don't worry, everything is going to be all right," he assured her. He broke branches and spread them out on the ground under a pine tree. It wasn't like the beds they'd left at home, but it had to do. They drank water and ate saltine crackers for supper.

The whole time they felt guilty about Jeannine's disappearance and wondered if she'd made it back to the cabin. But there was no means of communication, and it didn't make sense to try to return to the cabin just to see if she had found her way back.

That night, they snuggled on their bed of branches and leaves and wished for morning to come. They'd never slept outside before, except when Charles had slept in their backyard with his friends when he was eleven years old. But that was different. Bears didn't go walking in the city and climbing fences to look for someone sleeping in their backyard. This was definitely not their parents' backyard; this was God's backyard, the great outdoors.

Being city kids, they naturally were afraid. Jealissa constantly thought about the wild animals and insects that could be just feet or inches away from them. Suddenly, something tickled her arm, and she screamed.

"What's the matter?" asked Charles.

"I'm sorry, it was just a leaf rubbing against my arm."

"Jealissa, you don't want to go screaming for no reason. The wild animals will want to attack us. I don't think we need to see any animals tonight!"

She asked, "Do you want us to take turns keeping watch?"

"In your dreams," he replied.

The morning finally came, and the sweet chirping of birds awakened them.

Jealissa was the first to open her eyes. She looked around and thought, *Well, at least all the parts of our bodies are intact.* Then she whispered, "Charles, it's time to get up."

They gathered up their belongings and started on their journey again. They walked on untrodden paths until they finally came to a cabin.

"Hello? Is anyone there?" They knocked and called, hoping to find some friendly person who would help them, but no one came to the door. They tried the lock, but it didn't budge. Then Charles walked around the cabin, tapping on the sides, just in case someone was inside, sleeping.

"We've got to keep moving," Jealissa said in disappointment. "We should have followed the road we drove on to the main road as we had originally planned, instead of searching for another cabin for help. Now we don't even know which way to go to get to the main road."

For about an hour more, they walked until they stood in front of the cabin they had pounded on earlier. The cabin was distinctive, so there was no mistaking that it was the same one. Wild plants ran up its structure as if it were an abandoned old building.

"We've been walking in circles ever since we left our cabin," Charles groaned in disappointment. "Maybe someone's here this time." Again they knocked on the door and called, but there was no answer. Disheartened, they turned to leave but then heard the door of the cabin open behind them. They whirled around to find a man standing in the doorway.

"Yes?" he said, his face expressionless. They walked closer to him, and Charles took the opportunity to explain their plight, in hopes that he would have compassion and help them.

"We would appreciate all the help you can give us," Jealissa said.

Before they could fully explain their situation, the man opened the door wider, stepped back, and motioned with his hands for them to come in. Gratefully they stepped inside.

As they stepped into the cabin, their eyes fell on a man who was sitting on a pile of wood. His back was against the wall, and his face was covered in smoke from the cigar that was trapped between his lips.

"We really would appreciate your help." Jealissa gasped from the horrible stench of the smoke. The man who let them in looked at her questioningly.

As if they had to repeat their story for his companion, Charles began again. "We've lost our friend. Our cabin is…" He paused. "Somewhere around here, I guess."

Jealissa interjected, "It's hard to know where you are when you're surrounded by tall trees. We don't know if something has happened to our friend, but we need to get back to the city."

"What city would that be?" asked the man who'd opened the door.

"Milolta," said Charles.

The men's faces lit up. "We're also from Milolta," mentioned the man with the cigar. At the shared information, Charles's and Jealissa's faces creased into smiles, and they relaxed, because they now felt comfortable sharing their misfortune with these men from their city.

Charles continued, "Our friend witnessed two guys kill someone we all knew." The men exchanged quick glances. "We told her that it would be a great idea for her to get away because she would be safer out of the city, but now she's disappeared and we don't know what happened to her, and she doesn't know the area at all."

"That's really unfortunate," said the nonsmoker.

"Where did this murder take place?" asked the other as he fanned the smoke from his face as if to clear his vision so he could see who their visitors were.

"She said it took place in an alley behind Cranshaw Avenue. I suppose you heard about it on the news, since you're from Milolta?" Charles asked.

"Yes, we did. It was unfortunate for the young man. What was his name again?"

"Brendan," replied Charles. "Brendan Clark."

"Yeah, Brendan Clark," said the nonsmoker.

The two men exchanged glances again, but Charles was too busy talking a mile a minute to notice the change in the men's expressions. Then the two men began asking probing questions, as if they were more interested about Brendan and Jeannine.

"This girl that's lost in the woods is the same one that witnessed the murder?" asked the smoker.

"Y-yes," Jealissa stuttered. She noticed where the conversation was going and now became uneasy. The men's personalities seemed to have changed, and she became suspicious.

Charles began to feel the same way and read the expression in her eyes. Knowing his sister well, he knew she didn't feel right being there and that she wanted to leave. So he gave a half-hearted smile and announced, "Well, the main road shouldn't be too far from here. Sorry to have bothered you. The walk is good for us, anyways."

Jealissa's heart pounded rapidly as she turned toward the door. She was prepared to make a dash for it because she sensed the men weren't good, law-abiding citizens. *If only we had picked up on that before we actually stepped inside the cabin,* she thought.

"Don't worry, we'll help you to find her, because that's exactly whom we've been looking for!" The man with the cigar laughed as he slipped out his handgun and pointed it at them. Jealissa let out a shrill scream.

"It won't do you any good," he said as he crushed his cigar on a log and his lips curled into an evil grin.

His accomplice let out an evil laugh that sent chills up their spine as he announced, "We'll help you find your friend."

Then they laughed and joked about how they had killed the little pest (Brendan) and how lucky they were to meet these two young people who were going to help them get whom they had come there for in the first place.

Incensed, Jealissa bellowed, "Why did you kill Brendan?"

Charles nudged her to stay quiet. *The last thing you want to do is to get a gunman angry,* he thought.

"He had something of ours…a few disks. Do you know what he did with them? You help us and we'll let you go with no harm. Those disks are highly valuable. So you help us and we help you. Deal?" said the man with the gun.

"We have no idea," said Charles honestly.

"We hate being lied to!" He rose from his seat, and his hand brushed the cigar off the log and onto the floor. "But I bet your lost friend does, doesn't she?" said the smoker.

"What are you going to do with us?" Jealissa asked.

"You'll see." He laughed again.

She began to plead for their lives, saying, "We won't tell anyone that we met you."

They only laughed harder. "Sure. What do you think we are, stupid?"

They then proceeded to tie them up and dragged them to a room that was hidden behind a wall. A huge chest covered the small door. They gagged them before they left them for hours on end.

Since the cabin was old and squeaky, they knew each time the men came and how long they stayed before leaving again. Charles couldn't understand why they would just toss him and Jealissa in the hidden room and just ignore them. He even wondered, *Have they forgotten we are here? Didn't they need us to help them find the disks and Jeannine?*

Charles wriggled his body, but the rope held him tight. When he glanced at his sister, he saw her face was moistened with tears and could hear her muffled sobs through the gag. This spurred him to do some serious thinking. *Maybe no one will find us here, so we have to work up a plan to get ourselves out. We've got to do something. We can't just sit here and die,* Charles reasoned in his thoughts.

Jealissa sighed heavily and thought she would probably never see the light of another day.

Meanwhile, Remington was still alone in the cabin, and Jeannine hadn't showed up. He just didn't know what to do but was thinking it might not have been such a good idea for him to have stayed there alone. He felt lonely and afraid and wondered how much longer it would be before someone came for him.

Men were supposed to be strong and fearless, and he was embarrassed that he was afraid. He prayed for someone familiar to come and get him back to civilization. And that Jeannine was all right.

*****

While Remington, Charles, and Jealissa thought about Jeannine's safety, somewhere in the woods she lay on a little patch of grass with a throbbing headache.

"Oh," she moaned and blinked. "Where am I, and what am I doing here?"

Her vision was a bit blurry, and her mind was fuzzy, her mouth and throat very dry. Worse, she had no recollection as to how she had come to be there on the ground. She sat up and tried to think, but her head only throbbed harder.

No one was there to help her to understand why she was in the middle of nowhere all by herself. Gradually and slowly, she got up and began walking, to where, she didn't know. *I have to walk. Maybe I'll see something or someone I recognize,* she thought.

Raising her head to view the birds that were flying so peacefully in the air, she thought everything seemed to know where they were going except for her.

She'd only gone a few steps when she had to stop because she felt faint and the world seemed to be spinning. It was weird; every muscle in her body felt weak. Quickly she sat back down on the ground.

"Oh," she moaned faintly. "Someone please help me."

Again, she tried to stand on her feet. *I must get to somewhere… anywhere. How far is somewhere or anywhere?* she thought.

Overcome by weakness, she plopped back down on the ground again and lay down flat on her back.

Help! she thought. *Who can hear someone's thoughts?* She prayed for strength and for God to send someone to rescue her. Then, she shakily rose to her feet and took a few more steps. Her dry tongue seamed to stick to the roof of her mouth.

Then she heard something, and so she stopped and listened. It was a sort of rustling movement. Water? It sounded like the spring she used to visit where her aunt Eunice lived.

She hurried, or so she thought, and when she came to a little hill, stopped, and looked down. There was water, lots of water. Then she slid on her buttocks until she came to the bottom of the hill. The running water looked like gold.

Throwing herself down on the bank of the stream, she buried her face in the water and began to drink. There was no time to scoop, and she felt she needed almost all the water that was available. But she drank until her stomach tightened, and then lay down on the bank and rested until her body was revived.

After a while, she proceeded to wash her face, arms, and legs. As her thirsty body absorbed the water, her mind became refreshed and her thoughts cleared. And then she remembered. "Oh!" she exclaimed with a little more strength than when she had first awakened. "That's right, I'm lost and I've got to find my way back to the cabin."

She had no idea what day or what time it was, but she knew that it was the same creek she had found when she first went on her walk.

Just then, she heard a crackling noise behind her and quickly swung around only to find a man standing behind her with a rifle in his hand. "Hi!" he said. "A beautiful young woman like you shouldn't be out here alone."

While managing a little smile, she pondered whether or not to tell him that she was lost. *If I do, he might try to hurt me. Or if I do, he might help me. Should I let this man leave me here all alone? Yet he might very well be an angel in disguise.*

She smiled again and said, "I'm okay," and turned away from him.

When he drew closer, she began to really feel uneasy and fought the urge to run away. *He might just shoot me in the back,* she thought, so she turned around to face him.

Startled, she found he was standing so close that she could feel his breath on her face. When she tried to speak, nothing came out. He raised his hand to touch her face, and she took a step back.

"You're awfully pretty. Are you married?" he asked.

Uh-oh, the warning bell rang louder. *Run!* her mind said as the warning bell rang more urgently. But she couldn't. It was as though she were paralyzed from the neck down. Instead of running, she just stood there and stared at him.

He placed his rifle down on the ground, then said, "I could make you the happiest girl in the world." He smiled flirtingly and reached out to touch her again.

"Jeannine!"

"Remington!" she whispered. Her voice came back, and her body cooperated, and she ran into Remington's arms.

He held her tight, as if he'd never let her go, and then turned to the stranger and asked in a commanding tone, "Who are you?"

The stranger looked at him, bent and picked up his rifle, and just disappeared into the bushes.

"Are you all right?" he asked tenderly. "You sure scared us half to death!"

"I got lost and almost died," she explained as she sat down on a rock. "I went for a walk, but I got lost trying to find my way back. I must have fainted from the heat and dehydration. When I woke up, it took me a while to remember where I was. I'm okay now. I just had a lot of water to drink, and now I'm beginning to feel like myself again."

"Thanks, Remington. You found me just in time. The man only beat you here by a couple of minutes." She managed a smile and blushed as she continued, "I don't know what would have happened if you hadn't come by when you did."

"Well, I'm glad you're okay." Actually, he was overjoyed. Then on a grimmer note, he told her all that had transpired since she'd left. "You've been missing since yesterday morning, and I haven't heard anything from Charles and Jealissa since they went for help. I hope they're okay."

"I've been gone for more than twenty-four hours?" she asked incredulously. "I survived lying in the middle of nowhere all that time?"

Bowing her head, she thought, *Maybe God is watching over me.*

On their way back to the cabin, they suddenly heard something, and as they quickly crouched down behind some bushes, they saw two men carrying guns and coming from the cabin. Hoping they hadn't been detected, Remington held Jeannine and stilled her trembling body. "Don't worry," he whispered, "we're going to be just fine."

After the men left the area, Remington and Jeannine waited about a half hour before going inside the cabin.

Jeannine wasted no time in changing into other slacks and her hiking boots. They packed two small bags and were just getting ready to leave when she noticed something on the floor by Remington's feet. "What's this?" she asked as she picked it up.

"That wasn't here before," replied Remington.

"I don't believe so either. Those intruders might have dropped it." She held the metallike object up to take a closer look. It was a silver coin with jagged edges and what appeared to be a red dragon engraved on it. "Very interesting. I've never seen anything like it," she said, absentmindedly slipping it into her pocket.

They threw their backpacks on their backs and headed out the door. As soon as they had gotten through the door, they were confronted by one of the men that had been in the cabin a few minutes before. He cocked his gun and aimed it at them. Without even thinking or waiting, they took off into the woods. A shot was fired, but they didn't look back. They just kept running until Jeannine began to gasp for air.

"Come on, Jeannine," Remington called frantically as he ran back and grabbed her by the hand and pulled her through the woods.

Finally, they had to stop, and they slumped down on a patch of ground. They stayed crouched behind a huge rock and rested.

Remington's leg felt as if he had had a beesting, and when he rubbed his hand over the area, he felt moisture. Looking down at his bloodstained leg, he yelped, "I think I've been shot! I've been shot!"

"What?" asked Jeannine.

He pointed to his leg as he pulled off his shirt to use as a tourniquet to help stop the bleeding.

"I'll do it," she said, nervously tying his shirt around the gunshot wound.

He watched her face as she tied it and tried to joke by saying, "I don't think you'd make a good nurse."

"You're right," she confessed.

"Don't worry, I'm not going to die. It's only a graze." He laughed.

"You just got shot, and you're laughing?" she indignantly asked.

"It could have been worst. Thank you, Nurse," he said as she tied the last knot. He smiled.

She sighed and plopped down next to him and whispered, "Remington, I'm scared."

"Don't be. This wounded soldier will take care of you."

He had a distant look in his eyes and, after a few minutes, said, "The guy that fired the shot was one of the men that had just come out of our cabin."

"He probably came looking for the coin," she finished.

"Those hoodlums ran us off course. Too bad, because I had wanted for us to take the trail that led to where we'd parked the car. That way, we could have followed the little dirt road to the main road. Now I have no clue as to how to get to the SUV."

"It's really hard to have a sense of direction in these wooded areas," she confessed.

Remington's adrenaline had slowed down, and now he was beginning to feel the pain in his leg. Jeannine could tell that he was in agony, but they had no pain relievers and there was no telling when he would get to a doctor. She worried about him.

*****

Night had fallen again, and Remington and Jeannine had walked a long time, but now it was getting harder to see. Added to that, they had no idea in which direction they were going. Just then, Jeannine spotted a cave at the bottom of a mountain and asked uncertainly, "Do you think we should go inside?"

Without answering, Remington cautiously entered and Jeannine followed close behind. The cave was about six feet, eight inches high, which gave Remington about four inches of clearance without bending down. A few pieces of firewood lay half-burned in a corner. It looked as though the cave had been used the previous winter.

"This looks like a good place to camp," Remington announced.

"I don't think we should sleep in here," Jeannine protested. She didn't wish to take any chances, and Remington didn't object to her fears. So they made up a sleeping area behind a rock just outside and to the side of the cave entrance.

The night was musical, with the busy sounds of night bugs and small animals. Jeannine sat up and tilted her head as far back as she could and focused on the billions of stars that lit the sky. "Look at all those stars staring back at us," she said as she cast her eye in Remington's direction. "What do you think they're saying to us, Remington?"

"I think, if we could hear them speak, they would say to us, 'Don't give up.'"

Jeannine sighed and cast her eyes back to the earth and looked all around. Then she whispered, "Someone could be watching us right now. Do you really think we'll ever get back alive?" She mentally cringed at the thought.

"Yes, we will," he said firmly. "We've got to think positive and work together, Jeannine. Fear will cripple you. Just think of the good things, things that make you feel good. If you become worried, it'll drain you of your energy, and since we don't have that much to eat, we need to conserve our energy the best way that we can."

"I'm scared, and I can't help it," she confessed. "We're stuck in the middle of the woods, and who knows what'll happen to us?"

"Jeannine, you're not listening. Now, think positive! We'll be just fine, I promise." He pulled the jar of peanut butter from his knapsack and opened it and made them each a peanut butter sandwich, but she refused to eat.

"I'm not hungry. Save it for breakfast," she said with heaviness.

The day burst forth with the sun's rays emanating from the east, and a squirrel that scurried past them in the nearby bushes awakened them. Jeannine stretched and yawned. The night seemed short because they had slept like babies, which surprised her. She whispered, "We're alive!"

"Of course we are," said Remington sleepily.

A few minutes later, they had gathered their things and were ready to move on. "The sunrise is breathtaking!" said Jeannine softly as she threw her backpack over her shoulders. She wished she had her camera to capture its beauty. For a short time, they had totally forgotten about their plight and were enjoying being drawn into the beauty that surrounded them. "Moments like this ease the pain of our everyday lives," she confessed.

They followed the trail that ran before them, hoping it would lead them somewhere.

"I don't think I can take another step," complained Jeannine as she sat on the ground and stared into the sky, which shone brilliantly with the afternoon sun. She watched as energetic birds flew back and forth, and she wished that she were among them.

"If I had wings like a dove, I'd fly away."

"To where?"

"Jamaica, of course."

"Good choice. I hope to go to Jamaica someday. I've heard so much about it. What is Jamaica like?"

Jeannine took a deep breath and closed her eyes. A faint smile lit up her face, and she said, "Paradise!" She paused, smiled, and went on, "Well, it's not perfect, but there are a lot of beauties about Jamaica that keep the tourists flooding in."

She rambled on for a while before she realized she might have been talking to herself. "Remington?" she asked.

"Uh…yeah? Oh, I'm sorry, I must have dozed off."

"Well, you'll have to see it for yourself to believe it, anyways. Maybe one day you'll get the opportunity."

Shifting her gaze back to the sky, she noticed patches of fluffy white clouds resting just below its rich blue color. They looked so soft and cuddly. *I wish I could cuddle on one of them,* she thought.

They rested for a while until Jeannine felt she was ready to move on. The trail they had taken ran into another one that then took them into a meadow. Jeannine couldn't help but be fascinated by its beauty. As they continued to walk, they came upon another stream of water. An apple tree sat about four yards from the stream's edge, and they filled their backpacks with as many apples as would fit and, after drinking their fill of water, topped off their water bottles.

As they continued on their journey, it wasn't long before they came to the foot of a mountain. As they climbed up its rugged side, they witnessed the beauty of the valley below.

"What a sunset! It looks like a painted picture from here," said Remington. The sun's rays seemed to be cast in every direction.

"Wow!" exclaimed Jeannine. "What a beautiful sight! Nature is really awesome!"

They continued hiking and resting periodically until they came to a freshwater lake, where they saw birds, raccoons, and rabbits. Also, they encountered a great number of wildlife species that they'd never seen before.

"Nature sure knows how to take care of its own," commented Remington.

Jeannine stopped and placed her hands on her hip, asking, "Do you know in what direction we're walking?"

"Not a clue. We'll wind up somewhere as usual." Remington sighed.

"We should have at least made some kind of progress by now," she fretted.

They walked until their feet hurt, and Remington said, "I think we should find a place to camp for the night." His leg seemed to be doing better.

They heard a rustling noise just to the right of them. They looked at each other, and Jeannine huddled closer to Remington, a panicked look on her face. "Did you hear that?" she whispered.

He nodded and placed his finger on his lips to signal silence. He pulled her down to the ground, and they stayed in a stooped position for a while. "It probably was a small animal, but get ready to run," he whispered a warning in her ear. Just then, a shot was fired, and instantly he threw his hand over Jeannine's mouth. It had sounded pretty close, but they stayed crouched to the ground in a patch of bushes.

"I think it came from that direction," she whispered in a quivering voice as Remington released his hand from her mouth. Again, he placed his finger over his lips and shook his head to warn her not to say another word.

After not hearing anything else for about ten minutes, he asked quietly in her ear, "Do you know how to climb a tree?" When she nodded, he gestured for her to climb the tree that was about three steps away from where they were hiding.

"Be as quiet as you can," he whispered.

Luckily, the tree had many limbs that were close to one another and she was able to climb it with ease. While she climbed, Remington hid their belongings under some bushes and then made his way up behind Jeannine.

"Keep climbing!" he whispered. "Go all the way up to the top!" Then there was another rustling that came from the nearby bushes, and they flew to the top in seconds. They covered themselves with the limbs of the tree.

"Why are you way over there, Remington?" she whispered after a few minutes of silence.

"We can't be on the same limb, or we'll go flying to the ground," he whispered back.

"Do you think you can stay up here all night?" he asked. "It's safer up here from people and animals."

"I don't know, but I'll try," she answered.

"Try to wedge yourself between limbs so that when you fall asleep, you won't fall to the ground. We're a good distance from the ground, and if we fall, we could get hurt. And that is the last thing we want right now."

Jeannine took his advice.

The sky was now black above them, and patches of stars stretched from one end of the sky to another. Remington felt a greater presence than that of human, as if there were angels all around them. "Do you believe in angels, Jeannine?" he whispered.

"I do believe that angels exist," she responded without hesitation. "I've heard stories of them helping people get out of unusual circumstances."

"If there are angels, maybe we have a couple of them here with us. What do you think?" he asked

"Maybe."

Neither one of them spoke another word after that. They were being very cautious.

When the first rays of dawn finally broke, Remington whispered, "Jeannine?"

"Yes?" she whispered back.

"It's time to move on."

"I can't move. I feel like a truck just ran over me."

"I feel sore, too, but we've got to keep moving. My leg hurts bad, but I've got to be a man and endure."

Remington climbed down first. Then Jeannine carefully descended as he stood at the bottom to help her.

They pulled their bags from their hiding place and continued their search for the main road.

Later, Jeannine said, "Remington, look at this view! Look at this scenery!" They were on top of another mountain overlooking a valley. They could see more valleys and hills and rocks that stood before them.

When a helicopter appeared suddenly and flew overhead, Remington grabbed an orange T-shirt from his backpack and waved it frantically. Their hearts sank as it disappeared behind a mountain.

Was that a rescue helicopter that didn't see them? Had Charles and Jealissa made it out and notified the police, who, in turn, had sent out a search party for them? Maybe they would circle back and would find them before the day was done. Remington sighed and tried not to show his frustration.

They waited in the open in the hopes that the helicopter would return, but to their disappointment, it didn't.

"We've got to keep moving," said Remington.

They did, and it wasn't long before they stumbled upon a cabin. The old cabin was almost invisible, as it was almost hidden under wild plants that ran up and down its structure.

Carefully, they took precautions and tried the door. It was locked. They took the chance and knocked. There was no response, so they walked around to the back and scoped out the surrounding area.

"No one's here. Let's keep moving," Remington eventually said. "Which way should we go?"

"Let's go in the direction of the sun. That's east, and we did drive west to the cabin. Maybe we'll find the main road this way," Jeannine suggested.

The hill was steep, and they perspired, were hungry, and became exhausted and somewhat dehydrated.

"I know we have to save our water, but I really do need to drink. We might find a stream somewhere," said Jeannine wearily. "Have just a little to drink, Remington," she coaxed.

"No, I think I'll wait a little longer. We have no idea how much longer we will be in the woods," said Remington.

Jeannine looked at him, and he said, "I'm sorry. I didn't mean to discourage you. I just wanted to be realistic. Actually, I'm fine. You go ahead and drink some. If we find a stream, we'll drink our fill and top off our bottles."

"I don't want you to pass out. It seems as if it's going to be a very hot day," Jeannine said.

"Don't worry, Jen." She gulped down the water like a dry ground soaking in the rain.

After a while, they saw some footprints, and Remington pointed at the huge prints in the dirt, saying, "These footprints look like the ones we saw at our cabin."

No sooner had he said this and they were going to change direction away from the footprints than two men jumped out at them and demanded that they stop.

Instead, their reflexes took charge and they ran like lightning bolts in separate directions. Overcome by fear, they were driven by impulses to seek safety, but unfortunately, they went away from each other. They didn't have time to plan on what route to take; their feet had just started moving as fast as they could.

Jeannine ran until she came to a cliff. When she looked over and saw a great body of water, without hesitation she jumped over the cliff and into the heavy stream. She was carried for a while by the rough water before she was able to gain control of her body, and she grabbed ahold of a log and held on for dear life. Even though she could swim, she was tired, and it made it hard for her to maneuver her body. But she managed to muster up all her strength and made her way to shore.

She lay breathlessly on the bank. Exhaustion was an understatement, and she had nothing but the wet clothes on her back. Then she thought, *Remington!* She was scared, alone again, and the thought terrified her. She wondered if he was all right.

Then her thoughts turned to the two men who had startled them. She wondered, *Why didn't they shoot us? I don't remember hearing a shot unless I was too scared to hear anything.*

Her thoughts then turned to whoever had shot Remington in the leg, but she wasn't sure if he was one of the men that had just ordered them not to move. Once she had heard what was said, she didn't look behind, just took off and ran away.

Who were these men, and what did they want? Have they been after them, or were they just trying to scare them?

Looking up into the shining blue skies, she thought, *Where is God when I need him?*

She had prayed, but it hadn't seemed to work for her because she was still in the woods, lost, lonely, scared, and in great danger. It had been days of sheer horror for her.

"Mama, Dad, help me, please!" She vowed never to go camping again. Her life seemed to be in turmoil. "Why me?" she sobbed.

Jeannine had no idea how far away she was from the original cabin. Not that she would even dare go back there. Taking off her boots, she wrung the water out of her socks, then slipped them back on and started walking again.

When she heard a noise, she immediately hustled up a tree and pulled two branches toward her and covered herself with them. She waited, and soon a deer hopped by. Relieved, she climbed down slowly, still being cautious.

Wearily, she walked on. A patch of wild berries was like precious gold, and she buried her face in a handful of them. Suddenly, something overshadowed her, and before she could turn around to see what it was, a pair of hands grabbed her and tossed her to the ground. She struggled and screamed with all her might.

"Shut up! You're the little trouble we've been looking for all this time." She stared into the faces of the two men she had seen at the cabin. She'd never seen them before that day at the cabin.

"I think you have the wrong person," she quaked.

"You're Ms. Jeannine Shrouder, aren't you? You sure fit the description well."

Her eyes widened. "How did you know my name?"

She was about to die, and she knew it. One of them pulled out a picture from his breast pocket and held it up to her face. "Yep, it's her."

She gasped. Who were these men, and how did they get her picture?

"O God, please help me!" she cried.

"I said shut up! God isn't going to help you. Let me see God save you from my clutches," grunted the one who held her with his bare hands.

They tied her hands together with a coarse rope that bruised her delicate skin, then shoved her through the woods and back to the cabin that she and Remington had recently checked out.

"We've been waiting for this moment," gloated the one with a four-inch scar on his right cheek. He puffed on a cigar, and the smoke quickly disappeared into the air.

They seemed to know a lot about her, but she had no idea who they were.

When they opened the door, they shoved her onto the hard floor. "Ouch!" she cried in pain.

"Shut up!" yelled the scar-faced one. "Your little friend Brendan had something of ours, some disks that belong to us. If you don't hand them over, we're going to do to you what we did to him. I'm glad we finally found you. Now we can get a good look at the face that saw us when we killed that pest!"

She gasped and raised her head and looked at them. *That voice. It had sounded awfully familiar, and now I know why. I heard that unique voice the night one of the men killed Brendan!*

Scarface talked as if he had gravel in his throat and nodded with a grin. "Yes, we were the ones you saw kill Brendan Clark, and we've been looking for you."

"You're not very smart," added the other man. "Now, before we do to you what we've done to your boyfriend, we would like for you to cooperate and give us our disks, unless you want to die real soon."

She gulped, and her eyes widened, because she was puzzled about how they got her picture and how they knew her full name and that she'd gone camping. "Murderers!" she yelled.

"You've got a lot of mouth for a little girl," said Scarface's accomplice. He beckoned to Scarface, who then reached down and yanked her up.

"How'd you know I was the one who saw you? You only saw my back when I was running in the dark."

"We've got connections, little girl. A friend of ours pointed you out. Then you disappeared on us, but then we found out your plans, and voila, here we are!"

Who could have told them? she wondered.

Tears rolled down her face, because she was sure they were going to take her life. *They had killed Brendan in cold blood, so obviously they placed no value on human life. Oh, Lord Jesus, if You will spare my life and bring me home safe, I will serve You for the rest of my life,* she vowed silently.

She was about to tell them she had no clue about any disks that Brendan might have had, but then she had second thoughts and said to the men, “If you get the disks, will you swear not to hurt me or my family?”

“Sure.” They laughed hard. “Where are they?”

“Back in Milolta.” She ignored their jubilation.

“You know where they are?” Scarface asked excitedly. She nodded.

“Tie her up with this, Cooper.”

She raised her head and looked at them keenly. She remembered hearing one of them use that name the night of the murder.

“You idiot, what’d you say my name for?”

Scarface blushed with embarrassment and tossed the rope to Cooper. They gagged and tied her to a wooden table in the middle of the room and then went outside. They locked the door behind them. Then a few minutes later, they were back inside.

They moved a heavy chest and opened a door that was hidden behind it. Then they brought her through the door and into a room. It was dark, and she couldn’t see anything. Neither of the men spoke as they led her to a corner of the room, where they tied her feet to something wooden.

The noise from the night bugs was the only sound she heard, and she wondered if the men were still there or if they’d left. She hadn’t heard them leave, but who knew? They were sneaky men, and anything was possible with them.

She guessed it to be after midnight. The words of an old song kept running through her head. *Count your blessings, name them one by one, and it will surprise you what the Lord has done…*

So she counted, and she was surely surprised. She was surprised also that she had become positive through all of what had happened late in her life.

After all the days that she’d been in the wilderness, she was still alive and physically well. She prayed again and felt a surge of peace, although there seemed to be no hope. She felt as if a power greater than hers was there to assure her that everything was going to be all right.

Then she prayed a prayer of thanksgiving, and immediately her attention was shifted to a shuffling noise she heard coming from the corner of the room. Something was in the room with her. A snake? She held her breath and stayed still, hoping she wouldn't attract it to her. If bitten, then it would be over for her.

Dawn finally arrived, and she hadn't slept a wink. Then, something in the corner of the room caught her eye. She turned her head and stared in shock at a figure lying on the floor. *Another victim*? she wondered. She gave an all-around look to see if she had more than one person for company and saw another figure lying in a fetal position at the other end of the room.

She raised her hands to her mouth and removed the gag.

"Hello?" she called in a whisper. The first figure stirred and raised itself up and looked toward her. Jeannine's mouth dropped in complete shock. A small amount of light streamed through the tiny window, and Jealissa rubbed her eyes as if to clear her vision.

"Jeannine?" she asked questioningly.

"Yes, yes," replied Jeannine with overwhelming joy. "What happened? What are you doing here? Are you all right?"

"I'm all right. How're you, Jeannine?" Jealissa was equally excited about the reunion.

"Yes. I'm fine."

"We were worried sick about you. We went to get help, only to find that every wire in the SUV had been cut. Then we found this cabin and asked for help, but the two men kidnapped us and dragged us here, as you can see. After they left, we screamed for help, hoping someone would just happen to pass by. So they drugged us."

Just then, Charles moaned and Jeannine said, "Charles? It's me, Jeannine."

Slowly he opened his eyes, looked at Jeannine and Jealissa, and then hollered in fear.

"Charles, are you all right?" asked his sister. "I think it must be the drugs they gave him," she said to Jeannine.

Charles shook his head violently and then looked again at the girls and asked incredulously, "Jeannine! When did you get here?"

She told them about the morning she left for a walk and didn't return and all the experiences that she and Remington had encountered and about the men that brought her there.

"I'm sorry, Jeannine. We were just trying to help, but I think we've made matters worse," Jealissa said.

"Don't blame yourselves. You never know why things happen the way they do. I hope Remington is okay," she said as she changed the subject.

"So those men are Brendan's murderers," said Charles. "Did you recognize them the first time that you saw them?"

"No, but they knew me, my full name and all. They even had a picture of me. It was after they told me who they were that I recognized the voice of the one with the scar on his face. The reason they're here is to find me. What I can't figure out is how they got all that information about me. It sure is a puzzle, because I don't know them from anywhere. Obviously, someone informed them, but who? There is no obvious explanation as to how total strangers could know so much about me."

After they talked for what seemed like hours, Jealissa wearily asked, "What do we do now?"

Then Jeannine remembered the coin she'd found back at their cabin, and a light bulb went off in her head. Reaching into her pocket, she pulled it out, but it fell and rolled to the unoccupied corner of the room.

"Oh, man!" she said in disappointment. "I was going to try to cut my rope with it." Then her attention shifted to the men's whereabouts, and she wondered what their plans were and when they would be back to carry out those plans. Would they be back, or would they just leave them there to die?

"Remington is very smart," Jeannine said after a long pause. "I could bet you anything that he's all right. I believe someone is going to find us, and someday we'll look back on this day and laugh."

Jealissa could hardly contain her pessimism. "Remington could be in as much trouble as we are. We've got to try somehow to get out of here. We're all tied up and can't get to one another, so we can't lose ourselves."

"The only thing left for us to do is to pray to God for a miracle," said Jeannine.

"Well, if there is a God, I don't think He's going to help us!"

Jeannine sat up abruptly, her eyes widened with new hope, and she totally ignored Jealissa's pessimism. "Hey, guys, while they were bringing me in here, I secretly pulled some of my beads out of my braids and dropped them on the trail. I also dropped some in the cabin before they brought me in this room. If Remington comes looking for us, he'll know that those beads are mine."

"And if he doesn't come this way?" asked Jealissa.

Charles had been in deep thought and didn't hear much of what the girls were saying because he was trying to come up with a plan to escape. But he couldn't think of any, since he was helplessly tied to a wooden bench.

Jeannine hoped that Remington would come to the cabin again but feared he might not pass that way again.

It had been about nine hours since they'd been separated, and Jeannine was worried sick about him. She hoped fervently that he was all right and would be able to come to their rescue.

Just then, a crackling-type noise was heard from outside, disturbing their thoughts.

"They're back. Those awful men have come back for us," Jealissa whispered and began to tremble. They were all afraid for their lives.

One set of feet came into the cabin and moved hurriedly back and forth. *Someone's here, but who?* they all were wondering. *Maybe one of them has come back for something important.*

It was obvious that whoever it was was searching frantically for something. The three froze in fear, because if it was one of the men, there was no telling what he would do. After all, they *were* cold-blooded murderers, which meant they were capable of killing just for the thrill of it.

Jeannine begged God to help them. Suddenly, the pair of feet hurried out the door. They looked at one another in puzzlement, then waited silently to see what would happen next. But there was no sound of any movement for hours.

*****

Somewhere in the woods, Remington was diligently searching for Jeannine. He'd lost her once, and now he'd lost her again. Something told him he might never see her again, and he shuddered. Once, they had been lucky to find each other. Would luck be on their side again?

He grimaced as he pulled back shrubs and thickets and searched mountains and valleys in vain. Behind huge rocks and in caves, he also looked, but there was no sign of her. And calling her name was out of the question, lest he give himself away to the enemy.

When he checked out another cave that seemed to be west of the one that he and Jeannine had found, six baby rabbits scurried out.

"I won't bother you. Just looking for someone who means a lot to me." He blushed at the thought; he'd never told anyone about how he felt about her.

There was no lead to her whereabouts, nothing that could bring him to her. Discouraged, he wondered where she was and if she had been caught. He feared the worst, that he might not be lucky and find her in the nick of time again.

He hadn't gotten a good look at the men and so wouldn't be able to give a description of them if he were asked. He continued his search for Jeannine even though his body ached with fatigue and intense pain from the gunshot wound on his leg. It had been healing pretty well until he had poked it while searching through a thicket. He had ripped off the bottom of the T-shirt he was wearing and bandaged it up. He limped on in spite of the throbbing and continued to earnestly search for his Jeannine.

*****

The floor squeaked loudly. "Quick, put your gag back on," whispered Jealissa. Jeannine shoved the gag back in her mouth. The men opened the door so hard it flew open and banged against the wooden wall.

"If we don't get those disks by tomorrow, none of you will live to see the light of another day!" threatened Cooper.

Jeannine had thought it odd they'd left without even asking her to tell them exactly where the disks were located. She couldn't help wonder, *Where have those two been all this time? And why, all of a sudden, had they lost patience and become extremely furious?*

"You'd better tell us where those disks are! If you lie to us and we have to come back here without them, you're all dead!" said Scarface with disgust. "You hear me? DEAD!"

The trio's hearts seemed to melt with fear. Charles felt so helpless. There he was, the man in the midst of two ladies, and he couldn't even protect himself, let alone them. A surge of anger enveloped him, and he determined, *We* will *get out alive, if it's the last thing I do!*

"Where are the disks? All of them!" Scarface asked impatiently, yanking the gag from her mouth.

I've gotta think, thought Jeannine. She had no clue but knew she had to come up with something.

"Tell us, I said, where the disks are!" barked Cooper.

"They're at his grandmother's house. They're in a shoebox in the basement," Jeannine said straight away, the words flying out of her mouth. One second, she was trying to figure out what to tell them, and the next she found her lips moving and words just falling out.

"Are you lying to us?" asked Scarface as he bent over and stared her straight in the face. The stench of his awful cigar breath caused her to almost gag.

She turned her head to the side and said, "Brendan gave them to me and asked me to hide them there. He told me not to tell anyone about them. Not even his mother."

"Nobody knew he had them?" asked Cooper.

"Nobody. You killed him before he got a chance to figure out what to do with them," Jeannine explained.

Suddenly, the men's brows relaxed. They weren't in as much trouble as they'd thought.

"How do you plan on getting them?" she asked.

"Don't worry about that. Just tell us where she lives," Cooper said.

"Ah, 32 Lennox Street," she said, looking straight at them with her big brown eyes. She hoped they would believe her.

Scarface grinned, showing all his teeth, and Cooper said with a tight face, “They better be there.”

*****

The men wasted no time hurrying back to Milolta in order to retrieve the disks that they’d been trying so hard to recover. But they were due for a big disappointment. When they got to 32 Lennox Street, it was not a house but a vacant lot.

A neighbor saw them staring at the vacant lot and volunteered, “The city tore the house down that used to be here. It was in bad shape.”

The two furious men were prevented from returning immediately to the cabin by a pretty horrible storm.

During the storm, Jealissa, Jeannine, and Charles were all terrified. The wind and rain beat strongly against the cabin, and inside was pitch-black. They all feared the cabin would collapse, and it was so frustrating and fearful to know that there was absolutely nothing they could do to save themselves. Jeannine tried again to loosen her rope, but it wouldn’t budge. For days, they had to stand the horrifying ordeal of the storm and endure it in total darkness without food or water.

*****

Ben’s recovery was gradual. He had gotten comfortable living with his family even though he couldn’t remember much of anything. Periodically, something of his past would vaguely flash in his mind and he’d get excited, but then his excitement would diminish because it would amount to nothing but a vague flashback.

Ida had told him how much he used to like gardening, and she’d asked him to plant some tomatoes. But he didn’t remember a day in his life when he’d gardened. Picking up the fork, he dug up the ground in the backyard, jabbing the fork into the hard ground and then turning over the soil.

Suddenly, his eyes caught sight of a marble that glistened like a diamond in the sunlight. The sight of it put him in a daze and his face looked as if he had fallen into a trancelike state as he just stared at the glistening marble. His eyes stayed focused as if drawn into a captivating movie. Then suddenly, his expression changed, as if he were witnessing scenes that provoked different moods.

He saw a nine-year-old boy bending over and picking up the marble. The boy's bright brown eyes were dazzling as he held the precious marble in his hand and was just staring at it before he gave a broad grin. His soft, tender skin looked smooth and delicate in the warm sunlight.

Luscious trees moved softly in the gentle eastern breeze. Huge rocks that gave a sense of power, strength, and protection surrounded him. Vibrant birds and colorful butterflies brought the atmosphere alive, causing Ben's backyard to look like an animated color cartoon.

Ben? a voice called in his head.

"I know him," he whispered as he tried hard not to lose this precious moment. "Benjamin Thomas Shrouder," he whispered almost hypnotically.

Determinedly, Ben kept his focus on that little boy. The boy turned to search for the voice that had spoken his name. A woman stood at the entrance of the door.

"I found another one, Mama," he said with glee as he held up the marble between his thumb and index fingers.

Playing with marbles had been one of Ben's favorite hobbies. He'd flicked marbles at school and in his neighborhood, winning everyone else's prized marbles by the bagful. He was the best and had seldom lost. Now, he stared at the marble in the palm of his hand and repeated his name over and over. "Benjamin Thomas Shrouder. That's my name, and I know it!"

As Ben stood in the garden of the home he'd called his own, vivid, colorful pictures of his entire life flooded his memory, and he began to weep. He held up the marble in his hand and stared solemnly at it through tear-filled eyes.

Ben dropped the fork and sat down on the ground. His mind flashed from one scene to another. Suddenly, he stood to his feet and wiped his eyes with the palm of his hand. A warm smile softened his facial muscles as he stared in awe at an eighteen-year-old girl standing before him. She was the prettiest girl he'd ever seen. "Ida," he whispered in an even softer tone. "Ida Jean Charette."

His excitement bubbled, and a burst of renewed energy for life saturated his being. He turned and looked at the house that he and Ida had carefully chosen. With chest sticking out and head raised high, he mounted the steps with pride. He knew who he was, and he was proud to be Benjamin Thomas Shrouder.

He pulled up the blinds and opened all the windows in the house. Fresh, warm air blending with vibrant reggae music brought life and ecstasy into the house. Next, he went directly to the cabinet where Ida kept all the family albums, and page after page he studied each picture. Tears of joy streamed down his face.

He heard Ida's car pulling up into the driveway, and quickly he replaced the albums and lowered the volume on the stereo. His precious Ida was home, and he couldn't wait to see her again for the first time.

He stood to his feet and watched the door to see when she would open it and her face would fill his vision. As Ida opened the door, Ben's dark-brown eyes fell on her face, and his heart palpitated. *My Ida,* he thought. *How could I ever forget that face?*

She was in her usual cheery mood, as if all was well. "Hello, Ben. How was your day today?"

"Fine, Ida," he returned the greeting. Ida didn't notice anything, because he wasn't quite sure how he wanted to reveal to her what had happened to him earlier. He'd kept his distance with the family, because to him they were strangers and he felt as though he was intruding by staying in their house. But Ida had been very patient and understanding. She respected his desire for space.

When she ventured into the kitchen for a cold drink, Ben trailed behind. "I hope your day was better than mine," she said as she poured some ginger ale soda. He smiled, and she noticed it. It was a different smile.

"I suppose it was," she said and returned the smile. She picked up the bottle of soda and turned to put it in the refrigerator, but then Benjamin Thomas Shrouder said something that caused her to freeze.

"Tibbits."

Slowly turning around, she looked him in the face and stuttered, "W-what did you say?"

"Tibbits," he repeated with a broad grin. Her eyes widened.

"What do you mean by that?" she asked. Without a word, he walked over to her and took her by the hand. She looked at their locked hands, then at his face. Now she noticed the glow on his face. He wasn't the same Ben she'd left that morning.

He walked her over to the sofa and sat down with her. "Isn't that the name of our baby girl that she'd acquired in the country when she was just a little girl, seven years old, to be exact?"

Ida was speechless. They hadn't called Jeannine by her nickname since she was about thirteen years old. Of all the ways they'd tried to jog his memory, the name Tibbits never came up.

"Who told you that?" she asked, doubting he would remember the incident.

Gently he cupped her hand into his and looked her in the eyes. "Ida," he began, "something strange happened today." He said this in an almost-worshipping tone. "I was in the garden, turning over the soil, when a marble popped to the surface. Something about it triggered something in me. It brought me back to when I was a little boy and had a fascination for marbles. From then, my mind began to play back scenes of different stages in my life. Just like that, out of the clear blue, my life came back to me and I think it's here to stay. I am now the happiest man in the world! I am happier than I've ever been. I now appreciate life even more. My Ida, I love you so much!" he said and embraced her.

"Ben, oh, Ben," she murmured and began to weep. Every day Ida had dreamed about her Ben returning to her, and indeed her dream had now come true. Was there such a thing as dreams turning into reality? The Shrouders had defied nature. They believed that God loved the humans that He'd created, had pitied them, and had granted them their request and had worked a miracle that only He could have done.

Ida cherished every moment as she began life anew with her husband. She praised the God whom Mildred spoke so highly about. It was none other than Him who'd healed her husband. If she had any doubt about the power of God before, her husband's full recovery had eradicated it.

Once having his life back, Ben saw everything through a new set of eyes. He had a respect for everything, from the seemingly insignificant to the highly prized. Then going back to work brought on an even greater feeling of self-worth. He was independent! He was competent!

Things were going great so far. He hadn't lapsed back into the amnesia, which was a possibility. *I'm here to stay,* he thought.

The sun wasn't shining his first day back to work, but he himself was beaming with a warm feeling of renewed love for life. He shuffled through his desk and touched everything as if they had some magical power from which he sought an eternal strength.

Chapter 17

Revelation

The sliding doors opened slowly, and as the men walked through, they rolled up their sleeves, exposing tattoos on their right arms. The tattoo of a jagged-edged coin with a red dragon matched perfectly the coin Jeannine had found.

The gray-haired man behind the desk smiled, his glossy eyes twinkling as he nodded in confirmation.

Straight ahead and down the long and narrow hallway, the two men's feet disturbed the silence with echoes that carried to the other end of the hall. They knocked on the door with the heavy gold plate that read, "Edward Coons."

"Come in," a voice invited. As they entered the room, Ed whirled around in his chair behind his mahogany desk. Two pens in a holder, a sheet of paper, and a desk calendar were all that was on the desk. There were no family pictures of any kind. With both hands resting on the desk, he stared expectantly back and forth between the two men before grunting, "Yes?"

"We didn't find the disks," Cooper mumbled.

Without a word, Ed rose from his desk. His tall slender body gracefully glided toward the window, where he stared through the blinds, scanning the area subconsciously. His fist pounded in his palm, and his teeth clenched as he angrily asked, "What do you mean?"

But the two men just stood in silence and trembled. "That would mean a disaster if those disks were to get into the wrong hands!" he shouted. Then more calmly he said, "The next time that you come back, you'd better have all the disks!"

Scarface felt a surge of boldness and opened his mouth. "Your daughter might know something about the disks. She was very close to him."

Ed didn't answer. Scarface assumed the man hadn't heard him but didn't venture to repeat his statement.

As if he had been suddenly snapped back to the present, Ed hollered, "Get out and find those disks!"

The two men scrambled to the door and made their way out of the building. They wiped beads of sweat from their foreheads as they left.

Edward Coons slumped down into his chair and heaved a weary sigh. Then he flipped open his briefcase and withdrew a disk with a purple circular tab at the bottom right. Slipping it into his A drive on his computer, he then placed his hand on the mouse.

At first, he just stared at his hand as if it were leprous. *Password,* it requested as he clicked on the icon for the floppy disk. He punched in six digits, and the word *accepted* flashed across the screen. He double-clicked on folder *Y*. His eyes scanned rapidly as he scrolled through the files and thought, *How did that no-good boy get those disks? If I don't find them, I will wipe out everyone that belongs to him, if it's the last thing I do! Nobody crosses my path and gets away unscathed!*

Then picking up the phone, he dialed a number. "A31," he said to the person who answered the phone. There was a pause, and then he was connected.

"Code 21 VRS," he said slowly to the third party. Then he replaced the receiver on the hook and waited. In a few minutes, the fax machine in the corner signaled that a fax was being received. Getting out of his chair, he walked over and picked up a sheet of paper. It read thus: *9 PM Z-19*. He placed the paper in his briefcase and closed it. The intercom buzzed on his desk.

"Yes," he said almost peacefully.

"I have Memphis on the line, and he wants to meet with you tonight."

"I can't. I have an appointment. Tell him I'll call him."

Later, when he left his office, the moon was out, and he glanced at his watch and noticed it was 8:35 p.m., enough time to get to his appointment without undue rush.

The moon also shone brilliantly over the suburb of Milolta, almost outdoing the scattering of stars over the otherwise-black sky. Ed waited impatiently. He placed his left hand inside his suit jacket and adjusted the shotgun. Then he folded his arms and leaned back against the post, trying hard to be patient.

"Excuse me, do you know what time it is?" A voice from behind startled him. He looked at the beautiful young woman who had broken his concentration.

"Yes." He cleared his throat and smiled. "Yes," he repeated and stared into her face.

She gave him a shy look. "What time is it, please?" she asked again with a smile.

"Oh, I'm sorry, forgive me for staring. It's 9:35."

She thanked him and walked away.

It was on the tip of his tongue to compliment her on her beauty when a midsize car pulled up in front of him and three men got out. One of them pulled out a coin from his pocket and held it up in the moonlight as if to inspect it. Ed knew that it was his signal that those were the men for whom he'd been waiting. He walked over to the man who'd displayed the coin and showed him a similar one.

Then Ed handed him a burgundy briefcase, and he, in turn, was handed a large yellow envelope. "Six hundred and fifty thousand," Ed said as the man reached out and took it. The man just nodded in response.

Ed pulled out a sheet of paper from the envelope and glanced at it quickly. He smiled as he noted several columns of numbers on each page.

With his transaction completed, Ed drove down the dark streets of Milolta and found his thoughts shifting to Brendan's mother. *What if the disks are at her house? He could have hidden them there when he found out that I was on to him.* Ed didn't know exactly where she lived but knew he would have to find out somehow.

He glanced at his locked briefcase and beamed, knowing the envelope was in it. He was like a child with a new toy and couldn't wait to get to his computer so he could put the code numbers to the test.

At the warehouse, he locked himself in his office. On the piece of paper were listed thirty jewelry stores, and next to each one were their address, telephone number, and the hacker's codes. At the bottom of the list were step-by-step instructions on how to enter the stores' computer systems.

He tried the first store at the top of the list, R&S Jewelry.

"It really works! Yes! Yes!" Ed excitedly exclaimed as he continued to scroll through the files until he'd located the order files.

"Diamonds, pearls, and gold were just ordered three days ago. Hope they haven't delivered yet," he mumbled to himself.

He accessed the file for Proficient Parcel Delivery. Alt+Tab switched him back to R&S Jewelry, where he located the tracking number and tabbed back to the Proficient Parcel Delivery screen.

"Excellent!" he declared. "It's here and ready to be delivered tomorrow." With his ingenuity, Ed deleted R&J's file from the Proficient Parcel Delivery system. "No record of you, baby!" he said jubilantly.

He picked up the phone and dialed a number. It rang about five times before a groggy voice answered.

"Gizmo!" he said excitedly into the receiver.

"Who is calling me at two in the morning?"

"It's me, Ed. Wake up! This is important! Now, listen closely. You have a package there at your job for R&S Jewelry, and it's scheduled to be delivered tomorrow. I've deleted it from your system, so when you go in tomorrow to do your delivery run, first thing, drop it off at the warehouse. Don't have it in the truck all day."

"Don't worry, I'll take care of you. They'll never find out. It'll only be a mystery to them. I've got you covered, man. You gonna take care of me real good, right?"

"You bet!" Ed promised.

After hanging up with Gizmo, Ed tried all thirty stores, but only five of them had a delivery scheduled for that week. R&S was the only one that used PPD service, and Ed didn't have a guy at the other delivery companies. *But that's cool. I'll just keep checking,* he told himself. *Next time they'll use PPD's service.*

Three days later, R&S Jewelry called to check on their order. The manager was informed by customer service that they'd sent out the package the week previously by Proficient Parcel Delivery.

"Well, we haven't received it yet, but we'll call PPD and have them track it down."

PPD informed the manager that there was no record of the parcel. "It keeps saying 'Tracking number not found.' You need to call back to the place where you ordered it and let them know we never got the package, ma'am."

Ed had tried to keep his stealing transactions far apart. He hoped they would never find out and treat the problem as an "ordinary" lost package.

*****

Mrs. Clark had tried to get her life back in order after Brendan's death, but it wasn't easy. She tried to hold herself together and knew she wouldn't be able to deal with any more problems right now. Still, she had no idea who Brendan's enemies were yet never felt that she, personally, was in any kind of danger.

In any case, she longed for heaven and felt she was ready to go because all that had mattered was now gone. Brendan had given her hope and had been what had kept her going. But now that he was gone, she didn't see any reason to go on.

As she thought these thoughts, tears welled up in her eyes and everything looked distorted. She shut them tight and spilled the tears in her lap. Then she rose to her feet and walked over to the window and mused, *Time seems to be standing still. Nothing is happening. There is stillness in my house that seems to mimic the outside world. There are no butterflies or birds or squirrels or any sign of life in view. Even the trees are very still.*

She turned away and almost subconsciously dusted a piece of furniture. Then she looked around to scope out what she could do next. But basically, she'd done everything that needed to be done. *I have to find something else to do, or I'm just going to go crazy from too much thinking,* she told herself.

Taking a pen and paper, she jotted down a short list of things she could do. It wasn't long, and she was running low on ideas. *Well, at lease I haven't touched the basement and the attic yet. I could get started working on them. Then by the time I'm done, I'm sure I'll have come up with new things to do,* she thought.

The basement was where she had decided to start, and by the close of the day, she was done with her list. Seeing that night was falling, she felt she had accomplished something and realized she was both tired and glad. She decided, *Now, after eating something, I'll go to bed, and for a few hours, I'll be able to forget about my troubles until the morning, when I will awaken and my mind will recall my plight.*

She didn't eat much because she still didn't have any appetite, but she ate something just to keep herself from starving. A cup of coffee, a slice of toast with grape jelly was all she managed to get down for her supper.

When finished, she rose from the table and walked over to the sink, where she placed her plate, cup, spoon, and butter knife. They were the only items in the huge sink. Out of habit, she turned on the water, and as it ran aimlessly and noisily down the drain, she stood for what seemed to be ages with the sponge in her hand, lost in thought. She might have been standing there for an hour, or maybe two minutes—she couldn't tell. Coming back to the present, she turned off the water and walked away, planning to go to bed. Then she suddenly remembered she hadn't washed the dishes. Sighing, she picked up the sponge and tried again to do what she'd intended to do in the first place.

As she washed the few items in the sink, she tried to calculate her age on her fingers but was surprised she couldn't remember exactly how old she was. "You're too young to be forgetting things," she scolded herself in an almost-quivering voice, a voice that didn't sound like hers. "Another thing, I haven't talked out loud for a long time. My, I have almost forgotten what my voice sounded like."

Finished in the kitchen, she turned off the faucet, wiped down the counter again, then dried her hands in her apron. On the way to her bedroom, she momentarily cast her eyes on a picture on the wall: Brendan. She smiled and, trying to console herself before crying a bottle of tears, thought, *He's in heaven. I don't want to cry anymore, at least not tonight.*

In her bedroom, after she had pulled back the covers, she sat on the edge of the bed, clasped her hands, and bowed her head and prayed.

Almost reluctantly, she gathered her feet into bed and slowly placed her head on the pillow and then covered her head with the covers as her body shook. *Brendan. Oh, my son…*

Then she dropped off into perfect quietness and slept.

*****

The wind gushed noisily as it pounded unrelentingly on the building. The rattling noise disturbed Cecilia as she sat nervously at his side. She was alone with a stranger who needed help. She didn't know much about first aid or helping someone who was gravely ill. Her mother had wanted her to be a nurse, but she hated that idea. She couldn't stand the sight of needles or blood. She could hardly sit still to have her blood drawn even with a nurse holding her hand for comfort. Now she was playing nurse. *What a twist of fate,* she thought.

She stared at the helpless man on the bed. In one sense, he looked strong and energetic, yet on the other hand, he looked frail and helpless. "No one is invincible," she muttered.

She cast her eyes at the door. *Stedman, where are you?* she thought. She'd been at the cabin with her husband for a few days when the storm struck. They had no idea that there was going to be a storm until it started four hours after Stedman left to get some hunting equipment. She'd suggested that they bring the young man to see a doctor, but Stedman thought all he needed was plenty of fluid and some rest and that would restore his strength. As soon as they'd brought him to the cabin within a half an hour, Stedman was out the door. She wished he hadn't left.

She stared at the vulnerable figure who'd popped into their lives. Now she was alone with him. She was anxious about the return of her husband. *What if he gets worst?* she thought. *I wouldn't know what to do!* she worried.

He was worse than they'd thought. Stedman thought he was just a hiker who'd become weary and had fainted.

"How do you explain the lump on his head?" she'd asked.

"From his fall," he had replied and shrugged his shoulders.

She watched the door, hoping that he would open it any minute, but she knew that it wasn't possible.

The weather was bad, and it was impossible for him to make it in such a rough storm. How long it would last was unknown to her. She had neither a phone nor a radio. She tried to stay calm and think positively.

He groaned and shifted a bit. She sat upright, hoping he'd wake up and she'd at least know if he was going to live or not. On the other hand, she needed company.

Her hands clasped and lay lazily in her lap. Her eyes focused on his face, as if to read his condition. Something told her he was in no hurry to wake up. She waited.

A wooden bench sat at the far end of the cabin. It was sitting over against the fireplace. It was more comfortable than the little wooden chair she sort of squeezed herself into.

She took the two cushions that were lying on the floor and placed them on the bench to cushion the hard surface. She took a blanket that was folded neatly on the metal rack and threw it over her legs. She rested her head on a cushion. She took a deep breath, closed her eyes, and before she knew it, she was fast asleep.

When she finally woke up, it was dark as midnight. She couldn't believe it. She sat still for a moment to gather her thoughts. Her watch read 10:45 p.m. She'd been sleeping for six hours. The candle was now at the bottom.

Her shadow loomed on the walls as she moved about the room. She placed another candle on the candleholder and lit it. *That'll last through the night,* she thought.

She yawned. *Oh, Stedman…*

She walked over to the only window and peered out. It was still raining, but not as hard anymore. It was pitch-black.

She turned around to see her patient sitting halfway up and staring at her. His lips curled into a smile. She returned the smile.

"How're you feeling?"

He made a circle with his index and thumb to give the okay sign.

"Think you'll stay awake this time?"

He smiled. She sat down and took him by the hand.

"The storm just won't let up. It has been raining with heavy winds for a few days now. My husband isn't back yet, and I don't know when we're going to get out of here."

His eyes stayed focus on her face. He looked at her questioningly. She read his thoughts.

"We're safe here. This is a pretty good cabin. We do have enough food to last for a while," she said, thought a moment, then continued, "but I just don't know how bad your injuries are. You should be at a hospital."

His face relaxed, as if his unanswered questions had been answered. It was as if he was waking up for the first time since they'd found him.

"What is your name?" she asked in a tender tone.

He shook his head. "I can't remember it," he replied and lowered his eyes.

"It'll come back to you. That bump on your head must have been from a hard blow. In the meanwhile, I'm going to have to give you a name." She thought for a moment. "How about Angel?"

He nodded and smiled faintly. He knew that he was far from being an angel, but he wouldn't argue with that.

"I think I'll be all right," he muttered under his breath. "You've been so kind. God bless you."

God. He remembered his Creator. He remembered praying to Him and didn't know for sure if He would answer his prayer. After all, he hadn't been a saint. But it looked like He did listen to his prayers. He was alive. He was discovered and brought into a warm place before the storm came. He closed his eyes and thought, *You did answer. Thank You.*

The wind beat vehemently against the cabin. It sounded like they were swooshed back and forth in the ocean. She tried not to worry or even to let him think that she was the least bit worried.

He was hurting again, but he really didn't want to bother this kind woman. He'd been much trouble. He was going to bear the pain like a man and endure its intensity until it left. He threw the covers over his head and shut his eyes tight. He hummed a tune in his head to keep his mind off the pain.

I refuse to feel pain. I refuse to hurt. He repeated the words over and over. He thought of a television program that he'd seen where people walked barefoot on red-hot coals and sharp nails and shoved flames of fire in their mouths or had a truck roll over them. They felt no pain. If they could do all that, then he could endure a *little* pain.

It didn't work for him, though. His mind didn't listen at all. The pain grew more intense until he couldn't bear it any longer.

She noticed his restlessness. "Are you in pain again?" He admitted it, and she gave him another capsule. He hoped that pretty soon he'd be out of the woods and into a hospital, where he could get the treatment he needed.

She fed him again. This time, it was something different—scrambled eggs, bacon, and wheat bread.

It must be morning, he thought. "Do you remember any phone number of someone that we might call for you? Once my husband gets back and brings us into the city, we could call a relative."

He remembered a number vividly, but to whom did it belong?

"Yes," he said between bites. "Ah, 555-8456." He was beginning to be company to her. He stayed awake longer. They talked about everything until he got weary and fell asleep in the middle of her sentence. She smiled.

"I think you're going to be just fine," she muttered. The rain poured hard again. She wondered when it would be over. It had been too long. She longed for the sun and the outside world.

*****

Angel slept for hours, and now he looked pale in the face. She knew that something was wrong. He wasn't responding to her calls. She shook him, and he lay like a lifeless man on the bed.

The swelling on the left side of his head had gone down a bit, but it was still black-and-blue. She knew that his head injury had a lot to do with him going in and out of consciousness, but he was doing fine. *What happened?*

She paced the floor and hoped that her husband would walk in the door and carry this man to the hospital. She had no idea what the prognosis of his condition was, but she knew that he needed help. She couldn't understand why, after being up and talking, he would suddenly fall back into unconsciousness.

*****

The slender woman opened the door just a crack to see who'd knocked.

"I'm sorry to have disturbed you, but I'm lost here and I need some help," the voice stated from the other side of the door. "I beg you to please help me," he pleaded.

Hesitating momentarily, she then opened the door a little wider so she could see him better. She wanted to examine the stranger who was seeking help.

"My name is Remington, and I'm lost here in the woods. Please, I need help!" he pleaded again earnestly.

"My name is Cecelia. I'm sorry, but I have to take precautions," she confessed.

"I understand," he replied. She stepped aside, and he took two steps into the cabin. "I don't blame you for being careful," he replied. "I'm really sorry for intruding."

"No need to be sorry. You're no bother at all. Besides, I don't mind the company."

The cabin was warm. He felt relieved that she had believed his story. "I'm here alone." She paused. "Well, not exactly alone. I have someone here who is very sick," she said, pointing to the little room where Angel lay sleeping. He glanced in the direction. "My husband went into the city, and I'm just waiting for him to return so we can take him to the hospital."

Remington couldn't help but comment, "Mmmm, something smells good." He was hungry and couldn't think of anything else but food right then.

"It's chicken soup. Would you like some?" she asked.

"Oh, would I! Thank you," he said gratefully.

For the past few days, he'd been eating only dry crackers and had completely run out a couple of days previously.

Remington felt safe. He thought back on the storm that he'd sat through all alone. *It was a dreadful ordeal to be alone in a storm so severe,* he thought.

Cecelia enjoyed Remington's company and told him that her husband would be more than willing to help him find his friend. "He's a wonderful man," she said with a warm smile.

Then noticing how tired he was, she gave him a sleeping bag and told him, "There isn't too much room in here, but you can place it at the foot of the bed that Angel occupies."

Readily accepting her generous offer, it wasn't long before he was sound asleep himself. He hadn't felt this safe since he left his house in Milolta.

Before he knew it, morning had come and the little cabin was flooded with the natural sunlight that seeped through the window's curtains. He thought, *It's a brand-new day to start again to find Jeannine, but this time with the help of Cecelia's husband.*

Cecelia was already up and was preparing breakfast. Remington rolled up his sleeping bag and placed it neatly in the corner of the room, and then he stood to his feet and looked at Angel to see if he was awake. Angel was lying on his back, with his face turned slightly away from Remington. His face was partially covered by the sheet, leaving just his eyes and the bridge of his nose visible.

Remington walked over to the side of the bed where his face was turned and stood looking at him. He knitted his brow and frowned, watching a moment to see if Angel would move. *Is this guy even alive?* he thought. Then for some reason, he pulled the cover down gently until it revealed the face to the chin and Angel turned his head slightly to the other side.

"Oh!" A croaking sound escaped Remington's lips as he dropped the sheet as if it had burned him. His eyes widened, and his mouth dropped open, and he stood frozen over Angel like a mannequin. Suddenly he felt weak, and then all of a sudden, hot flashes ran through his body like episodes of lightning. He bent over, as if he were nearsighted, to take a closer look.

Brendan? he thought. "Can't be," he whispered. *Brendan is dead. It isn't possible for a total stranger to look so much like someone I've known for years...or is it?*

He sat down in the corner for a few moments, trying to collect his thoughts. Then he got to his feet and leaned over the bed again and whispered, "Brendan?" He didn't know why he'd called the young man by that name. It wasn't as if he really expected him to respond and say that he *was* Brendan.

Angel fluttered his eyes open and searched the room for the voice that had spoken. He raised his head slightly off the folded sheets that were used as a pillow so he could get a better look at the figure that was standing over him.

Remington gingerly pulled the covers away from Angel/Brendan's chest, as if it hindered him from seeing his face clearly.

"Brendan?" he croaked.

"Hello, Remington," Angel replied in a weak but clear tone.

"Oh my god! My god!" whispered a shocked Remington, who slowly began to pace back and forth in the little room.

Just then, Cecelia walked into the room, saying, "I see you two have met."

"Oh my god!" cried Remington again. It seemed he could find no other words to express his reeling emotions.

Cecelia looked at him, puzzled, and asked, "Are you all right, Remington?"

"That's Brendan Clark," he said incredulously, pointing at him as if he were a monster, a look of disbelief covering his face like a mask. "That's Brendan Clark," he repeated. "He just spoke my name, so that tells me I haven't suddenly lost my mind."

"So you know him. What a coincidence!" replied Cecelia with joy. "There is a God!" she squealed with overwhelming joy.

"No!" Remington blurted out.

Cecelia looked at him, puzzled. "There is no God?" she asked.

"No. I believe there is a God. I just can't believe this is Brendan. We buried him!" he said, pointing down at Angel with a shaky hand.

By this time, Angel was sitting upright. "Yes, I am Brendan Clark."

Cecelia turned and looked at the man that had been totally helpless up until a moment ago and said, "Something about you did something to him, Remington."

With weakened knees, Remington sat down in a corner on the floor as he said, "I just don't understand. We buried you, man! We had a funeral and you were lying in the coffin, dead, dead, dead! I don't feel too good." He said the last part so suddenly and raised his knees and put his head between them and placed both hands on his head.

Cecelia went from being surprised to being puzzled. Brendan was even more puzzled than either of them and asked incredulously, "My mother thinks that I'm dead?" Remington nodded. "You had a funeral and buried someone that looked like me?"

"No!" said Remington in a fearful voice. "We had *your* funeral and we buried *you*! How did you do it, man? I never believed in reincarnation until now…unless you're a ghost! Jeannine saw you get shot, your mother identified your body, and I saw them lower you six feet deep into the grave. I watched them cover the grave with cement! One of three things is happening right now," Remington said solemnly. "I'm either dreaming, dead, or dying!"

"He has no gunshot wound," said Cecelia. "My husband checked him over," she added quickly. "Just a head wound and possibly torn ligaments."

"Remington," Brendan said. "You're okay. I'm really Brendan, and I never died. I almost died, but I wasn't the one you guys buried."

Remington lay down on the hard floor and covered his face. It was almost unbearable to handle the sight of Brendan. Cecelia brought him a cold glass of water.

"How is my mother?" Brendan asked after Remington had finished his glass of water.

"She wasn't doing too well last time I spoke with her."

Brendan began to feel uneasy. *My mother needs me, and I can't help her. But I have to somehow let her know that I am all right...and soon.*

"How are Kim and everybody else?"

"I don't know. I haven't spoken to them in a while. Man, I don't know how your mother is going to take this. If your death didn't kill her, your resurrection will!"

As the minutes ticked by, Remington became more accepting and was getting over his shock of seeing Brendan alive. He explained everything that had happened since Brendan had supposedly died and how he'd come to be in the same cabin as Brendan.

"Let him rest now for a little while," said Cecelia.

Brendan didn't have an appetite to eat when Cecelia brought him a light snack an hour later, but she coaxed him into putting something in his stomach.

The bandage around his head had come loose, so he pulled it off and placed his hand over the spot where a lemon-size lump had been. He didn't know what to think. *Who was the dead guy that looked so much like me that he fooled my own mother and close friends? Dead people usually don't look like themselves, anyway, so maybe the person had a minor resemblance to me,* he thought wearily. *We'll understand this big misunderstanding later.* He closed his eyes and took a short nap.

Someone nudged him, and Brendan woke up to find Remington standing over him. *So I wasn't dreaming. It was real.* He couldn't tell where he was and what had happened to bring him to the condition he was in, but he could tell that Remington was standing over him. At least he knew something that was fact. It was someone he knew, and he remembered the conversation that had taken place earlier. He felt there was hope after all.

The front door opened, and Stedman walked in. Cecelia squealed with joy. She was thrilled to the bone.

"Guess what?" Before he could answer, her lips flapped a mile a minute. "Our little stranger is doing much better, and we found out who he is."

She led him to the room where Remington and Brendan were quietly conversing and said, "This is Remington. He happened to find us and happened to know this guy. Isn't that exciting? What an awesome day it is today!"

"That is great news!" Stedman said as he gave his wife a gentle squeeze. "So you made it through the storm all right. I was so worried about you and the young man." He turned to Remington and held out a hand, saying, "Nice to meet you, Remington."

Remington gave him a firm handshake, and then Brendan added, "Nice to meet you too, Stedman." He hadn't had the chance to officially meet the man who'd saved his life.

Stedman then suggested they called Brendan's mother and handed his cell phone to Remington, who dialed Mrs. Clark's number. But there was no answer. So he called Kim to tell her the good news, but there was no answer there either. He left a message on Kim's machine and told her, "Your beloved Brendan is indeed alive! He's at a cabin not too far from ours." He added the last just before the beep ended his call.

*****

Ed Coons was appalled upon hearing the news that Brendan wasn't dead, and immediately questions flashed through his mind. *How could they have had a funeral if it wasn't Brendan? But what if it really wasn't Brendan they buried? No...no, that couldn't be. Surely, the police and then the family would have known it wasn't him...wouldn't they?*

Shaking his head and not wanting to leave anything to chance, he searched the map diligently with a magnifying glass and, finding what he was looking for, circled a tiny spot. Then picking up the phone, he made a few phone calls. "I think I know where it is. Meet me at the Brick and we'll go over specific instructions and details," he assured whoever was on the phone with him.

Actually, he was frantic. To say the least, he was hot with anger. He made another call and ordered Scarface and Cooper to get back to the cabin where they were. "Bring those wretches to the Brick! Do it immediately!" he hollered before slamming the phone onto the hook. *I'll dispatch a couple of men to seek out that Brendan character. This time, he'll really be dead, because I will do it myself!* Ed folded his map and rose from his chair, his eyes blazing. Without another word, he walked stiffly out the door.

Scarface and Cooper headed toward their mission with a passion. "Maybe she honestly doesn't know anything about the disks," commented Cooper. "We've tried several different people, and nobody who associated with him knew anything about the disks. They didn't know who we were, so they weren't on their guard either."

*****

Meanwhile, Stedman discussed their plans to help find Jeannine as they walked down the path to Stedman's Jeep. "Do you think you could find your way back to your cabin from here?" he asked Remington.

"I'm not sure," he confessed embarrassingly. "I've never been to it from this direction, so I really don't know if I can find it from here or not."

As Brendan's body slumped between Stedman and Remington's strong bodies, they walked firmly but carefully down the long winding path to the vehicle.

With the description of the surrounding area that Remington gave him, Stedman, who was familiar with the area, drove two miles east and parked in a clearing. There he and Remington got out. "We'll be back," he said to his wife as he kissed her lightly. She turned and smiled at Brendan, who was propped up comfortably in the front seat.

Remington wasn't lucky enough to find the cabin. He was treading on new trails that weren't at all familiar, and if truth be known, he didn't know if their cabin was east, west, north, or south.

He looked at Stedman in disappointment and embarrassment. "Which way do we go?" he asked. "Follow on in front or turn around and go the other way? Up or down?"

Stedman suggested, "Let's just keep going this way. If it leads to nowhere, then we'll turn back and go the opposite direction." Remington agreed.

Suddenly, out of nowhere, a cabin appeared in front of them. "This is the same cabin that Jeannine and I stumbled upon when we were together. There was no one here. Two days ago, I was able to search the inside, but I didn't find anyone or anything. But I knew someone had been here since, because when Jeannine and I tried the door, it was locked, but when I found it after we'd been separated, it was unlocked. I looked to see if Jeannine had been captured and taken here."

"Shhh!" Stedman whispered as he motioned for Remington to be quiet. Then with caution, they approached the cabin and inspected all around it. There was no sign of life, but Stedman cocked his hunting rifle as he knocked on the door. No one answered.

With the handy tools he had in his backpack, Stedman pried the lock open. They stopped at the entrance of the door, ready to defend as they pushed it open, but nothing happened.

They entered cautiously and searched every possible corner. Meanwhile, on the other side of the big chest that Remington was leaning against, Jeannine and her friends waited breathlessly as they expected Cooper and Scarface to enter the little room any second. They knew those two didn't have a spot of softness in their hearts, especially after they learned that Jeannine had lied to them.

They waited, not moving a muscle, then suddenly, Jeannine had a thought. *There is no need for us to keep quiet now. Even if it is the two men that have returned, they already know that we are here, and I'm quite sure they haven't forgotten us. I don't want us to blow any chance of being rescued. But if Remington has come looking for me, I can't risk letting him leave. He might not come back again. It is a chance I have to take.*

So she began kicking on the wall as hard as she could with her feet and calling loudly, "Remington!" but there was no response. When Jealissa and Charles joined her, she hollered his name even louder.

"Shhh." Remington motioned to Stedman. "I hear something." They could hear the faint sound of a voice and a banging sound.

"Remington!" the voice yelled again. Both Stedman and Remington froze as they listened.

Remington gasped. "That's Jeannine. She's here!"

Looking around, they saw it was one huge room and couldn't figure out where the voice was coming from. "Outside, maybe," said Stedman, leading the way. Out there they pressed their ears to the walls of the cabin, and Remington heard a muffled male voice. It sounded like Charles. He turned and looked at Stedman, puzzled.

Back inside, Remington said frantically, "We've got to hurry! The sounds seem to be coming from behind the wall." They moved everything that was leaning against the wall until they got to the chest and, after moving it, found the door that led to where the three friends were. Stedman pulled the latch and entered the room to find Charles and the girls each tied up in a different corner of the room.

Unexplainable joy, relief, and excitement filled the room. "We've got to go right now! We'll explain later," Stedman said, reminding them of the danger they were still in.

"I was in here a few days ago, searching for a clue to your whereabouts, Jeannine," said Remington as he hurriedly tried to untie her.

Jeannine glanced at Jealissa and her brother and said, "That was you? We heard one set of footsteps moving, and then all of a sudden, they hurried out the door. I thought maybe one of the men had forgotten something and had come looking for it."

"No, that was me. I thought I heard a noise outside, so I got out as fast as I could. And to think that you guys were here all along. If only I had known."

Within seconds, they were trying to get on their feet. All three suffered from severe muscle cramps and shooting pains in their arms and legs, but they had to make themselves ignore the pain and make their limbs move.

"Well, we better get out of here, because I think those awful men will be back any minute," said Jealissa. "Jeannine sent them on a wild-goose chase, and I think when they come back, they're coming back mad. As horrifying as the storm was, it worked in our best interest, because it hindered them from coming back sooner."

They were about to leave when Stedman, who was the first one at the door, saw some movement in the shrubs a few feet away. Quickly he placed his finger to his lips to motion them to be quiet. Then he stepped back and closed the door quietly, and they all took cover.

They could hear footsteps and then voices. "You stupid idiot, you left the door unlocked again!" said one of the men.

"No, I didn't. You were the last one out." They swung the door open, and immediately Stedman stood with his rifle cocked and aimed at them.

"Lie down on your stomachs and put your hands behind your back. And if I were you, I wouldn't try anything!" Stedman threatened.

Remington and Charles stripped them of their guns as the men obediently did as they were told, and they tied them up.

Jeannine and her friends stepped out of the cabin into the spacious world of the great outdoors. At first, they cringed and squinted as their eyes adjusted to the beaming light from the sun. Then, as their eyes adjusted, everything looked so bright and lovely as compared to the dark dungeon from which they had just emerged. Forgotten were the aches and pains their bodies had felt and now were as nothing when compared to how fortunate they felt to be alive and now safe.

The ground was still moist from the storm that had passed through, and they could see where some giant trees had fallen. There were many shrubs that had literally been flattened by the force of the storm. It was obvious to see that the weather-beaten ground bore mute testimony of the force of the storm that had passed through the area while the friends had been locked inside the cabin.

Cecelia was shocked to see Steadman and Remington coming toward them, accompanied by five others. There was no doubt in her mind that the two men with their hands tied behind their backs were the kidnappers. *Thank goodness,* she thought. *Evil can't always prevail. Sometimes there's just got to be a reward for the good at heart!*

"Yes!" she breathed out as she lightly pounded her fist in her palm.

Just before they got to the vehicle, Remington announced, "I hope you guys have strong hearts. I've got a surprise for you that will knock your socks off! This surprise is for everyone…actually." He looked at the two captives and sneered, "Murderers too!"

"Is it a good surprise?" asked Charles. "We've been through too much to hear any bad news right now."

Remington replied as he cast a cold glance at their two prisoners, "Some of us will like this one."

As they got closer to the vehicle, Remington increased his pace and stood by the passenger door, held out his hand, and said to the group, as they got closer, "Okay, wait right there." Then, smiling at Brendan, who was sitting in the passenger seat, he slowly opened the door and continued, "There has been a terrible mistake made. Something awful that we thought had happened actually didn't, and it is to our benefit but to these men's doom."

Then he nodded and beckoned to the group to come closer. "Take a good look," he said and pointed his finger at the figure in the front seat.

At first, the group of five didn't know what to think or say. Sheer shock froze their minds. Each wondered if everyone was seeing what he or she saw.

Charles looked from Brendan back to Remington. He tried to read Remington's expression to see if he'd played a sick joke on them. Things like this only happened in the movies. It was hard to accept that he was looking at Brendan Clark and he was alive.

Cecelia watched with tears streaming down her face, and Steadman kept a close guard on the two murderers.

"Hi, Charles, Jealissa, and Jeannine. It really is me, Brendan Clark," Brendan said with a weak smile.

Jealissa beat on her chest with the palm of her hand and then let out a high-pitched screech. It was as if the ability to release her emotion was lodged in her chest.

Charles's knees were not able to hold him up any longer and wobbled as he went down to the ground.

Jeannine? She flat out fainted, and Remington scooped her up and held her like a baby.

"Jeannine?" Remington called her name and gently shook her a few times in order to get her to respond. When her eyes fluttered open, he assured her, "It's all right. It's all been a terrible mistake. We can't explain, but we'll find out what happened when we get home."

"I need to see a doctor, now," Jealissa declared matter-of-factly.

"I'm sorry for all that I put you guys through, but it's really me, Brendan. I didn't die." As if to convince them he was not a ghost, he added, "I never died. It's a long story I will have to share with you later."

Jeannine's composure was returning, and Remington stood her back on her feet. She reached out and touched Brendan's fingers, and her hand didn't go through them. "Brendan?" She looked in his face, needing reassurance.

He smiled and said, "Yes, Jeannine?"

"Brendan!" She grabbed him, giving him a squeeze as he winced in pain. "Oh, you've been hurt," she said apologetically. "I saw you the night you got shot by these two monsters." She turned and gave them an icy stare. "They…"

"I've never seen them before in my life," Brendan interrupted. "It's all been a big mistake. They must have killed someone else that looked like me."

Charles was at a loss for words and couldn't help but wonder, *So who, then, did we bury?* He rubbed his temples and gave up on the whole situation, at least for the moment.

The two criminals expressed obvious confusion. They had absolutely nothing to say.

Steadman interjected the need to get going so they could turn in the thugs to the police. He supplied Remington's friends with water, fruit snacks, and some chips. They drank down the water like rain on parched ground.

After everyone got into the vehicle, Steadman drove to the police station. "Remington, you come with me. The rest of you, wait here," he said as he slid from the driver's seat.

"What about these guys? What if they try to escape?" Jealissa stated with concern.

"Don't worry, they'd be lucky to move an inch," Remington assured them.

Remington and Steadman entered the police station, and within about five minutes, they emerged with four policemen in their wake.

"Everyone, get out of the vehicle, please," ordered one of the police officers. He was wearing a short-sleeved white shirt with stripes on the right shoulder.

He must be in charge…the captain? Jeannine thought.

Then he asked, "Which one is Brendan Clark?"

"I am," Brendan softly replied.

"You can stay in the vehicle, sir. We'll be right with you."

The other officers helped Cooper and Scarface out of the vehicle and, seeing they were already well restrained, didn't bother cuffing them, but two of the lawmen escorted them into the police station.

After that, another policeman escorted Jeannine, Charles, and Jealissa inside, where they were all subjected to hours of harsh interrogation that also involved the FBI. Evidently, Cooper and Scarface were no strangers to the police. Their pictures and fingerprints were in the system, nationwide, and both were wanted for a string of crimes in addition to the kidnapping of Jeannine and her friends.

During her interrogation, Jeannine identified both the criminals as the men she had seen at the murder scene. Even though Brendan had *not* been murdered, they *had* killed someone. She also told the police about the report on file in Milolta and that Jake Schennenburger was the officer working on the case.

The police called Milolta and spoke with Detective Schennenburger, and naturally, he was elated. He asked to speak with Jeannine and, after hearing what she had to say, was delighted at her contribution to the case.

Steadman; his wife, Cecelia; and Remington were deemed heroes, yet they also were questioned for hours for even the most intricate details that ordinarily would have seemed insignificant. Then, hours later, the same questions were asked, but in different terms.

From the day Jeannine was missing up until that point was a weary and exhausting experience for all of them. But each held on, knowing that this was the last and yet very necessary phase of their nightmare and that they *would* win in the end.

Brendan was not as intensely interrogated because the police had no idea yet that, originally, he had been the intended murder victim. Neither did his friends, because they had not a clue that he had even been in danger.

As a matter of fact, Brendan thought, *I'm not sure if those guys had intended to kill me…as I have never seen them before today. The fact that Ed* did *threaten to kill me and that someone looking like me* has *been killed gives me the distinct feeling that I really might truly have been the intended target.* But he kept those thoughts to himself.

Not up to revealing Ed Coons's involvement just yet, Brendan figured he'd do all that at home, because right then he had nothing concrete on which to go. His thought was that he would take the disks and passwords to the police station in Milolta and then explain his story.

Actually, Brendan didn't have much to tell the police, because he could not remember too much about how he'd gotten to Cecelia and Steadman's cabin or recall being kidnapped. The police didn't push him too much, as they realized he needed to be hospitalized and had called for an ambulance shortly after everyone was inside the station, and they had ascertained his condition.

As far as the police were concerned, Brendan was basically just a hurt kid that was lucky to have been found. To them, he was not much of a significance to the case. They promised that they would follow up with him once he had received the necessary medical treatment at the hospital.

*****

While the friends were enjoying their reunion 150 miles away, Ed Coons was waiting impatiently in the bushes as the men broke into Stedman and Cecilia's cabin with guns drawn. There wasn't much to search, and minutes later, they came out, embarrassed.

Ed kicked the rock in front of him, then hollered in agony. Brendan had slipped from him again. He began to feel his doom and was becoming desperate.

So close and yet so far, he thought. It hadn't been a problem finding the cabin. *I knew exactly where it was. As soon as I'd found out where he had been hiding, I had been on my way there, but apparently, I didn't get there fast enough.*

He threw his hands on his head and made a deep groan. He was nervous and didn't know what to do, but he knew that he had to come up with something fast, very fast.

*****

Mrs. Clark didn't believe what Jake Schennenburger was telling her even though he was standing in front of her and looking quite sincere. *News like this has to be told in person for reasons such as her doubts,* he thought.

The detective looked at her and told her where Jeannine and her friends were and that he had spoken to Brendan himself.

"Well, I need to talk with Jeannine myself, because it's hard to believe what you're telling me," she insisted. "I don't like people playing with my emotions," she said flatly. Then eying him suspiciously, she suggested, "We could use my phone." Afraid to hope, she thought, *News like this is just too good to be true.*

Jake dialed the number of the police station where Jeannine and the others were still being detained and questioned. After about a two-minute conversation, he handed her the phone and began to say, "Mrs. Clark—"

Grabbing the phone from him, she said, "Jeannine, is that really you?"

She recognized the voice as Jeannine's and closed her eyes as the young woman said, "Yes, and you know I wouldn't play any kind of trick on you. Brendan really was here with us. Trust me, Mrs. Clark, I fainted when I saw him with my own eyes."

Mrs. Clark began to feel weak all over and began to tremble so hard she could hardly hold the phone. "Are you sure?" she asked tremulously. "Please, Jeannine, don't do this to me. I can't take any more hurt and disappointment."

"Mrs. Clark, I am positive."

"Dear God, I thank You!" the mother said with tears seeping from her eyes. "Can I speak with him, Jeannine?" she asked in a pitiful voice.

"Well, actually, he is not here right now, as an ambulance came and took him to the nearest hospital. He's been hurt, but it is not life-threatening. He will be fine," Jeannine said, trying to reassure the understandably distraught woman.

"Jeannine…" She spoke her name softly. "You did see him and touch him and he spoke to you?"

"Yes, I did. You won't be disappointed this time, I promise."

*****

The freshness of the morning air seeped through the window. Brendan felt warm, and the fabric touching his body felt soft. When he opened his eyes, he saw a figure standing next to his bed. He rubbed them to clear his vision. Standing there was his weeping mother.

"Mom! Boy, are you a sight for sore eyes!" He could remember everything that had transpired not too long ago but couldn't remember how many days had passed since he'd seen his friends. For all he knew, it could have been the same day.

Mrs. Clark cried uncontrollably. She didn't try to stop the tears from rolling down her cheeks. It was unbelievable. God had pitied her, she knew, and had worked a miracle in her life. Just like the prodigal son that the Bible talked about, her son, who once was dead, was now alive.

"The surgery went well," she said softly.

"Surgery?" he asked. "Why? I mean, why did I have a surgery?" No wonder he felt a little groggy and couldn't tell how long he'd been in the hospital.

"Minor surgery just to correct a few things. We'll talk about it later. Right now, I just want to love you. Oh, it's really you, my Brendan." She hugged him as tight as she could without hurting him and thought, *I haven't really lost my son like I'd thought. Life is grand.*

She let him go suddenly, as if he'd burned her. She stepped back and looked him over. She rubbed her face with the palm of her hand. "I don't understand!" she said solemnly. "We buried you." It was as if it had just dawned on her that they had actually had a funeral and had buried someone.

"Don't worry, Mom, we'll figure this out later," Brendan tried to reassure her.

Kim now looked at Brendan from a new perspective and was now sure she wanted to marry him.

"Yes...," she said with a glowing smile. He waited for her to complete her sentence, but she just held his hand and stared into his eyes.

"Yes what?" he asked curiously.

"I will marry you. I will! I will! I will!" she said excitedly.

If what I went through was what it took for her to be ready to marry me, then the suffering was worth it all, he thought.

"Oh, Kim, I'll be the best husband in the world!" Brendan was too happy for words. His Kim was finally ready to make the commitment with him. She was going to be his forever. He didn't care much about all that had transpired in his life lately, because Kim had made him the happiest man alive.

Mrs. Clark hadn't lost her curiosity about the whole thing and wanted to get to the bottom of such a mystery that had occurred in her life. *Was this all planned?* she wondered.

*****

Officer Schennenburger looked at her from across his desk. He tapped the desk lightly with his pencil. "I'm as baffled as you are," he told her.

"How do we go about finding out what happened? Jeannine saw him get shot. I went to the morgue and identified the body. No one could tell me it wasn't my son," explained Mrs. Clark. "Apparently, it wasn't him," she added quickly.

He massaged his temple and said, "I honestly don't know." He ran his fingers across his closed and weary eyes.

"I tell you what?" he said suddenly. "Let me get back to you. I have to do a little homework."

She rose from her chair. *At least he was going to do something about it,* she thought. *I will make sure not to let up on him until he has solved the mystery,* she promised herself as she left.

Detective Schennenburger scribbled a few things on a sheet of paper that he'd wanted to check out. Then he got up from his desk and walked to the locker area, where he picked up a plastic bag from one of the lockers. The label read, "Brendan Clark."

After putting on a pair of latex gloves, he rummaged through the bag that contained all the things that had been found on the body. There was a three-by-seven notebook, a few pictures, a few bills that amounted to fifty dollars, loose change, a handkerchief, a pen, a telephone book, and a wallet that had its contents neatly intact, indicating that no one had opened it.

Schennenburger frowned. *Evidently, no one even bothered to look in the wallet.* He shrugged his shoulders. *After all, he had been a victim, not a suspect, and a close friend had witnessed the murder, his body identified by his "mother." Evidently, the police felt they needed nothing more. It must have seemed insignificant to rummage through the man's wallet for any form of identification.*

A driver's license fell to the floor as he pulled out the wallet's contents. He held it in his hand and inspected it, which caused the detective's brows to knit, because it was a Clarksville license. It showed it had been renewed only a week before the man had been killed.

He looked at the picture, then read the name out loud, "Daniel Applegate. What? Daniel Applegate!" He bellowed the last part. The words tumbled from his lips almost uncontrollably. He was stunned. "The dead kid's name was Daniel Applegate? Something is very wrong," he said in a soft whisper.

How on God's green earth could Brendan's mother and friends have thought that the body that they were looking at was Brendan Clark's? This is one stinking mess is what this is! He was fuming.

Reaching for the phone, he dialed Mrs. Clark's number. He was relieved when she answered, because he wanted to get to the bottom of things as soon as possible. In a calmer voice than he felt, he asked her, "Can you come down to the station right away?"

"Certainly," she replied. "Did you find out anything?"

"We'll talk when you get here. Oh, I would appreciate it if you would bring Brendan with you."

Mrs. Clark and Brendan drove to the police station. Upon entering the detective's office together, they found him sitting in a trancelike state, a few items sprawled out on his desk. He raised himself to an upright position when he sensed their presence.

"These items were found on the body," he said without preamble. He handed them each a pair of latex gloves to wear so they wouldn't leave any fingerprints on any of the articles. "Recognize any of it?"

Mrs. Clark shook her head after picking up each item and examining it carefully. She shrugged her shoulders.

Next, he handed her the driver's license. She stared at it for a few moments and frowned. "This sure is Brendan's picture, though. The date of birth confirms it. But Clarksville?" She turned and looked at Brendan. "You went to Clarksville and got a driver's license?"

"No, Mom, I didn't," he replied as he then came and stared over her shoulder at the license. "My god, what is this?" He gasped as he studied the picture. "I've never been to Clarksville! Who had this?"

"I don't know what to make of all this," his mother confessed, quite baffled.

"Dear God, this picture looks just like me!" Brendan said in some confusion.

Mrs. Clark had grown silent as she studied the name on the license. For some reason, the last name on the license seemed familiar, and she was trying very hard to figure out if she knew or had ever known anyone with that last name. "Daniel Applegate. I'm afraid I don't know anyone by that name," she confessed.

But for some reason, the name Applegate struck a chord; she just couldn't put her finger on who it could be. *Maybe one of my husband's friends had that last name,* she thought. *When he was alive, each day after work he used to relate to me all that had transpired on his job. He would always tell stories about his coworkers. My husband never had a dull moment at work.*

"I've been here in Milolta all the time," Brendan stated, looking puzzled into the detective's eyes. "There's got to be some logical explanation for all this." Brendan picked up the driver's license and studied it. "This is too spooky."

Mrs. Clark now studied the driver's license over Brendan's shoulder.

Detective Schennenburger excused himself while he responded to an officer who had motioned for his attention.

"Applegate…Applegate…" Mrs. Clark closed her eyes and repeated the name over and over. Suddenly, something snapped and she became frozen in place, as if she were almost in a catatonic state. She felt numb from the top of her head to the soles of her feet, as if some spiritual force had entered the room and was pressing her into her chair. There was nothing she could do but stay seated, motionless and speechless.

Brendan looked at her and immediately knew that it must have been something from the driver's license that had triggered a memory.

"Mom?" He wanted to know what she was thinking or had remembered. "Mom?"

Evidently, his voice snapped her back to reality. She cleared her throat and finally spoke. "Applegate. I remember that name," she said softly. Then she grunted as her thoughts ran back to Mrs. Dunns. "Madeline Applegate went looking for me at the old house. Mrs. Dunns had a message from her to give to me, but she died before she could give me the message. Oh my god!" she cried vehemently.

Brendan could have sworn that his mother had lost her mind, and he knew that he was the cause. He'd caused her too much grief, and now this was the result.

"Mom, I'm here." He was afraid for her and thought how it must have really stressed her out when she thought he had died. Now it seemed it was taking a toll on her. He trembled at the thought that his mother might have totally lost her mind.

Then she turned and looked at him and suddenly remembered where she was. "I'm sorry," she apologized rather abruptly yet avoided her son's gaze.

He looked into her eyes and saw a hollowness. *Oh, Mom,* he moaned silently. He felt compassion for her.

"So?" asked Detective Schennenburger as he walked back into the office.

Mrs. Clark cleared her throat and said as she stood, "I'm sorry for all the mix-up about this case, Detective. I'm glad that my son is alive. I wish you luck." She reached for her purse and clutched it under her arm.

"Well, I'll keep you informed of any new information," he replied as he sensed her desire to leave. He turned to Brendan. "None of these things belong to you, right?"

Brendan shook his head. He removed his gloves and laid them on the desk. "Thank you, Detective," he said.

"Thank you for coming," the detective said.

She turned and walked out of the office without saying another word. Brendan trailed behind her.

Letting Brendan drive, she sat quietly in the passenger seat, fastened her seat belt, and stared blankly out the window. Brendan flipped the channel on the radio to reduce the intensity in the car as he glanced at her. She had such a vacant look in her eyes.

After a few minutes, she removed a tissue from her purse, and her hand shook as she raised it to her face. She dabbed the teardrops that were silently trickling down her face.

"What's all that about, Mom?"

She shook her head and mumbled, "Nothing."

Arriving at the house, she got out, but when she walked to the house, it was as if she had a chronic case of arthritis. Later, she carefully sipped the coffee that Brendan had made for her, but she still hadn't spoken since she had left the precinct.

"Mom, you've been acting very strangely. What is going on with you?" he asked.

She placed her coffee mug on the table and walked over to the couch, where Brendan was sitting, and sat next to him. Placing her hands in his, she said very slowly, "I remember the day so well as if it was yesterday…"

Across the street, standing on his front lawn was Mr. Stavis. He watched Mrs. Clark and Brendan through their open window and wished that he had a son. How he wished that he could have shared in the joy of having a child call him Dad. While Brendan had been missing, he'd prayed for him. He prayed for Mrs. Clark, too, that she would have good news on her son. Now, his prayer had been answered. He was happy for them. But oh, how he wished God would answer his prayer and bless him with a son.

He watched as they conversed intently. Every now and then, Mrs. Clark would dab her eyes with a tissue. *How she loves her son,* he thought. *They must be catching up on missing times.*

Then he saw Brendan stand to his feet with an expression of bewilderment. Mrs. Clark then slowly walked over to him and gently rubbed his shoulders.

Oh, I'm being nosy, Mr. Stavis scolded himself and walked back into his house.

*****

Two hours after leaving the precinct, Brendan picked up a black bag that he'd placed on his bed and walked out of his old room. "Mom?" he called. She opened her bedroom door and gave him a half-smile.

"I've got to go see Detective Schennenburger right away" was all that he said. He had very nearly forgotten about the disks that had almost cost him his life.

"Be very careful," she warned. "I want you to come right back, okay?"

"I will. I promise."

Detective Schennenburger was surprised to see him there so soon. Brendan handed him the bag, then said, "You'd be surprised to know what is on these disks."

Detective Schennenburger gave him a questioning look. Brendan sat down and then explained everything from the beginning up to the time he had been found by Remington.

"So these are the disks Jeannine heard them ask about. Wow!" exclaimed the detective.

"It took me a long time, but I was able to get the passwords." He handed him a sheet of paper on which written were the passwords. Brendan shuddered at the memory of the day he had opened the safe and retrieved them. If he had been caught that day, he knew his life today would have only been a memory.

"We've suspected this guy for the longest time but didn't have anything with which to nail him," said the detective. "I'll call you if I need any more information. You've made my day, kid."

Brendan walked out of the detective's office feeling lighter than he'd felt when he walked in. He paused at the door and asked, "Do you think I will need police protection?"

Detective Schennenburger smiled at him and said, "You better believe you do, and you're well deserving of it. Those hoodlums might already know that you're alive. I also have a feeling they know that they're going down."

After Brendan left, Detective Schennenburger popped the first disk into the floppy drive on his computer, then picked up the sheet of paper Brendan had given him and ran his finger down the list until he got to the password for the disk with the green tab. He typed it in and hit the Enter key. Ten columns of meaningless numbers and letters appeared on the screen. He closed out the file and popped in another one. He ran his finger down the list again and typed in the password for the yellow tab disk. That one had a list of names with codes that were similar in format to the first disk he'd scrolled through.

Finally, after a few hours, the detective began to notice a pattern to the information on the disks. The information on each disk was connected to the others like a jigsaw puzzle and, when placed in the right order, seemed to make a whole picture.

"Oh my goodness!" Detective Schennenburger was stunned. "This man is highly intelligent."

"What?" asked a fellow coworker overhearing the jubilation in the detective's voice.

"I've finally figured it out," he said with pride as he stacked the disks in the order of their files, shocked at what he'd found. "The man is a thief!" uttered Schennenburger in disgust. "Thousands of serial numbers that belonged to a computer company were put on computers this crook had assembled at a warehouse right here on the outskirts of Milolta. Those computers were sold within the US and also to other countries as property of the computer company, but he pocketed the money. This Ed Coons is also the ringleader of the biggest drug ring we've ever tried to bust."

Then, glancing at his calendar, he scrolled through the files that had dates of past and present activities and found that murders and money laundering were on the disks in full detail. Everything Detective Schennenburger needed to put Ed Coons behind bars forever was on the disks. The real names and presumed names of all the criminals were also on them.

Schennenburger glanced at his calendar. "We've got to get to the warehouse tonight." Ronnie and a few other officers peered over his shoulders in amazement as he scrolled through the files.

*****

"Right under our noses!" exclaimed Ronny. Secret Service men were in the vicinity of the warehouse, just watching the building. Detective Schennenburger adjusted his toupee as he kept his eye on the redbrick building. It looked deserted, and there was no real sign of activity, but all his men were ready for action.

After a while, a limo pulled up to the back of the building and a stocky man slithered from around the wheel. He looked around as if to make sure that no one was watching, then he unlocked the door and entered the building. Detective Schennenburger motioned to one of the detectives, who, in turn, motioned to another.

They rushed the limo, and Schennenburger hollered, "Get out of the car!" He held his cocked gun at the man's head. The man, who was in his early thirties, shakily exited the back of the car and leaned against it with his hands in the air. The detective flashed his badge before his face before they searched him for weapons. But all they found in his pocket was a silver coin key ring with a jagged edge and the picture of a red dragon.

"Are you a devil worshipper or something?" Detective Schennenburger asked. But the man said not a word.

They pulled him to the side of the building, handcuffed him, and read him his rights. Then they waited for the stocky man to reappear. Minutes later, he walked out the door.

"Police, don't move!" Detective Schennenburger handcuffed his hands behind him and gave him a search. He, too, had a similar coin. After reading him his rights, they transported them to the police station.

Detective Schennenburger and eight other officers entered the warehouse cautiously, with guns cocked. No one was found in the building, but at one end of the huge warehouse were hundreds of computers that had been assembled and were packed and ready for shipment. Then at the other end were stacked crates in which the police found drugs.

Back at the station, Detective Schennenburger waited for the two arrested men's cell phones to ring. He knew that sooner or later, they would receive their business call. Fernando DelaRacco and his partner had refused to give any kind of information to the police, but the detective knew it wouldn't be long before they would get another lead.

One of the cell phones finally rang. Fernando answered it, cleared his throat three times, then said, "And, Jeremy…" Quickly the detective snatched the phone to see what number showed on the screen, but the phone was already dead. Schennenburger pounded his fist on the hard table, as he was positive Fernando had given the caller a secret hint.

Schennenburger immediately checked the airport, and just as he had suspected, Ed Coons had booked a flight.

*****

Meanwhile, Ed sat nervously in his seat on the plane as they waited for takeoff. A little boy watched him as he fidgeted nervously.

"Excuse me," he said to the stewardess, "what's keeping the plane from taking off?" He tried to keep his voice from quivering.

"I don't know, but we will be taking off shortly. The pilot has to get the okay from the tower before we can take off, and he hasn't received that yet." She smiled warmly at him.

His eyes roamed the aircraft. He knew he wouldn't feel safe until the plane was in the air. The police had already caught Fernando and Jeremy, but he had confidence in Fernando that he wouldn't give them any information. He just hoped that Jeremy would also keep his mouth shut.

"May I have your attention, please?" Ed's heart skipped a beat at the sound of the voice over the speaker. "We're sorry for the delay, but we will be taking off shortly."

The longer they waited, the more Ed knew he was in danger of getting caught. He knew that Brendan was a clever kid, and worried if he'd turned the disks over to the police.

I'm not going to get caught and spend the rest of my life behind bars. I've just got to slither my way out of this. I know I can by using my other ID. Thank goodness I have it with me, he thought.

Feeling a little more secure, he carefully slipped off his shoe and slightly leaned down and tucked the ID he didn't need in the bottom of his sock. Then he slipped his shoe back on and slipped out his driver's license. He looked at it to make sure it was the right one. He placed it in the front of his wallet.

He felt dizzy. *If they are on to me, I figure I have a good chance to escape, unless they do a strip search.* He shuddered.

Just then, there was another announcement from the cockpit. "May I have your attention again, please? There is no emergency, but will everyone please exit the aircraft in an orderly fashion? You do not need to bring your hand luggage with you. We are sorry for any inconvenience this might cause you."

It's the police, he thought. *I've got to keep my cool.*

As the passengers exited the aircraft, the people complained. The police escorted the men to a designated room in the building. Ed wasn't the least bit surprised when he saw them. He gave a friendly smile as he entered the designated room.

*****

"According to our computer, Ed Coons checked in at 10:50 p.m. His luggage and everything else is on the aircraft," said the man behind the counter.

"What happened, then?" asked Detective Schennenburger in despair. He was desperately looking for answers. *How could they have come so close and yet have missed catching him?*

"That must have been him that called Fernando on the cell. He knew that there was trouble. Since he is a very cunning man, he must have known we were hot on his heels," explained the detective, more to himself than to the other officers. The disappointed Schennenburger had no choice but to have the passengers released to reboard the plane.

Ed was happy because the way was now clear. *I've beaten them again!* he thought. *Paris, here I come!*

While in the air, he decided, *I'll stay in Paris until everything has cooled down. With the help of my acquaintances, I'll be able to come back to the US and move to a different state. It will be no trouble for me to get an alias, and I won't have trouble living under another presumed name.*

He had an idea. *I will tell my family that it was all a lie but I had to be in hiding because if I couldn't prove my innocence, they would think I was guilty. I'll just convince them that I was framed. They'll believe me.*

*****

While Ed was in the air, Jake Schennenburger had gone to Mrs. Clark's house. But before going to the door, he first exchanged a few words with the private detective who was keeping guard in a black car at the front of the house. Mrs. Clark answered the door, and immediately Schennenburger said, "I need to speak to Brendan right away, please."

"Do you have a picture of Ed Coons?" he asked Brendan.

"Sure," Brendan responded with a smile. "I have a picture of him right here." He reached into his wallet and pulled out a picture, saying, "That's him and his daughter."

"Great!" Schennenburger responded. "I'll be in touch." He proceeded to put on his jacket as he headed out the door.

*****

"Please buckle your seat belts. We will be landing in fifteen minutes."

Those were the sweetest words in Ed's ears. The landing was smooth, and as the plane came to a complete stop, the passengers clapped happily.

Though delighted to be safely in Paris, Ed had no time to show gratitude. He quickly unbuckled his seat belt and was one of the first ready at the door to exit the aircraft.

What the passengers didn't know was that a squad of French Police was awaiting the aircraft. It had been arranged, once again, for the passengers of this particular flight to be escorted into a special room.

What a nightmare! Ed thought. *But I'll slip through their hands yet another time.*

Just then, one of the officers asked, "Are you Edward Coons?"

He swallowed hard before stuttering, "W-who?"

"Ed Coons," repeated the officer slowly in precise English with a French accent.

"Oh, no, I'm not," Ed hastily replied.

"May we see some identification, please?"

He gulped before saying, "Sure." Then he reached for his wallet and pulled out his driver's license.

The officer took it and then pulled out a picture that had been faxed from the United States and intently studied them. Looking up, he said to Ed, "Looks like the same person to me."

Suddenly, Ed dashed down the hall toward the exit door, with the officers in hot pursuit. It was really no contest, and seconds later, they caught up with him and immediately placed him in handcuffs.

"Marshall Futon, a.k.a. Ed Coons," said an officer as he shook his head in disgust. "Do you have something to hide, Marshall?" asked the officer sarcastically. "Or should I say Ed?" he added coldly.

"I have nothing to say to you. I want to speak to my lawyer. You're going to be very sorry!" he snapped.

"You *are* going to need a lawyer, Mr. Futon/Coons. And a very good one too," retorted the officer.

He was escorted to a holding cell there in the customs office of the De Gaulle Airport. They gave him no opportunity to escape, and four hours later, accompanied by a US Marshal, he was boarded on a flight to the USA. The French Police guarded the plane carefully and watched until it soared into the air and out of their jurisdiction.

When Marshall's flight finally landed him at the Milolta Airport, the plane was not taxied up to the regular dock but first escorted to a remote area, where a squad of police personnel surrounded it. After all was secure, Marshall was personally escorted from the plane and promptly placed under arrest and read his rights along with a string of charges against him.

*****

To say that Kim was in shock was the understatement of the year. She stared at her handcuffed father on her television set as he was led to a police car. *A phony, a murderer, a thief? No, not my father! It's all a big mistake, and I know it will be cleared up and they'll apologize to my father for the misunderstanding. There has to be a legitimate reason he would try to flee the country and why he didn't tell me that someone was trying to frame him,* she reasoned in her mind.

But as the news progressed, she was dumbfounded to learn that he had an alias. There, shown side by side on the television set, were his two IDs, one with his real face and the other with a different-looking face. Yet it was obvious that Ed Coons and Marshall Futon were one and the same person.

Before the night was over, Kim painfully realized that there had been no misunderstanding surrounding her father's arrest. Marshall had confessed to some things and denied being involved in other criminal acts. It was one of the most heartbreaking news she had ever received.

She cried and cried, and balls of damp tissue were scattered on the floor of her room. After a while, she stood before her mirror and looked at the mess she was and clenched her teeth. Her anger boiled. "If he is what they say he is, then he might as well forget that he has a daughter!"

The doorbell rang. She didn't want to see anyone, so she went to sit on the couch in the dark and wept silently. But whoever it was was persistent, and they kept ringing and waiting for her to come to the door.

The incessant ringing became irritating, and she finally rose to her feet and walked toward the door, quite angry with whoever was intruding on her grief. It was the police. "Is this the home of Marshall Futon?" one of them asked. She nodded numbly. "We have a warrant to search this house." With that, they barely gave her time to get out of their way as they swarmed into her home.

Feeling violated, she went into the family room, where she lay on the couch and just cried and stared unseeing at the ceiling while they rummaged through the entire house.

They confiscated his computer, her computer, the safe, and all disks he had in his study.

When they finally left, Kim bolted the door after them and sat in the dark. She was lonely, angry, and now afraid.

"I lost my mother. Now I've lost my father too. I've lost everything that ever had any meaning to me," she sobbed out loud.

After a while, the doorbell rang again. She was reluctant to answer it but thought, if it was the police, they wouldn't go away. Peeking out the window, she saw it was Jeannine. Calling through the window, she said rather harshly, "I'm sorry, I just want to be alone right now." But deep down, she knew she really didn't want to be alone.

"I won't say anything. I'll just sit quietly next to you," replied Jeannine.

Kim opened the door, and Jeannine took her friend into her arms. Together they cried, and cried some more.

"I'm sorry," said Jeannine with empathy and sat in silence until Kim was ready to talk.

*****

As Kim and Jeannine sat in the huge solemn house, Zaire walked out of jail and breathed the fresh air of freedom. "I'm free!" he shouted to the world at large.

Kim was all that was on his mind now. He wondered where she was and what she was doing. He couldn't wait to see her.

All charges had been suddenly dropped against him, and he had yet to find out that Brendan was alive and Kim's father was not the man everyone had thought.

*****

The K-9 barked and sniffed briskly as he pulled the police officer to the area where Brendan said the helicopter had sat. Nothing had been found hidden in the bushes, but Schennenburger believed that something might be buried in the area.

The beep of the sensor got louder as they went over the area by a rectangular object. "No doubt this was used as a marking spot," said the detective. He dropped the object into a black bag and proceeded scanning the area.

"Over here!" called one of the police from about ten feet away.

It didn't take much digging for them to hit something hard. "Try to dig around it," said Schennenburger excitedly.

Brendan watched as he had that night, but now he was a little bit closer and had much more visible light. "What is it?" he asked curiously as the digging exposed what appeared to be a huge black chest.

Once the police hauled the object out of the hole, they cracked the lock and opened it. Detective Schennenburger whistled as he stared incredulously at the contents of the chest.

"I have never seen that much money in all my life!" exclaimed Ronny.

"My guess is that there's at least ten million dollars in this fat baby!" added Schennenburger.

"I think there might be another one!" called another police officer who hadn't been able to resist the idea that the one chest was not the only one. Sure enough, another chest was dug up and pulled from the earth. As they opened it, the sun shone on the objects inside and reflected the glistening diamonds, pearls, and gold.

Brendan was ecstatic. They patted him on the shoulder and complimented him on the great work he'd done. He'd done a great deal for the police department, and it was then that he thought that maybe he might want to join the police force. Something of that magnitude of victory gave him a great sense of pride. He tried to imagine what he could do as a police officer if he could do such great work as a civilian.

He thought about the Jeep that had almost ran him off the road that night. *Now I understand why they had been so frantic. They had been the lookout men. Too bad,* he thought. *You lost this time, Ed.*

Chapter 18

The House of Doom

It was a dark and gloomy day. A slight drizzle dampened Marshall's head as he stepped out of the county jail and walked the few steps it took to the paddy wagon. Stopping, he took a deep breath and filled his lungs with the fresh air he once hadn't thought much about. How precious those few moments were when he walked out of the building toward the waiting van. He looked up into the sky. There was no sign of the sun, as if it didn't even exist. Dark clouds invaded the sky, bringing a sense of dullness over the land.

It was court day. His heart felt faint because his fate would be placed in the hands of a jury. Naturally, this weighed heavily on his mind.

Marshall Edward Futon, a.k.a. Edward Coons, walked in front of the escorting officer down the hall and to the courtroom. He held his head rigidly, as he seemed to focus on the desk that was reserved for the defendant and his lawyer. The gloomy weather seemed to intensify the gloom that he felt in the room. *Right foot, left foot.* He'd almost had to think about each step he took, as if the weight of his circumstance altered his natural ability to walk. Each step had seemed to bring him closer to his doom. His body felt heavy, as if he were carrying a man twice his weight. Each agonizing step he counted as he headed down the aisle for the defendant's table. *Twenty-four in all. Twenty-four steps to the chair of condemnation,* he thought.

As he sat down carefully, his lawyer leaned over and whispered something in his ear. He nodded in response.

The jurors' chairs were neatly lined against the wall on his right. Slowly he looked at each juror, chair by chair, as if to read each personality. They all sat perfectly still, waiting for the trial to begin.

Marshall took a quick glance at the back of the room, where his daughter sat. With her left elbow on the back of the bench and her hand supporting her head, Kim Futon clutched a tissue in her right hand and dabbed at any escaping tears.

Her father stared at her as long as he could without meeting her gaze. As long as her head was down, he could look at her. He thought, *She looks weak and frail and very stressed. I've put her through a lot, too much for such a loving daughter as she had been.*

The huge room was crowded mainly with people he didn't know who were there for the trial. *Curious people,* he imagined. *Nosy people, for that matter.*

Marshall felt chilled to the bone. *Was it the room, or was it just me? This is an ugly room,* he thought. He could almost feel the coldness of death itself, the death of his character, his personhood, his very being.

During the past few months, it seemed he had aged ten years. Evidence of his lack of sleep could be seen in the red of his eyes and the dark circles and huge bags under them.

Leaning slightly forward, he pulled the tail of his jacket from under him. Then he straightened his tic and waited.

*****

Kim hoped that any minute she would wake up and find that it had all been a bad dream. *Not my father! He is not a criminal! How could he be guilty of all the ugly things of which they accused him? Marshall Futon is a good father and a law-abiding citizen. I'm not the daughter of an evil man, but of a good man!*

She had a distant look in her eyes as she looked back to her childhood. She had been happy as a child and had lacked nothing.

Her father had always been there when she needed him. Nobody was perfect, but he was close.

Staring at nothing in particular, she clenched her teeth, as if by sheer will and determination alone she could refute the accusations against her father.

"I'll always be here for you, Kim." Jeannine's whispered promise brought her back to the present as her friend threw an arm across her shoulders.

"I know," Kim sniffled.

"You know, Brendan hasn't taken his eyes off you since the moment you walked in. Why don't you talk with him when we break for recess?"

She shook her head back and forth. The last time she had talked with or seen him had been in the hospital, because he had wanted to keep a low profile and stay away from the public until he'd informed the police of his findings and received some kind of protection. She was angry with him because she had found out *he* was the one who had been responsible for her father's arrest.

Brendan's heart was also breaking, and he thought, *If only I could just have the chance to explain everything to Kim, I know she'd understand. But I suppose she no longer wants to have anything to do with me.*

The DA was harsh and ice-cold, showing no sympathy for Marshall. He pounced on him with every string of evidence that would ensure Marshall got the maximum punishment for his crimes. Schennenburger was there to testify against Marshall. He had had a computer programmer investigate the entire computer system in order to pull out even more evidence on Marshall. The disks and Marshall's warehouse computer system proved how he had duplicated some serial numbers from Dimension Computer Galaxy Corporation and had used those same serial numbers on the computers he'd assembled at his warehouse.

Schennenburger had gone through DCGC's inventory files and checked out the companies from whom they'd ordered parts and found out that for almost every order they'd placed, Marshall had ordered ten or more duplicate serial numbers. Hundreds of computers had been produced at Marshall's warehouse that had matching serial numbers to those of DCGC. Luigi Rice thought he'd covered his tracks, but not well enough to avoid being discovered.

The disks Brendan had stolen and files both at the warehouse and DCGC complemented each other in nailing Marshall.

It was shown that Marshall had sold his computers for one-half the going market price. Of course, he was able to do that. If he had sold each computer for just one hundred dollars, he still would have made it good, because he hadn't paid a dime for them.

The gold, diamonds, and pearls that had been discovered by the K-9 dogs were found to have been the stolen orders from area jewelry stores. Just cracking the codes on the disks and running through the files along with the warehouse files spilled out everything about Ed.

Detective Schennenburger happily said to anyone who would listen, "He thought he was so clever, which he was, as he had covered his tracks well. But then when the disks were discovered, it showed he had not been clever enough."

*****

All the men that worked with Ed were eventually also captured and stood trial. Juan Rivera, Ms. Abbey, and some other murders that had once been unsolved were linked to Ed and compounded his wickedness.

Schennenburger figured, "If you're going to be a criminal, you should keep some things to yourself, that is, in your head, because sure as I'm sitting here, the truth has a way of coming out."

The men that were caught in the cabin, Cooper and Scarface, both confessed to dealing with Marshall and led the police to crucial information regarding Ed in exchange for lighter sentences.

The next day, Brendan stopped in to have a little chat with Detective Schennenburger. "I'm glad it's over for this man," said Brendan. "Now, I finally can feel safe again."

Brendan held out the coin for the detective as he said, "I forgot to give this to you. This is what opened the safe in Marshall's study."

"Jeannine had one similar to this," said Schennenburger.

"Evidently, it was his men's ID. That was what they used to let one another know they were working for the same guy," Brendan explained.

"How're you doing, really?" asked the detective with concern.

"I'm a survivor. I'm gonna make it," Brendan replied.

Schennenburger smiled and said, "That's the spirit."

*****

"This man is so clever it's unimaginable. With a brain like his, he could have used it to better society. He's a modern-day Einstein, with the title of 'fool,'" the DA uttered.

"These disks are incredible," added the DA concerning the six disks he held up in his hands. "It's funny how someone could actually lay out their rotten life plain and simple so others would have no trouble figuring out the details, or the evidence, for that matter. Everything there is to know about this man and his scheme is here in meticulously kept records. You couldn't ask for better details.

"We have the names of people he'd ordered killed. Some of these names have been on the news and had been listed as unsolved or mysterious crimes. Now, eight unsolved murders are solved. They are all here in great and unmistakable detail on these disks.

"His coworker Harry, who died in the parking lot at his job, was killed by his hit men because he'd stumbled upon a forbidden file. Daniel Applegate was another one that was also murdered by him. Marshall Futon has been known for years as Ed Coons. He's fooled people for too many years. He's an animal and should be put away from society for good." At last, the DA concluded.

*****

Glancing around the room, Kim saw Michael R. Dustin III sitting across the aisle from her. She'd met him once a few years ago when she'd visited her father on the job. He was the owner of Dimension Computer Galaxy Corporation. There were a few well-dressed men and two women sitting in the row with him. She noticed Mr. Dustin had a frown on his face, but who wouldn't if you've been robbed out of millions?

Kim looked coldly over at her father, and their gazes met. Father and daughter at the county courtroom, locked in gaze for the first time since he'd been arrested, paused time and spoke clearly with their gazes.

For a brief moment, his eyes showed her his bare soul, his inner self. Beyond his dark-brown eyes she caught a glimpse of what was in his heart. She saw guilt, shame, remorse, and disappointment. Then, as if to let her know her time to view had come to an end, he had closed his eyes and turned away.

In his brief glance into her soul, Marshall saw the disappointment and anger clouding her eyes as she briefly stared at the man whom she'd once thought of as the perfect father.

He knew what she was feeling and saw the hurt that was within her. He even knew that she might never forgive him, and he couldn't blame her. She had trusted him with all her heart, and he had let her down. Because of her trust in him, she had been oblivious to signs that things weren't right. He thought of the day she told him Remington had left a message on the answering machine stating that Brendan was alive. When he had stumbled for a chair to sit in, she had anxiously asked, "Are you okay, Daddy?"

Marshall had the best lawyer money could buy, but deep inside he knew he was doomed. Even his lawyer had said to him, "Only a miracle can help you. But that seems very unlikely."

*****

During the trial, the tenseness in the air intensified, especially when the DA accused, "You've even murdered your wife!"

Kim's eyes had widened, and a chill ran up her spine. The thought had never once entered her mind that her father had had anything to do with her mother's death. It made her feel sick to her stomach.

On the stand, all eyes now focused on Marshall. His voice quaked as he spoke. He couldn't think clearly and didn't know if he was coming or going. Words fell from his lips haphazardly. He couldn't remember the statement he'd made just three seconds earlier.

The DA pounded away at him with his accusation. "She was sick of your messes and threatened to leave you and turn you in to the police. She knew too much, and you couldn't risk being exposed, so you had her killed!"

To Marshall, it seemed the room became darker. Beads of perspiration popped out on his forehead as he sat in the witness stand. He felt as if someone had stripped him of his clothes and hung him on a pole naked for the world to view.

"Objection, Your Honor! That's implying something of which he has no proof," interjected Marshall's lawyer. Marshall felt relieved as all eyes, it seemed, turned away from him and to his lawyer.

The judge, tapping his pen on his chin, replied, "Sustained."

"Your Honor, we would like to introduce exhibit 2." The judge nodded.

The DA read a single statement that had been taken from one of the disks Brendan had given the police:

My wife was getting in the way. She made me nervous. I had to kill her.

Kim let out a shrill scream. "Order in the courtroom!" the judge commanded as he hammered his gavel. But Kim couldn't contain herself.

"Recess until 2:00 p.m." The intangible sound of judgment was heard as the judge's wooden hammer connected with the desk.

"I should have told her," Brendan whispered to his mother as an officer escorted a distraught Kim out of the courtroom.

"She wouldn't have believed you. She had to hear for herself. If you had told her, she probably would have told her father. Then he would have quickly initiated your murder and you wouldn't have been given your opportunity to hide."

"You're right," he said matter-of-factly.

"How did you ever get those disks if his office was always locked?" asked Jeannine as she and Brendan strolled down the street to a nearby restaurant.

"I picked the lock. It was easy," he said, a smile on his face. "I was curious. The day I saw him with a mask on set my curiosity on fire. So I just had to see what he was up to, because I didn't trust him as far as I could throw him. He was always too secretive, and his eyes gave him away. He had evil eyes, and I could see right through him."

"You have good intuition. I never noticed anything odd about him," she commented.

Recess was over, and Marshall resumed the witness stand. He sat motionless, his head hung down. It was midafternoon, and the sun beamed through the east windows. It did nothing, however, to lessen the intensity of the gloom that permeated the walls of the courtroom.

The stillness of the room was unbearable to him. He watched the people gathered for the trial. He knew there were reporters waiting anxiously outside the courtroom, and he wondered how many more days it would take before the trial would be over.

He really hadn't noticed before, but because he hated to look into the faces of people, he hadn't realized some of his ex-coworkers were there, not for support either, but because they were angered and shocked.

The DA spoke, and it startled him, as if he'd forgotten that he wasn't alone. "Harry Genre died by his hand…"

Brendan looked back at Kim with compassion. She now seemed a bit calmer, yet he knew she had to be keeping a tight rein on her emotions. Deep within his heart he felt bad about the whole thing but knew that he had done the right thing. He hoped that someday she would forgive him.

Then he remembered something Jeannine had told him previously. "She's not really angry at you, Bren. She's just trying to let out all her anger, and she is throwing some of the blame on you. But trust me, she'll understand after it's all over."

Since the reporters had been bombarding Marshall's house, Jeannine had been staying with Kim and they had many discussions about all aspects of the case.

At the end of another day of the trial, Brendan walked out of the courthouse. His heart gripped him as he thought about how it all was affecting Kim.

"Brendan?" Ben had caught up with him as he was heading to his car. "I think you need to talk to someone." Ben Shrouder pointed to a teary-eyed Kim as she hurried from the courthouse, her face buried in a tissue.

Brendan took a deep breath and hurried over to her side. As she raised her head and saw him coming, she quickly turned and headed to her car.

"Can I talk to you, Kim?" he gently called.

"No!" She wasted no time in driving away, leaving Brendan standing in the spot where her car had been a second ago.

Kim wanted to get away and be someplace really quiet, and her mother's grave was the only place she could think of; she wanted to talk to her mother.

As she stood by the grave site, she just stared at it. Her eyes were blurry from the tears that had welled up in them. In her hand she loosely held a single rose. Now she was alone again with her beloved mother. The last time she had been there was the day she and Brendan had become officially boyfriend and girlfriend. She had been happy.

She remembered having planned to come back and tell her father about their wedding plans, but before she had gotten the chance to do so, he had been arrested.

Today was the third saddest day of her life. The first was the day she'd learned her mother had died. The second was when she discovered her father wasn't who he portrayed himself to be. And the third was when she learned her mother's death was at the cruel hands of her own father. These three days, engraved in her mind, traumatized her so much that she feared healing might be impossible. She had no idea how she could ever get over such trauma.

Falling to the ground, she placed her head on the tombstone. "Mom," she cried bitterly. She lay quietly under the dark clouds, clouds that were as dark as the ones that invaded the skies the first day of her father's trial. *The sun didn't rise that morning. Evidently, it didn't see the world as worthy of its beauty,* she thought.

Death. How somber, how still, how pain-free. Right then, she welcomed the idea and wanted to go to heaven and be with her beloved mother. All she wanted was to live in tranquility and be free from pain and suffering.

"God, where are *You* when I need *You*?" she cried. She rested her spirit in the name of the God above. "Please help me," she murmured.

The stress of everything that had happened all weighed heavily on her mind. Then a Bible verse came into her thoughts as she lay motionless: "Surely He hath borne our griefs and carried our sorrows." She allowed the words to flow over and over in her thoughts as she rested quietly on her mother's grave.

Finally, she rose to her feet, surprised she felt okay. She felt at peace. Looking up to heaven, she whispered, "Thank You." Then she realized the tightness was gone from her chest and her body actually felt lighter. She thought, *God heard me, after all, and He has given me strength. I'll get through this, with Him by my side.* Then she walked through the graveyard back to her car with a faint but serene smile on her face.

"Brendan," she whispered. For the first time since her father's exposure, she now actually wanted to talk to her Brendan.

It was much later that day, and Kim was rummaging through the piles of boxes that had been stored in the attic. She had no idea what she was looking for, but she wanted to go through her parents' past to see what might surface. Mentally, she braced herself for the worst, telling herself that whatever she found, she could handle it, no matter how hard it might be.

She didn't really find anything of interest except for a little rose-colored notebook that had her mother's name on the inside cover. *The Diary of Charlene M. Futon* was printed in her mother's pretty handwriting. With natural curiosity, she opened it, and page after page, Charlene gave an account of the significant things that surrounded her life.

Kim gulped as her eyes stayed glued to every word on the pages. "Unbelievable," she groaned when she read what her mother had written:

> *I am so afraid that someone will tip off the police and tell them that my husband deals drugs. I'd hate to know that they'd find the drugs in my house and arrest me on drug charges.*

Kim had only read a few pages when she decided to put it away in her purse to read later. Then continuing to rummage through the rest of the boxes, she didn't find anything else that was significant. She sat on the floor among the things of her past, and as the tears welled up in her eyes, Kim Marie Futon wished fervently that she had never been born.

*****

That was it. The weary court days were over. Her father was found guilty of laundering money out of the country. It was an easy thing for him to put thousands of dollars inside some of his specially marked computers and to ship them off to various drug dealers oversees.

The computers he'd made were innumerable, and for two years he'd been able to use the name and logo of Dimension Computer Galaxy Corporation without anyone suspecting the fraud. He'd earned over five million dollars from his computers alone.

Kim was still in shock. She could hardly believe some of the things that her father had been involved in. She had taken her mother's diary and burned it, but that hadn't stopped the police from finding out the things about which her mother had written.

She thought, *I hope I will be able to put all this behind me and start my life afresh.*

Brendan smiled as he walked out of the courtroom for the last time. The nightmare was finally over and he could finally give a sigh of relief. Marshall and all his men were behind bars for the rest of their lives.

Kim. The thought of how much the whole ordeal had affected her brought a surge of pure guilt. He was, in part, the reason for her suffering. If he hadn't exposed her father, she might never have known all her father's dirty secrets.

She was still angry with him, he knew, because he either hadn't told her or because he'd caused her father to go to jail. Himself, he had mixed feelings. Yes, he was happy that Marshall's evil business was no longer in operation, but he was unhappy as well for all that Kim had had to suffer. Since it had been so long since he had talked with her, he had no idea how she was feeling anymore.

"Let's celebrate this wonderful victory," said Charles. "We're all safe, and those menaces to society are behind bars, for good."

"We've been through a lot together, and it only pulled us closer," Jealissa said as she threw her arms around her brother and rested her head on his shoulder.

Brendan was silent as they drove to Stephanie's place to celebrate.

"It's pizza time!" Jeannine grinned from ear to ear, exposing her deep dimples.

"How can I celebrate when Kim's not okay?" Brendan said sulkily.

"She's okay, and she wants more than anything to talk to you," Jeannine told him.

"She does?" he asked, surprised. "Are you sure?"

"Girl talk," replied Jeannine with a grin.

"Anchovies, mushroom, green peppers, and pepperoni—now that's pizza!" said Remington as he sniffed the vapors that ascended from the delicacies.

"That was the most horrific ordeal I've ever experienced," said Jeannine as she bit into a slice of pizza. "You know," she added with sincerity, "Kim was so naive and innocent that whatever her father asked about me, she unsuspectingly told him. Kim and I are so close that we basically know everything about each other. It was no problem for Marshall to supply those kidnappers with my picture and any information they needed about me. Before we had left, I had told

Kim exactly where I was going. I'd even given her a copy of the map I'd copied from you, Jealissa. Too bad I didn't copy one for myself, but I figured the one was good enough for the group."

"I probably made it even worse when I left a message on her answering machine telling her that I was with Brendan in a cabin not far from our cabin," Remington added.

"So, Brendan, you never told us how you got to the cabin where Remington found you," Charles said with curiosity in each word.

"Well, I had a fight with Zaire, and I was angry." His face tightened, and he had a distant look in his eyes, as if he was recapturing the emotion he had felt the moment he saw Zaire at Kim's house. He cleared his throat and continued, "I wanted to clear my thoughts, so I went for a long walk. On my way back, I took a shortcut through Alex's backyard. As soon as I had jumped over the fence and was walking through the back street, I heard what sounded like a shot fired, so I quickly jumped in the dumpster that was in the middle of the dead-end street, knocking myself out."

"That must have been the shot I witnessed when I saw those men with the guy that looked like you," added Jeannine.

"When I came to," Brendan continued, "the dumpster was moving, but then I realized that it wasn't the dumpster but a dumpster truck. They must have carried me to a remote place where they dump garbage. By the time they dumped the garbage from the truck, I was badly hurt. I drifted in and out of consciousness. I remember pushing a lot of garbage off me and then trying to get up and make my way through that huge heap of garbage. But what happened after that, I just couldn't tell you. Parts of my memory are coming back, like waking up inside a little room where you found me, Remington."

"You're lucky to be alive."

"I know," he replied.

Jeannine suddenly turned to Remington and asked, "How did you manage to make it through the storm?"

"I went back to our cabin and nailed the door shut." He laughed.

The celebration was okay for the others, but not for Brendan. It was no celebration knowing that things weren't all right between

Kim and him. His hope was that things could be cleared up and they could put it behind them and move on together.

*****

Mrs. Clark closed her eyes as Brendan drove down the freeway. After six hours of driving and asking directions, Brendan finally pulled up at the house whose address had been on Daniel Applegate's driver's license.

A woman was hanging clothes on a clothesline at the side of the house, and her back was turned toward them. Walking up to the fence, Mrs. Clark softly said, "Madeline?"

The woman whirled around to see who had spoken and looked at Mrs. Clark without saying a word. After all the years that had passed, Mrs. Clark knew that it was her midwife, Madeline Applegate, and Madeline knew that it was her patient Estelle Clark.

Madeline let the clothes fall freely from her hands into the clothes basket.

The look on Madeline's face compelled Estelle to relive the moment when Madeline had told her that her son had died. It was the same look that had carried the message that had saddened her for years.

Estelle buried her nails into her purse as she thought, *Madeline is a good actress. What sadness? She isn't sad!*

Estelle took a few steps toward the fence, and Madeline cautiously walked to the gate and opened it. "It's good to see you, Estelle. I know that we need to talk." She motioned for her to enter the yard, but Estelle stood firm. "I went looking for you back in Milolta," she continued.

"I know!" Estelle interrupted impatiently. "Mrs. Dunns told me on her deathbed. I had a feeling it was you that came looking for me."

Estelle's eyes narrowed, and she asked in an authoritarian voice as she changed the subject, "Did my son really die? Did the hospital really bury my son?"

Madeline gripped the metal bars of the gate until it left an impression on her hands. She raised one hand and covered her face, and she leaned against the fence for support.

"What did you say happened to *my* son that day I gave birth to him?" Estelle asked angrily between clenched teeth.

Madeline was weeping. "I'm sorry. I...I...," she stuttered. "I... wanted a baby. I took your son, and I'm really sorry."

Estelle felt no compassion. How could she feel compassion for a woman who'd stolen her child?

"That was horrible of me...please, Estelle, please..."

Estelle threw the driver's license at Madeline's feet as she said, "He came looking for us and was murdered!"

Madeline's sobs stopped abruptly, her eyes widening. "What?" she asked faintly. "What are you talking about?"

Surely, Estelle must be lying. She wanted revenge, and this must be the way she had chosen to do it. Danny wasn't dead. He couldn't be! Biologically, he was Estelle's son, but the bond we share is a strong mother-son relationship, Madeline tried to rationalize.

"You killed him twice! You stole his identity and gave him a pretend family, then you caused him to come looking for us at the wrong time. I should have you arrested, you...thief and murderer!" The words sent chills up Madeline's spine.

"I've never been so deeply hurt by anyone, Madeline!" Estelle spoke her name in disdain and spat on the ground.

"Danny? My Danny's dead?" Madeline's voice echoed.

"No!" Estelle angrily retorted. "*My* son Brandy Clark is dead!" She emphasized the word *my.* "When I looked at his face in that morgue, he had a disappointed expression on his face that said, 'Why? Just why did I have to miss out?'"

Madeline's arms dropped to her sides. The baby she'd raised to be her own had been snatched away from her in the worst way possible. A terrible churning wrung her stomach.

"The evil you've done to me has returned on your head. I'd been grieving and empty for years because of you. Now you're experiencing the grief you've caused me."

"I'm sorry. I'm really sorry. Oh, Daniel, Daniel, my son," she cried bitterly.

Brendan sat and watched from inside the car until he finally decided to get involved. Madeline hadn't noticed that Brendan was there, because all her focus had been on Estelle. When he walked toward his mother, she stared at him a moment, then said, "Daniel!" For a few seconds, she thought Estelle had really fooled her.

"No!" he said angrily. "I'm Brendan Clark. You hurt my mother, and I hate you!"

She gripped the fence again with both hands as she bawled, "I know, I know. I shouldn't have done that."

"You are a thief and a liar, and I hope that God casts you into hell!" he said with anger.

"I laid my son to rest because of you," Estelle said.

"I'm sorry, Estelle, please find it in your heart to forgive me. I'm sorry."

Without another word, Estelle and Brendan got in the car and drove away. Madeline stood on the lawn with her hands on her head, weeping vehemently.

*****

Estelle's body literally shook from her soul-wrenching sobbing. She and Brendan were on their way back to Milolta. Somehow, confronting Madeline and giving her a piece of her mind just hadn't made her feel any better. She fervently hoped she would never see Madeline again and that the rest of the woman's life would be full of misery.

Brendan slipped in a tape and depressed the Play button. The vibrant music perked up the dull, somber atmosphere in the car, but not Estelle's spirit. She was quiet during the long, weary ride back to Milolta.

The next morning, Estelle Clark woke up bright and early. Surprisingly, she felt better than she had the day before. She walked into Brendan's bedroom, as if she needed to check to see if he really was still in her life. Gently she rolled the covers from his shoulders to get a better view of his precious face. "Oh, BJ," she murmured softly and planted a soft kiss on his face. Then she thought back over the years, *You defied death once again. How you scared me with that infected vaccination when you were just a baby, and how you scared me terribly once again. But now all is well. If only Cedric were here to see how you've matured. If only...*

*****

Estelle walked into the police station and inquired about Detective Schennenburger. "He's out but should be back any minute," an officer told her.

"I'll wait," she said.

"As you wish," the officer said.

A few minutes later, Schennenburger was surprised to see Estelle Clark at the station. He reached out his hand and shook hers, then escorted her to his office.

"About the young man that we buried..." She paused. "He was my son."

The detective raised his brow in interest.

She went on. "His real name was Brandy Clark. He was an identical twin to my son, Brendan Clark."

Jake Schennenburger leaned forward and placed both elbows on the desk and clasped his hands together. Estelle lowered her head and went on, "I had a midwife deliver them in my house. She told me that Brandy didn't make it, that he had died. While I slept, she left with the baby and returned only to inform me that she'd taken the 'dead baby' to the hospital and that they would take care of the burial." Estelle sobbed softly. "He came looking for his family, obviously at the wrong time. The men that were after Brendan got to him before he found us." She sniffed and dabbed her eyes, Schennenburger listening to every syllable.

She raised her head and stared into his eyes, then rose to her feet. "Detective, your mystery is solved," she said.

He stood and leaned forward on his desk. "I'm sorry, really sorry," he said with compassion.

Estelle nodded.

"Did you want to press charges against your midwife? We could. She committed a crime. Kidnapping is against the law."

"No," she said, interrupting his words. "I want this chapter of my life closed for good. It'll hurt more to relive the trauma. I just want closure. I've accepted my misfortune and now need to let go."

She turned to leave, and Schennenburger escorted her out. He placed a hand on her shoulder and said, smiling, "You're a strong woman, Mrs. Estelle Clark, very strong. I'm inspired, truly."

She smiled, nodded, and walked out.

Chapter 19

On the Wings of Love

Casey had already been in labor for eight hours. It ached Ida to know that her daughter was in such agony.

"I need a drink," Barry said faintly to the nurse. "I mean a drink of water," he added quickly as he left the room.

Barrington Taylor strode down the hall to the waiting area to join his father-in-law, who was pacing the floor from one end of the room to the other. He felt as if he were betraying his wife, and he felt kind of guilty that he just couldn't go back into that delivery room.

He sat down without saying a word to Ben. "How are you doing?" asked Ben.

"I can't handle it," Barry confessed.

"I understand," Ben replied. "But you've got to tell yourself that you *can*." Without another word, Barry stood up and walked back to the delivery room.

At eleven fifteen the next morning, Casey gave birth to a baby girl. They named her Chelsea Marie Taylor. She'd hoped for a boy, but Chelsea was a perfect baby, and she was happy. She cuddled her close to her, and they both drifted off to a contented sleep.

*****

Jeannine stood by the crib and watched as Chelsea fiddled with her toy. *So tiny. How precious. So fragile. So beautiful you are, my little pumpkin,* she thought as she gently touched her arm with her finger. *So delicate.* Chelsea looked into her eyes and smiled. She kicked her legs friskily and cooed.

"Oh, my darling. Oh, my darling. Oh, my darling, Che-el-sea. Oh, my darling. Oh, my darling. Oh, my darling, Che-el-sea," she softly sang. She picked her up and gave her a gentle squeeze as she said, "You are so huggable and squeezable. Oh, you are so beautiful!" She held her close to her and gently stroked her face. "You are a precious gift."

Jeannine walked over to the window and sat in the rocking chair and hummed her another lullaby. Chelsea snuggled in her arms.

"Ah," Jeannine sighed as she looked out the window. "My favorite time of the year. Just when it seems as if there is no hope of life, spring proves us wrong. Fresh, new leaves, green, green grass, birds chirping, blue skies, and a radiant sun."

As she rocked contentedly, her mind wandered back to her country. "Mmm, Jamaica," she whispered. There was a warm tingle in her stomach as she thought so fondly of her country. "Home sweet home." It hadn't been that long ago since Jeannine had visited her home, but she was homesick again.

"You know, Chelsea, I was born on a beautiful tropical island called Jamaica…" She paused. Chelsea was fast asleep.

A bird flew by the window and circled around and then disappeared into the sky. *Such a beautiful day today,* she thought. There were no clouds. Pleasant memories of the beach illuminated her mind. It was a day like today that she would go to the beach. She could almost hear the rustling of the waves. Her mind played scenes of the times she'd spent at the beach.

The pictures she saw in her mind were as clear as if they'd happened yesterday.

Just a few months ago, she had revisited her childhood home. Jamaica had been as pleasant and beautiful as she had remembered it.

"I'm back, Jeannine!" called Casey.

"I am too," Jeannine whispered to Chelsea, who was sound asleep in her arms.

"Up here," she called softly to Casey. Cautiously and slowly she rose from the rocking chair and gently placed Chelsea in her crib.

Casey was busy putting the groceries away. "Mmm, I smell fresh strawberries," said Jeannine as she descended the stairs.

"How's my angel?"

"Your angel is an angel. She's sleeping right now."

"Thank you. You're such a wonderful auntie," said Casey with a grin.

"I'm sorry that I have to leave so soon, but I have a lot of errands to run," Jeannine said as she picked up her purse.

"I really appreciate you babysitting for me."

"With a baby as wonderful as Chelsea, I don't mind at all."

"Yeah, but will you also do it when she hits the terrible twos?" Casey grinned.

"We'll see," said Jeannine as she walked out the door.

As she drove around the city, running the errands she needed to do, her mind drifted to thoughts of Remington. He had asked her out a few times, but she had always had a reason she couldn't go. Remington had persisted, and she had run out of excuses.

She'd never been on a date because she had never really been ready to date, but Remington had won her heart.

He got down on his hands and knees and, with tenderness in his eyes, stuttered, "J-Jeannine, will you marry me?"

Without hesitation, she answered, "Yes, I will, Remington. I love you, yes."

His eyes opened wide, and he grinned from ear to ear as he said, "Jeannine, you've made me the happiest man in the world!"

Ben and Ida had liked Remington from the first day they'd met. They were happy for their daughter and looked forward to having him in the family.

*****

Jeannine and Kim giggled on the phone as they talked about their great wedding plans.

When Zaire heard about Kim's engagement to Brendan, he became literally sick to his stomach.

"I'm sorry, Zaire, but Brendan and I are going to get married. Kim's words cut through his heart, and his first thought was, *I've lost her forever.*

Her mind was made up, and he knew she was set to do just what she wanted to do. So her choice was Brendan, and there was nothing he could do about it.

*****

"We love you all!" said Jeannine as she and her husband waved goodbye. They then climbed aboard the airplane that would take them to Jamaica. Ben and Ida stood proudly as they watched their daughter's plane disappear into the skies.

"It seems like just yesterday that I held her tiny body in my arms and sang her a lullaby," Ida said with tears in her eyes.

Not able to speak, Ben just held his love in his arms.

"Jamaica, here I come," whispered Remington as he cuddled his new bride and looked forward to his first trip to Jamaica.

Brendan and Kim were looking forward to their wedding day, which would be in a few weeks. Jeannine's wedding had been splendid, and Kim couldn't wait to experience the same happiness she saw on Jeannine's face as they had walked out of the church as man and wife. She loved Brendan with her whole heart and knew they would be happy together, no matter what came their way.

Kim couldn't wait for Jeannine to return, so she could tell her all about how great their honeymoon had been.

Ben and Ida heard from Jeannine and Remington almost every day. The young couple was floating on cloud nine, and Ida wished that her daughter would always be just as happy. She couldn't wait for her to come home. She missed her terribly.

Jeannine was the last one to leave home, and Ida knew it was going to be hard not having her around as often.

Ben counted the hours until he would see his Tibbits. He looked at his watch and said to Ida, "They should be in the air by now."

Shortly after, while watching TV, a news flash interrupted the program they were watching. "An airplane coming from Jamaica to the US has crashed, and all aboard are presumed dead."

"NO!" hollered Ben.

Ida sat next to him in a state of shock. As they listened to the fate of the 130 passengers aboard the airplane, Ida exclaimed with bitterness, "That's their flight. Dear God!" She then groaned. Immediately, they prayed desperately for the lives of their daughter and son-in-law.

Ben called the hotel where Jeannine and Remington had spent their honeymoon and, to their greatest dismay, found out that they had already checked out, which confirmed to Ben that they had indeed boarded the scheduled flight.

"They were on that plane!" Ben gasped in sheer horror.

Rescue teams worked around the clock looking for survivors and had recovered quite a number of the bodies. Grief-stricken, the Shrouders cried bitterly.

It had been twenty-one hours since the plane had gone down, and Ben and Ida still sat glued to their television set, desperately hoping for a miracle. When the front door opened, they didn't bother to look who it was that had entered their house, because nothing else mattered right then. Nothing could take away the horrible feeling they had over the loss of their precious daughter.

"Hi, Mama! Hi, Dad!" came a familiar voice.

Shocked, they whirled around to match the body with the voice and found Jeannine and Remington standing in the doorway.

"My god!" exclaimed Ben and Ida together. God had been good to them once more.

"We thought you were on that flight!" said Ben, now crying and laughing and grinning from ear to ear.

Remington and Jeannine had had no idea that there had been a plane crash, because they had been so in love and too engrossed in each other to care about current events.

"We met a woman that reminded me so much of Grandma. She was the sweetest little lady I've ever met. She invited us to her church because they were having a revival. It was a Pentecostal church. We couldn't refuse her and so decided to see if we could catch a later flight back to the US. The airline told us there were available seats the next day. We also wanted to stay a little longer in Jamaica." Jeannine laughed. "We went to the church and enjoyed it a lot. Remington and I gave our hearts to Jesus. I thought I was happy when we got married, but after that, there was a different level of joy. I felt light and free. Jesus Christ is living in our hearts. We've experienced His salvation, and we've never been happier."

Ben and Ida could see the difference in their faces. They looked *good.* "Well, for whatever reason you missed your plane, it was good, because you could have been on that plane."

"We are grateful to God that He saved us from sin and from dying on that airplane," said Remington.

Ida said, "You know, Ben, one thing we failed to do was call the airline and ask if Jeannine and Remington were actually on the flight."

"We would have known then that they never made the flight, and it would have saved us from a lot of worry," said Ben. "You don't know how you've made my day," he told them.

Well, that was that. The Shrouders were one big happy family again. Looking back, they realized the milestones that they had accomplished.

*****

God has really been good to the Shrouders, thought Ben. "Oh, Ida, I forgot to tell you I found those disks for which I had been so frantically searching. Guess where they were?" Before she could answer, he went on to explain, "I found them in my desk drawer at work. I knew I'd searched that drawer a hundred times, but Sandy told me I had given them to Mike Cuisack to edit and then to have Aladdin and Timber verify my work."

He laughed. "After she told me, then I remembered doing that. I don't need them anymore because I had to recreate the entire database for Cornell's Department Store. They weren't happy that I lost the disks and missed the deadline, but they gave me a couple more months. I worried the disks might have fallen into their competitor's hands, because they would have revealed their prices and very personal business matters."

"I've been restored back to life, and I am so grateful." He smiled and said, "I could have lost my job, my family, and my whole life. Now I look at life differently. I am more patient." He suddenly remembered Phil Demi and felt bad about convincing Marcus Guerie to get rid of him. Even though there was a legitimate reason for firing him, if the decision had come up after he'd recovered from his accident, Ben felt he would have given him yet another chance. Now he was more compassionate, more tolerant.

Just then, the phone interrupted his reverie. It was Jake Schennenburger, and he wanted to talk with him. "Ben, I apologize to you for my interrogation and accusing you of murdering Brendan. I was just doing my job." He sounded quite sincere.

"That's okay, Detective. It doesn't bother me, anymore, at least. I'm just glad the truth finally surfaced."

*****

"So you still want to be an actor, Rem?" asked Jeannine.

"Where did that come from all of a sudden?" he asked.

"I just remembered how much you used to crave an acting career."

"Well, that was just a phase. I'm all grown up now."

Jeannine chuckled and said, "Isn't it funny how we go through these stages of our lives where we gotta have something and a little ways down the road we disdain what we used to crave?"

"Such is life, Jeannine. If we all remain at the same point in life, then we'd know for sure that there's been no growth in our experiences. I've made leaps and bounds." He smiled wryly. "I've gained a wife. 'He that findeth a wife findeth a good thing.'"

Jeannine smiled and felt a warm peace fill her soul.

Brendan and Kim's wedding was just a couple of weeks away. Kim couldn't wait to be Mrs. Brendan Clark. Sighing, she thought of leaving her childhood home. The thought always seemed to be lingering in the back of her mind. *I'll miss this place. I've never lived anywhere else, and the house holds sweet memories. On the other hand, I can't wait to leave here, as there is too much of my father here as well.*

She was still trying to find herself, still shaken and confused about her father. Love, hate, and anger still warred with her emotions. Just thinking about him and the whole ordeal always seemed to open up wounds that were still raw. Yet she loved him. He was her daddy. She wished she could speed up time so that she could look back at the situation and smile, knowing that by then time would have healed her. She had no idea how things were going to turn out with her and her father.

Brendan wanted her to visit him in prison so she could confront him and begin the process of her healing, but so far, she hadn't been able to bear to face him, even though he was the one who should be ashamed. Often, she'd wake up gasping for air and crying hysterically.

"You have that look on your face again," Brendan told her. She shook her body as if to snap out of it. "I know. I just can't help thinking about it. It's just horrifying, and it's as if it just happened yesterday."

"We'll walk through this together." He promised to do everything he could to help her keep her mind off her troubles.

*****

Meeghan walked into the family room with a look of compassion on her face. She held out a disk with a rose pink-colored tab on it as she stated, "Your father called earlier." Kim sat upright and looked at her in anticipation. "He wanted me to give this to you."

Frowning, Kim asked, "Why? What for?"

"I really don't know. He just told me the general area where to find it. I went looking, and there it was," Meeghan explained.

Out of curiosity, Kim asked, "Where *did* you find it? In the attic? I tore that place apart after he had been arrested, and there were no disks up there."

"Well, there really was no way you could have found it even if you had been looking for it. Behind that old antique bookshelf is an area that was marked, about three and a half feet from the floor. You have to gently run your hand over the wall, and then you would feel a slight change in the smoothness of the wall. Once you feel that, there is an area on the wallpaper that is marked with an X. To be truthful, you need a magnifying glass to see it. Once you peel the wallpaper away from where the X has been marked, exposed is a small ring attached to a little box in the wall, rather like a circuit breaker box. I pulled on the ring, the box opened, and there I found the disk."

Surprised, Brendan asked, "You mean the attic was wallpapered over the spot?" Meeghan nodded in the affirmative. "And he told you all this over the phone?" Again, she nodded.

Kim said hesitantly, "I'm almost afraid to see what's on it."

"I'm curious," said Brendan.

She popped the disk into the A drive on the computer, clicked on the My Computer icon, then clicked on the three-and-a-half-inch floppy disk icon. A gray box with a blue bar appeared that said, "Enter password to open file." Kim and Brendan looked at Meeghan, but she just looked puzzled. Then she said, "Oh, I almost forgot. He said to tell you that the password is your nickname. I never even knew you had a nickname, Kim." Meeghan smiled. "I've never heard him call you any other name than Kim," she added.

"Now it is up to you, Kim. I have to get going." And just like that, Meeghan was gone.

"You have a nickname?" Brendan asked after Meeghan had left.

"Yeah, but he doesn't call me that too often."

She typed the word *princess*. Brendan smiled and said, "That's a nice nickname. Now you're *my* princess." But Kim kept a serious expression.

A yellow folder named Velocity appeared. She hesitated. "Click on it," coaxed Brendan. She double-clicked on Velocity, and a file opened up showing a cheetah in motion at the top of the page. Kim bit her lip and held back tears as they read what was on the page:

> *My darling Kim Marie Futon:*
>
> *I have neglected the finer things of life. I've neglected the one treasure that I had that is irreplaceable—you! I'm sorry. Forgive me for your sake, not for my*

sake, so that you can move on with your life. I don't deserve your love, but for your sake, let me go.

For a short time I felt invincible, unstoppable. And I was...for only that short moment. But then reality set in. I'm just another man. I'm so sorry.

Daddy

Kim cried as she read the note, and Brendan comforted her. With mixed emotions, she had read her father's message with eyes filled with tears. "Daddy," she whispered, "I can't believe you did all that." She clenched her teeth and cried vehemently, and all the while, Brendan offered her comfort. The well of tears released what had been bottled up within her through the whole ordeal, and then out loud she read and reread her father's message. Then she finally cried out, "Daddy, I love you! You were all I had!"

"And me," whispered Brendan in her ear. She grabbed his hand and held on tightly.

It was a simple note of apology, but to Kim, those words were no ordinary words; they carried power. The power to touch her heart and cause her to rethink. Kim's healing had finally begun.

Contact Info:

LWCOG
P.O. Box 66397
Albany, NY 12206

Website: LWCOG.org
Email address: LivingWaters2018@gmail.com

Other books by Sharon E. Harris:

Intercessory Training of Gatekeepers, Prayer Warriors, and Watchmen on the Walls

My Dog Gizmo

Understanding Spiritual Warfare

About the Author

Ever since she can remember, Sharon E. Harris has always loved reading. When she gets ahold of a good book, she will not stop reading until she has read it from cover to cover. Beginning with her favorite children's books as a little girl, she spent endless hours engrossed in her favorite mystery books and remembers the excitement and all the emotions that were stirred within her when an intriguing book caught her attention. As an adult, she says her passion for reading has not waned. She believes that books are powerful and are medicine to the soul. They inform, intrigue, motivate, stir, and push you to your wildest dreams. Because of her passion for books and reading, she has dedicated her life in painting pictures, through her books, that cause her readers to go, "Wow!" Mysteries, adventures, and all the passions that a book brings can distract a person, even for a moment, from the worries and cares of life so that they can take a retreat and replenish the soul from the power of a good book.

CPSIA information can be obtained
at www.ICGtesting.com
Printed in the USA
LVHW032323220420
654155LV00001B/60